Rock 'n' Roll
Rectory

Rock 'n' Roll Rectory

John Elmes
The Tiercel of the March

Rock 'n' Roll Rectory
John Elmes

Published by Greyhound Self-Publishing, 2017

Designed, printed and bound by Aspect Design
89 Newtown Road, Malvern, Worcs. WR14 1PD
United Kingdom
Tel: 01684 561567
E-mail: allan@aspect-design.net
Website: www.aspect-design.net

All Rights Reserved.

Copyright © 2017 John Elmes

John Elmes has asserted his moral right
to be identified as the author of this work.

The right of John Elmes to be identified as the author
of this work has been asserted in accordance with
Section 77 of the Copyright, Designs and Patents Act 1988.

This book is sold subject to the condition that it shall not, by way of trade or otherwise, be lent, resold, hired out or otherwise circulated without the publisher's prior consent in any form of binding or cover other than that in which it is published and without a similar condition including this condition being imposed on the subsequent purchaser.

A copy of this book has been deposited
with the British Library Board

ISBN 978-1-909219-52-6

Dedication

In my introduction you will meet Chris, a very special friend, who first planted in me the seed of writing about my adventurous life. That seed took root and has finally blossomed. My 'little mate' is sadly no longer with us and it is to Christopher John Fletcher that I dedicate this book.

FOREWORD

This book had a rocky passage from its completion to its appearance on the bookshop shelves. John Elmes, its author, took six and a half years to write this fascinating work of art. Being the only son of a vicar, he attended eight different schools in areas ranging from the beautiful Hampshire heathlands to the poorest part of Newport Docks in Wales. He processed a wonderful memory and had the ability to transfer incidents of importance with accuracy and humour.

I had known John for just over seven years and was a fellow poet although not in the same league as John; he was a master wordsmith and already had a book of his poems published under the title *Beneath the Wings of the Falcon*. At the age of seventy-four he became ill with heart problems and during the time of his illness he confided in me that he was worried that his book which took up so many years of his life would never get published. By this stage, his work was in the hands of his editor, Valerie Ball, who had advised and supported John for several years. It was then that I assured John that his book, of which I was privileged to read every chapter as he wrote it, would get published.

John finished his school life at Presteigne from where he was expelled because he refused to change his wonderful DA haircut. He was a Teddy Boy all his life and proud of it. He lived in the Vicarage at Gladestry in the shadow of the Hergest Ridge.

John died on 21 May 2017 and a few weeks later, the proof copy of *Rock and Roll Rectory* was with us. I have no doubt that you will enjoy reading this book; do please recommend it to your friends so that they may also take pleasure from it. One pound from each copy sold will be donated to the Midlands Air Ambulance Service; all the proceeds from this book will serve good causes close to John's heart.

Denis R. H. Teal
Fellow poet and countryman who
was privileged to have known John.

The following poem is a snapshot of John which I wrote on his passing:

Elmes of Leominster

Now John goes up to Heaven and knocks on Peter's gate.
'Hi there, my friend, I know I'm early, not one for being late.'
St Peter had a problem opening this massive gate
John at once saw the fault, one hinge was out of line
'Hang on, Pete, me old pal, it happened to one of mine.'
After a shove a kick and a gentle push the gate swung open wide.
'Welcome,' said Peter, 'you old reprobate, we can do with you inside.'

'Up here, John, our second-in-command has need of a new gavel,
He would have picked one up but of late has had no time for travel.
I'll take you down to the carpenter's shop for you to have a look
The boss whose name is Noah had a write-up in your dad's big black book.
That boat he designed and built was some great hunk,
Had he made the Titanic it never would have sunk.
The last job he did was to build a stable for Santa Claus's deer
With a cosy little hut for his elves nestling at the rear.'

'Carpenters are well respected up here I'm sure you will fit in well.
We don't have the risk of fire they have down there in Hell.'
'But Pete me old pal I don't have any tools;
A chap just cannot work - not without his tools!'
'John when we heard you were on your way
A box was found and in it every tool did lay,
Chisels with hickory handles and blades of Sheffield steel
And a rule that was wound on a fine oak reel.
Oh and John we found a lathe that you would wish to die for
(Sorry, we don't use that word up here any more).'

'Well thanks for making me so welcome Pete, I'm very happy to stay.
I'll miss my Joan, my family and friends I've mixed with every day.
But if they buy my book and read a chapter every night,
I'll be with them for years to come, and that will be just right.

From Teal of Bromyard
(one of your many mates, Denis, June 2017)

My First Radnorshire Winter

The late autumns grass now shows crystalline white
Hedgerows shrink back and seem to hide from sight
Moving fingers of mist swirling around the trees
Now standing gaunt skeletal black, bereft of leaves

The sky leaden, ominous with the spits of icy snow
A piercing wind shrieking with an eastern blow
Lookout tomorrow or so old men are heard to curse
A foot of snow come daylight, or could be worse

I the merest fool, ears flapping, wrapped in total awe
A half smoked woodbine burning my fingers raw
Eyes out on stalks, imagining the village in the morn
My first Radnorshire winter's now approaching storm

Etched in my memory those glorious summer days
Following the streams as they wound on their ways
Frothing over the boulders beneath that summer sun
Wading waist high in deep pools, memories of such fun

Standing neath a churchyard wall in the bitterest cold
Listening to countrymen, and the stories that they told
Walking across the hedgerow tops for a loaf of bread
Nineteen forty seven, when snow was snow they said

I rushed headlong back home to tell the folks the tale
The snow that was coming later with that eastern gale
Mother worried endlessly, father pooh-pooh'd it all
We didn't have any snow in Wales, maybe a tiny fall

So finally to bed I went with a last look onto the lawn
The wind soughing in the trees, I hoped if in the morn
Maybe if an inch of snowfall to prove he'd got it wrong
As local men who lived the years, got it right all along

Roused from drowsy lumber as mother opened the door
I've let the dog out for his wee, seems it's snowing more
Don't worry, I told her it will all disappear in the night
And then a hint of sarcasm, I'm sure father will be right

Six the following morning, blowing on the window pane
Finally a spy hole and a quick look before it froze again
Gasping for breath I staggered back and sat upon the bed
Never seen a sight like this, must be the day to go for bread

INTRODUCTION

Over the years people have said to me that from reading my poetry it is obvious that I loved the county of Radnorshire above everything else; that it shows up in my poems and sometimes can make me emotional. So yes, I have to admit that the six years I spent living there endeared me to its beautiful countryside, its wonderful wildlife and its marvellous people. Although many changes have taken place, many people have moved away and saddest of all, many people now sleep in the old churchyard. I still have good friends living in the village and deep down I feel a glow when I walk up the road and find it not that different but also remember it as it used to be. Finally, I settled in the small town of Leominster after living around the country and it was there, one winter's night in the Rankin club, that I was introduced by a dear friend, David Strangwood, to Christopher John Fletcher.

Chris became a very close friend of my wife, Joan, and me and together with his wife, Judith, we used to go out for meals in different areas. Apart from this, he came with me to Radnorshire and I showed him the secret places of my youth. He loved the tales of long ago and made good friends with the locals. We camped in Alman's field on a regular basis and he became good friends with Joe and Kim Alman, also with Marion and Roy Ingram. We were sometimes asked to go and have a cup of tea with people and talk over the old times to bring back cherished memories of those times. It sometimes became a bit emotional, but Chris loved it.

One morning, after one of these visits, he said to me that I should put it all down in a book. This bold statement took me by surprise and I thought long and hard about it, explaining that it would contain a lot of bad language, not to glorify it but that was how it was at the time. I apologise to readers if they are offended by some of it and I stress that it was not written to offend in any way. One of my favourite poets is Robert William Service and two lines of his poem Prelude, seem to sum up my style of writing:

> My fingers were not formed I fear to frame a pretty pen
> So please forgive me if I veer from virtue now and then.

This book is written from the heart and its story is told as it actually happened and is as true as my memory serves me.

We lost Chris in late July of 2009 and I truly believe the world is a poorer place without him. He loved life and fun and it was a pleasure to walk with him, be his friend and show him a different world away from the humdrum of life. His respect for the natural world and the people he met along the journey, his compassion and interest in everything, endeared him to all.

All of the folks that he met along the way always asked after him, if he was missing, and I personally still miss his companionship and good humour terribly for he was a good man and a total pleasure to have by your side. I was honoured to read a small eulogy to Chris at his funeral and I chose the words of A. E. Houseman's Shropshire Lad which is more or less the same as that first morning when we stood up on the ridge looking down on the village and up onto the Caety Traylow, when he wanted to know all I could tell him about the hills, the farms and the village.

> Into my heart an air that chills
> from yon far country blows.
> What are those blue remembered hills,
> what spires, what farms are those?

> That is the land of lost content,
> I see it shining plain,
> those happy highways where I went
> and cannot come again.

To try and sum up how much Chris was liked up in Radnorshire, the fact that on the day of his funeral, both Joe and Kim Alman left the haymaking that day to pay their respect and also Roy and Marion Ingram came down to Leominster to pay theirs, says it all for me.

Without his friendship and companionship and his earnestness in asking me to write it, this book would never have been written.

AS IT WAS IN THE BEGINNING

Was it really that long ago? Looking out of my caravan window on that glorious June evening, the sort of evening that sticks in your mind, the sort of evening that brings a smile of remembrance to the lips on those dark, cold winter days, where old men sit huddled around the fire, lost in memories and contemplation.

Looking out, I see myriad shades of green; the green of the freshly mown meadow hay; the greens of the new shoots of bracken pushing up through last year's rust brown tangle; the greens of the sun-scorched mountain grass and the lush greens of the oak, beech and horse chestnut beneath which the white-faced cattle find shade and the demon horseflies swarm.

The screech of the swifts as they hurtle past, showing off their aerobatics, now heading back to their chicks nestling safely beneath the centuries old grey stone church. Following close behind are the swallows and martins, chasing after the clouds of insects, their forms casting a fleeting shadow across the mellow walls of the long redundant chapel.

My gaze is drawn upwards to the skyline and there, dwarfing everything, smiling down over the village, its cottages, farms and barns that make up the parish is the mountain. Clad in his new summer mantle of greens and golds, dotted here and there with the white smudges of sheep as they graze steadily upon his sweet upland grass.

Smiling now, I have seen him in all his moods: sullen and half-hidden in the mist and rain when the soft drizzle of early spring seeps through the clothing and the raindrops hang like jewels from the budding branches awaiting the thin, watery sun to warm them and bring them into fresh green leaf. Angry, with black and purple thunder clouds chasing around his head, the icy rain plastering your hair to your skull and icy droplets unerringly finding their way inside your collar as you race for shelter. Then standing there cold and distant, stark white against a leaden sky. Ice cold his stare with the black skeletons of leafless trees girding his lower slopes like dead sentinels, guarding against all. While there below him lies the village deep in snow, hushed save for the far off bellow of a cow, safe in the byre or the occasional bleat of a sheep as they mill around the hay cratch seeking out mouthfuls of sweet-smelling hay saved from last year's harvest.

This, then, is my village, my home and the place of my dreams, where I grew through adolescence from boy to man, made my many mistakes and, I hope, learned from them. Through the years it has held me in its spell. Returning as often as I can, my love for it and my respect for its people has never diminished and I have sat and had a drink with several generations of villagers and shared many a joke around the hearth on a winter's night. When I left as a young man, I had my race to run and my dreams to fulfil. Looking back, I wouldn't change a minute of it. Whichever path I took was my decision and no one else's and I stand by that.

Sitting on a bench in that lovely old churchyard, I look around the generations of folk lying asleep down through the years. Many of those folk I shared a laugh with and my thoughts always stray back to that wonderful, spell-binding poem of Thomas Gray's Elegy, 'Beneath those rugged Elms that Yew tree's shade.' Nothing changes and yet everything changes.

Peace reigns here; that wonderful deepening peace disturbed only by the song of the blackbird and song thrush. A peace that today is so hard to find, far away from the busy streets, the stress of the frenetic office and the nerve shattering race home through the miles of commuter traffic. Where are they all now, I ask? Far, far away from this tranquil place and I sigh contentedly.

But yes, it really was that long ago!

BOOK ONE

Learning the Game
(Buddy Holly and The Crickets)

CHAPTER ONE
Movin' and a Groovin'
(Duane Eddy)

September 1954 and here I was, perched in the back of a furniture van, en route to my destiny although I didn't know it at the time. Thirteen years old me and knew it all, at least I thought I did. After seven moves in seven years I had lived both in towns and villages from Newport to Nottingham via Hampshire, Warwickshire and Breconshire and had that arrogance that only comes with youth, just waiting for someone to come and knock me down a peg or two. Been in love more times than I care to mention, left mates behind all over the country and here I was 'back on the road again' clutching a bottle of water with which to top up my two goldfish, Hitler and Mussolini, a gift from my parents bought from a pet shop in Nottingham, should the water level drop and the need arise.

The furniture van swayed as it travelled along the country lanes, the engine making a fearful noise as the driver went up and down the gearbox. Sitting close by my side was Kim, our faithful Collie cross for whom my father had paid the princely sum of five shillings from the gypsies who lived down the lane from us in Hampshire. Hemmed in on all sides by rolls of lino, carpet squares and furniture of all descriptions, I sat there and contemplated my recent past and my most important future.

My thoughts drifted back to my recent friends I had left behind and I wondered what they were doing now. Had Len managed to climb up to the Squirrel's drey yet? He had been trying for several weeks. Was Megan missing me already? Only last Sunday we had promised to keep in touch, but at my age promises were like pie crusts and meant to be broken. As to the future, all I had been told was that we were moving some seventy miles across country where my father was to be inducted as vicar. The house, I had been told, was a lovely big house standing in its own grounds, but I had heard all this nonsense many times before.

Uphill and down dale we travelled, mile after mile and I began to wonder if my persistent nagging to travel in the back with the livestock was such a good idea. The monotonous roar of the engine was dulling my senses and Hitler and Mussolini hadn't lost a drop of water, but it was too late now and I would have to stick it out. My eye slid over the different pieces of furniture, seeing them in their past settings and memories of times past came flooding back to me. The smell of Mansion polish, my mother's soft singing as she worked around the house, my large collection of books displayed on the shelves in my bedroom.

The van was slowing down considerably with the driver changing down through the gears. We appeared to be going around some very sharp bends, slowing down all the time until finally it came to a gentle stop. I heard the slamming of doors and I could hear my mother's voice and my father's deep booming laugh. Eyes wide open, I stood there with Kim on the lead waiting for the back doors to open, For heaven's sake hurry up, I thought, the most important person on the planet has just arrived. There was a grinding noise and as the doors swung open I shielded my eyes against the autumn sunlight which flooded into the van. Refocusing I took a deep breath and jumping down, looked around at my surroundings.

I was standing on the edge of a long, curved, gravel drive. To my right was a sunken tennis lawn surrounded by tall pines. Clearly visible through the trees were the grey stone walls of an old church tower with the algae covered tombstones of long dead forefathers standing in lines to the forefront. Long lawns stretched all around me, disappearing around the sides of a large double fronted, grey, roughcast house. There it stood, welcoming in the late afternoon sunshine. Framed by huge sash windows on either side was a large open porch with a curved brick arched lintel, giving access to a large imposing front door.

I can see today as I could then, the pleasure in my mother's face on that long ago September afternoon, as she took my hand and we did a little jig in front of the removal men who, though smiling, must have thought that we had completely lost the plot. Hands clasped, we mounted the steps together, waiting for my father who, with the importance of the head warder of the Tower of London produced a large bunch of keys and with a flourish, unlocked and threw open the large front door.

We entered a spacious quarry tiled hall with a large oak staircase halfway along the left hand wall, ascending up to the first floor where I supposed the bedrooms would be situated. Immediately to our left and right were two large panelled doors which led into two substantial rooms looking out over the drive. Both of these rooms had huge fireplaces with carved wooden surrounds. The windows inside each room had big panelled shutters covering them over.

Further down on the left was another generous sized room with French doors leading out onto a side lawn and further on, an extensive untended vegetable garden. At the end of the hall on the right was a door which led into a large kitchen with a Rayburn and some built-in cupboards. Off this was a scullery and large cold room with two smaller rooms leading off it. The back door opened out onto the rear lawn and a fence with a wicket gate.

Quietly edging past my parents who were oohing and aahing over the downstairs rooms, I slipped silently up the stairs. Somewhat nervously reaching the landing, I approached the door leading to the room which I had been told would be mine and furtively, like a thief in the night, I turned the heavy brass knob.

Looking into the room I felt all my fears melt away; it was perfect. Crossing to the window I looked down on the drive and the sunken tennis lawn with a big Larch tree directly across the drive. I just knew I would be happy here and once I had my possessions around me and my parents happy, I suddenly felt as though I had been here before and taking a long, deep breath I turned around and went back down the stairs. Both of my parents were deeply engrossed with the removal men, so it was out the back door me. After slipping the lead on Kim, across the back lawn we went and through the small wicket gate and into the paddock which my father had told me about earlier. Old Kim was delighted with this adventure and every couple of yards had a pee over every tussock of grass he could see, marking out his territory for future reference. At last we came to another gate and I knew from my father that this was the end of our property. Hearing the sound of running water I looked down the bank and there, lined with alders, was a stream, bubbling and gurgling over the stones. My thoughts flitted instantly to a fishing rod, little realising that before very long I would be taught the magical art of tickling the glorious mountain trout that live abundantly in these clear waters. Retracing my steps, I put Kim back in the outside room and went back into the front room of my new home.

The men had obviously finished the offloading and were sitting on some upturned tea chests with cups of tea and plates of biscuits, no doubt fortifying themselves for the journey home. I pictured them in my mind's eye, driving back along those narrow lanes, their headlights picking out the occasional rabbit on the side of the road and high above, the gibbous moon peeking between the racing clouds. Far, far away now, maybe someone else would sleep in my old room tonight; far, far away and already slipping from my fading thirteen year old memory. Covertly I slipped my hand into the biscuit tin and eased a handful of biscuits into my jacket pocket, taking the proffered cup of tea from my mother and yet more biscuits from the plate. Uttering my thanks I slipped out of the door and back upstairs to my room. Sitting on the iron frame of my bed which had not yet been made up, I quickly devoured the biscuits and washed them down with the tea. I heard the shouted goodbyes of the men and the thank you from my parents, the roar of the van's engine as it receded down the drive and then the crunch of the gravel from my father's footsteps as he returned from closing the drive gate.

The door opened and in came my mother with an armful of bedclothes and I swiftly helped her lift the mattress onto the bed.

'Well, son, what do you think of it so far?' she asked.

Replying that I thought it was marvellous and I hoped we would stay here this time, she assured me that we would and asked me to go and give my father a hand.

Downstairs my father was filling the Tilley lamps. Grabbing a handful of candles, I put them in their holders. No strangers to the frugal lifestyle, our family. My father had lit the Rayburn and I let Kim into the kitchen. It would soon be dark and with a good feed of sausages and beans on toast, we would all be warm and comfortable in our new home.

I awoke with a start, looking around the unfamiliar room and I suddenly remembered where I was. So this was my new room! I couldn't even remember dropping off to sleep last night and I lay there relaxed as my mind flitted back to the happenings of yesterday. Busting for a pee and clad in just my pyjama bottoms I slid out of bed and crept past my parents' room heading for the toilet.

'Morning, Sunny Jim!' boomed my father's voice in my ear.

Nearly jumping out of my skin, I turned around and there he stood, freshly shaved and clothed and looking as fresh as a daisy.

'I've got a nice hot cup of tea waiting downstairs for you, so come and have it while it's nice and hot.'

Bullshit, I thought. He will be especially nice today because there is a mountain of work to do and I am number one gopher, labourer and general dogsbody. But to be fair, I didn't mind as after all the moves and repetition I was quite handy. Also, today was Friday. That left one more day and my freedom would be terminated by school. Walking into the bathroom I was dismayed as there was not one drop of hot water but never mind, a quick rub down with the flannel would have to suffice. Glancing through the bathroom window I looked out across countryside I had never seen before. The fields on all sides seemed to stretch away as far as the eye could see while on the horizon, those ever present purple hills seemed to be climbing into the sky. The weather had all the appearances of being a lovely day, and I would have loved to have gone exploring, but I hadn't a snowball's chance in hell for the next few days, so I got dressed and leisurely descended the stairs for breakfast and orders for the day.

As mornings go I have had worse, and apart from the wranglings of my parents who wanted everything moved around a dozen times, we managed to get two rooms presentable. In those days there were no such things as fitted carpets, but carpet squares with either a linoleum or polished floorboard surround. Our squares had seen more use than a cricketer's crease and so much time was wasted by my mother wanting to try it this or that way for best effect. All gobbledygook to me, I'm afraid. But thank God, the floorboards passed muster.

Dinner on a Friday was normally fish and chips, but today it was going to be egg and chips as I was told there was no time to cook the fish. This was a downright lie because we had no fish in the house. There were no fridges or freezers then . . . come to that, we had no electricity anyway. My father always cooked the chips on his primus, this being a major operation just to light the bloody thing, never mind the chips.

I took Kim down the paddock. He was safe there and wouldn't run off and I picked a pocketful of Hazel nuts I had noticed yesterday. After what I thought was time to cook a few chips, we returned for dinner. Egg and chips have never tasted so good, washed down with two mugs of scalding, sweet tea and we were away again.

I should point out that from then on, Father was referred to as 'the old man'. Strangely, everybody called him that with no disrespect intended, but my mother hated it. Well, the old man smoked the most obnoxious pipe you could imagine which he hardly ever put down, so I was working in clouds of acrid smoke for most of the time. No elf and safety lunatics around in those days!

As time rolled on, I got the call I dreaded but knew would come. We had broken the back of the downstairs and in came my mother with the magic words, 'John, I want you to run down the shop for me please.'

Looking at the mantle clock, it showed four-thirty. The village kids would be home from school now, no doubt playing, and I was fair game so if the worst happened I would have to run the gauntlet. The old man, who seemed to know everything, told me to go down the church path, straight down the road and the shop was opposite the pub. Off I went with written instructions to get this, get that and nothing else would do. Being an old hand, I totally ignored everything and set off. Thinking back to those years, I do not think my mother ever went in that shop the whole time we lived there.

Rounding the corner of the church path I stopped dead in my tracks as I saw him in all his splendour, towering over all and I stood stock still, lost in awe. This was the mighty Hergest Ridge that the great Mike Oldfield was to write about many years later. I couldn't wait to climb up his sides and look out over the countryside. Tearing myself away, I marched resolutely onwards, but horror of horrors, out of a farm gate came a gaggle of geese led by the most vicious gander I have ever seen. Hissing fiendishly with neck arched, he came straight at me. Sidestepping, I ran past him and slowed, trying to regain my dignity but hearing muffled laughter, looked back to see three small girls sitting on a gate.

'Who's afraid of a little goose, then?' they chorused.

Glaring back at them, I received hoots of derision as I marched on and up the steps into the sanctuary of the village shop. Served by a friendly lady, I paid for the goods and taking a deep breath, headed for home. However, the return journey was uneventful as both girls and geese had vanished, but I was sure this was not the last I would hear of it.

Returning home, I dumped the shopping in the kitchen. Hearing voices, I crossed the hall and realised they were coming from the sitting room. Opening the door, I entered the room to find my parents talking to a little old man who had white hair, moustache and beard.

'This is our son, John,' said the old man. 'John, come and shake hands with Mr Evans.'

I grasped his outstretched hand, afraid to squeeze too hard, but my hand was held in a firm and strong grip.

'Pleased to meet you,' he said in an ancient, quavery voice.

I looked into his steady, ice-blue eyes and saw the experience of years, the summers and winters, the sorrow and the laughter.

'Nice to meet you,' I replied and left the room, somewhat overawed.

The following days passed both quietly and quite quickly, for as the old man was being inducted on the Thursday evening, it was thought to be respectful that we would keep a low profile until then and keep to the grounds as much as possible. However, my mother thought that I should accompany her to church for the Sunday

Evensong while Father stayed at home. Another fly in the ointment was that I was starting school the next day. How low profile is that, I ask?

Sunday night and scrubbed to perfection Mum and I, clad in our Sunday best, set forth. Mum clasped her prayer book and her little paisley bag holding her collection money as we set out through the drive gate, through the church gate and along the path to the church. At her side, I glanced right and left with lidded eyes, like some aspiring Mafia Don.

As we entered the church, you could almost hear the whisper, 'That's them,' echoing around the walls. The little church was gloriously beautiful with extensive stained glass windows. It was also quite full, including the choir stalls and I thought, good singing tonight, John bach. The congregation all turned in their pews for a glimpse of us as we looked for a seat as near to the back as possible, our intention being to slip out quietly as the service finished. As the nights were drawing, in the verger had lit all the oil lights and candles. These added to the ambience of the place and hung, chandelier-like, all the way down the church, each side of the aisle. I found out some time later that they were hung on chains and pulleys for ease of lighting them. The service, as always, droned on for me but finally we were into the last hymn and left quickly and quietly, or as I would remark, like a thief in the night. In fairness, I believe the congregation understood and come Thursday, we would be meeting all concerned at the school room, which appeared to be the place where it all happened.

Walking in through the drive gate we could see the old man had got all the lamps lit and we could see the warm glow through the curtains. He had the kettle on and was firing questions, none of which we knew the answers to. After listening to the Sunday night play I bade them goodnight.

'Goodnight son,' was the reply. 'You've got a busy day in front of you tomorrow and thanks for all your help.'

I gave Kim a cuddle and headed up the wooden hill, knowing that tomorrow was indeed, Another Day.

CHAPTER TWO
School Days
(Chuck Berry)

The alarm on my bedside cabinet woke me at 6.45 a.m. What sort of time of day was this for a human being to have to get up? I thought. Rubbing my bleary eyes, I headed for the bathroom. At least there was some hot water; the old man must have got the measure of the Rayburn. Stepping back across the landing, the smell of burnt toast invaded my nostrils so it looked like the deputation was up. Hastily scrambling into my clothes which had been laid out on a chair for me, and knotting my tie, I glanced at myself in the mirror and hurried down stairs to meet the day.

Grunting a mumbled, 'Morning,' I headed for the breakfast table but my mother was too quick for me and was on me like a cat on a kipper, patting and brushing me and straightening my tie as only mothers do. Then the questions:

'Have you brushed your teeth? Washed behind your ears?' Finishing with, 'You look very smart this morning.'

To my mind I was looking anything but smart, but who the hell was I? Firstly, I was the only one in the village going to this school. Secondly, I would be the first to get aboard the bus, for all to stare at as they entered and no doubt I would be sitting in someone's long claimed seat. Thirdly, my new uniform of maroon and yellow had not arrived, so my parents had the amazingly bright idea of sending me in my previous uniform, which was bright blue and yellow. So I had this vision of myself sitting in the seat like some strange Macaw, trying hard to make a good impression on my fellow students. To add insult to injury, the old man insisted on walking down to the bus with me. Luckily, my bus left three quarters of an hour earlier than the other school bus, which would save me from the pitiful looks of any future friends and acquaintances. So with a hug and good wishes from my mother, off we went, my satchel slung over my shoulder, empty except for some sandwiches my mother had packed for me.

The old man was clad in his clerical grey, his new dog collar gleaming in the early half-light of dawn. As we descended the church path into the village, I couldn't help but think we must look like the forerunners of some ancient carnival to some unseen observer. The lights in the windows of the houses showed that we were not the only ones up at this ungodly hour. Down past the Plough and Harrow and the shop and post office we trudged, man and boy with never a word between us and no sound except the wheeze of the old man's heavy breathing. We finally reached the little iron bridge at the bottom of the village, where the bus would turn for the return journey and although only thirteen, I thought to myself this must be some hell of a journey to leave at this time and get to school at nine o'clock.

Suddenly I could hear the roar of the bus as it rounded the last corner and with a squeal of brakes, rolled to a stop. Bidding a hasty goodbye to the old man I clambered aboard and with a clash of gears we were off up the hill.

The driver shouted to me above the noise of the engine, 'Bloody hell, old chap, I thought we would never get here. God alone knows how we are going to get here in the bloody winter, old chap, What in God's name made your pater move out here?'

I found out later that he was a retired army colonel, hence the old chap in every sentence. However, his last words cheered me up instantly . . . perhaps I would have every winter off due to bad weather? Shouting to each other, we managed to hold a conversation above the noisy engine.

'Your Pater is one of those bloody sky pilot chappies then, old chap?'

I confirmed this was indeed the case.

'Bloody hell,' he said, 'I would keep that to yourself if I were you; little bastards will give you a dog's life!'

Shouting agreement, he started to brake and I realised we were making our next pickup. This continued for mile after mile, on the side of mountains, down in valleys, at farm gates and little hamlets and lanes leading to seemingly nowhere until the bus was full. Thankfully, everyone seemed too preoccupied with their own business to take any notice of me. I observed that we were entering a main road lined with trees and there were lots of pupils clad in maroon blazers walking along it. The clamour in the bus was horrendous as we pulled up outside a grey stone building and I knew this was it. A general rush for the door ensued, which always amazes me. Whilst I can see the sense of rushing to get away from a school, I cannot for the life of me see the sense in rushing to get into it.

As I got off the bus and walked up the path, a funny thought struck me. This lot must think I'm going to another school in my fancy dress. On entering the building I was instantly met by a hovering member of staff and I saw his eyes flick briefly over my uniform. Holding out his hand he introduced himself as Mr Jones, Art and Woodwork.

'You must be John Elias the new boy? I'm to take you to our headmaster who wishes to welcome you to our school before assembly.'

I followed him down a long corridor to a door at the bottom which was obviously the Hall of the Mountain King. Jones Art and Woodwork knocked the door and in we went.

'John Elias for you, Headmaster,' he said and was gone.

Getting up from behind a large desk was a tall, thin individual with thinning hair and broken bottle glasses, holding out a long, thin, bony hand. I shook it to find it felt like a piece of old flannel and felt an overwhelming desire to wipe my hand on my trousers.

'So you are Elias! Welcome to our school. You will be going into the second form and will have to work hard; we are very proud of our reputation here.' He had this habit of spitting with his 'S' and rubbing it in vigorously with his clenched fist. I wondered if he would do the same to me, should I offend him in some way.

Dismissing me, he said, 'Remember my door is always open.'

I half expected him to say 'trap door', but that was the end of the conversation. Back outside I was confronted with Jones Art and Woodwork. He must have been waiting for the end of the interview like a naughty boy. We took another silent walk down another corridor until we came to a classroom door with Form Two on it, whereupon Jones Art and Woodwork knocked the door and entered with the words, 'Elias for you, Miss Grant.'

I found myself looking straight into the eyes of a middle-aged friendly looking lady.

Asking for attention, she said, 'This, everyone, is John Elias. John has come to us from two other grammar schools many miles away and I know you will all make him welcome. John, my name is Miss Grant and as well as being your English teacher I am also your form teacher for this year, so if you need some advice or help settling in, come and see me in the first instance.'

I glanced across at a sea of strange faces; some guarded smiles from the girls, either disinterest or hostility from the boys. Again that old feeling of, 'This isn't going to work.' Perhaps I had been here too many times before; too many times trying to make new friends; too many times answering what my old man did for a living, but whatever, I was totally trapped and would have to stick it out.

I was given a seat next to a lad called Brian, who seemed a totally cold fish, but told me he was on my bus and it appeared we were having a period of double English. Hurray, my favourite subject, but after ten minutes it might as well have been Serbo-Croat. I hadn't got a clue what it was all about and wearing what I thought was my most intelligent face, I managed to stumble through, nodding and shaking my head until the bell rang for break.

Heading outside, it appeared I had raised some interest, for a small crowd had gathered and the usual questions were fired at me yet again.

'Where do you live? What school is that?' pointing at my blazer.

One lad, stinking of tobacco, sidled up to me and asked 'What's your old feller do for a job then?'

Quick as a flash, I replied that he was a boxer. Giving me a knowing smirk he disappeared into the crowd, no doubt to finish off his fag. Funnily enough, we became friends after we left school and he went into the Navy some time later.

The day passed relatively problem-free and my satchel was once more stuffed full of literature to copy up. I boarded the bus knowing my worst nightmare, my favourite subject was totally different to anything I had ever done. Yes, it appeared English was going to be a nightmare.

The journey home was much more interesting than the morning one, with several people talking to me and I enjoyed the beautiful countryside we passed through, recognising several places we had stopped at this morning and began to put faces to the drop-off points.

As soon as the last pupil left the bus, my friend the driver started talking to me so I moved down to the front seat. It seemed to be the safest thing to do for both of us as he wasn't exactly a top driver. He was good company and gave me a good insight as to who could be trusted and who couldn't.

As the bus pulled in at the bottom of the village, I prepared myself to meet a gang of the local lads but it was deserted and within minutes I was walking up the churchyard path. I went through the drive gate and opened the back door and Kim was there as always, tail a-wagging and furiously licking. It is a nice feeling to be home at the end of a frustrating day. The place now had the old familiar smell of mansion polish and tea was cooking on the oil stove. As I opened the hall door my mother looked up from arranging some flowers in the big brown jug and, giving me a delighted smile, came with arms outstretched to give me a hug. I hurriedly ducked out of the way, too old for kisses and hugs now.

'I had a good day, Mum and will tell you both everything at teatime, there is nothing exciting to tell anyway.'

She told me that Dad was in his study, sorting out his papers and books. We both knew better than to disturb him and he was probably asleep now, anyway. I ran upstairs to get changed and stopped dead as I opened the door. My carpet was down, my books were all put on shelves and all my pictures, framed photographs and other treasures were all in place, but best of all, there on the bed lay my new school uniform. At least now I would look the same as everyone else and wouldn't have to throw a sickie tomorrow.

I ran back downstairs and gave my mum a hug and she told me how hard Dad had worked to get it ready for my return and to make sure I thanked him. I called Kim and together we went exploring the grounds, Kim sniffing everything in the shrubbery and me mulling over the events of that day. The days seemed to be getting shorter and the ground was covering over with golden, russet and yellow leaves. Standing there looking over the Cwm wood which was almost bare, I felt a cold shiver running down my spine and wondered how far away was this winter everyone spoke about.

I was still standing there in the silence, alone with my thoughts when I heard the old man calling, 'Tea's ready, Sunny Jim!'

Calling up Kim, we raced for the back door and into the kitchen where I knew the interrogation would start.

'Well, son, don't keep us in suspense!'

So I told them all about it. No, I did not make friends with the bishop or the archdeacon's son. Not even a lowly doctor or a solicitor's son. Other than that I told them everything they wanted to hear, but I didn't tell them that the headmaster was a total prat, that I was way behind in their curriculum, that once more I had a mountain of copying up and had no intention of doing any of it. Little did I realise how all this was going to work out and how much my feelings would lead me into a no return situation which would be just fine and dandy. But all that was to come along much later.

CHAPTER THREE
When the Saints Go Marching In
(Fats Domino)

Home from school, run up the churchyard path, in through the back door, kick the shoes off, never mind the laces because tonight's the night. Far more important than Christmas Day, or so you'd think if you'd been listening to the old man for the last few days. This was the big one; from tonight he'd be vicar of this church and another smaller church about three miles away. This made up the parish and he would be able to start his priestly duties with immediate effect. Great stuff! That would let me off the hook and I could wander at will and make friends with whoever I wished, that's if they would accept me in the village, of course.

My parents were sitting at the tea table when I got in. Also there were my uncle and auntie from Croesyceiliog, a little village outside Newport – at least it was then. Now it's part of the new town of Cwmbran and far removed from the little village of my boyhood, where the trees used to meet over the road and we used to play down by the Afon Llwyd. The river then ran black on the stones from the many works further up the mountain.

I was genuinely pleased to see them both, as they had always been good to me and I always spent some of my summer holidays with them. Shaking hands and reluctantly pecking my auntie's cheek, I sat down to tea amidst, 'Gosh! Hasn't he grown?' and, 'How's he settling into his new school? Doesn't he look smart in his new uniform?' All this as if I wasn't there, but I didn't mind, I was too busy cramming as much food down as I could so that

I didn't have to eat anything at the dreaded tea which was laid on in the village school after the service. Strange how the mind of a lunatic adolescent works. The old man commandeered the bathroom first, as you'd expect as he was Numero Uno tonight. Clad in his best dark suit, he had to go early to meet the bishop. I was last in the pecking order so the water was lukewarm and the towels all damp. Still, no matter – everybody was happy tonight, except yours truly. Finally, with the last bell tolling and the mantle clock showing seven twenty-five, we left the house and took the short walk towards the church, looking to my mind like a funeral procession.

Walking next to my mother, with my uncle and auntie close behind, we all entered the church porch. We were met by two smiling men holding the door open and escorted to our pew right up at the front of the church. Talk about royalty, they couldn't hold a candle to us that night. As we walked up the aisle I could see that the place was packed and I could feel the pairs of eyes, looking me up and down. As a youngster I always felt strange kneeling down and praying as soon as we got into church. My mum, for example, took ages so I thought in my small mind she must have a lot to pray about. I could never think of anything to say, only that the coconut matting was playing hell with my knees and I hoped that she'd soon finish so I could get up and rub them. However, I had a kneeler and I also didn't want to let anyone down so I stayed there, watching the choir girls through splayed fingers. I must have lost track of time because I felt my mother kick me in the back of the leg, and so red-faced I clambered back onto my seat. Trust me to cock it up, but fair play, the whole of the village must have thought I was the most religious boy they'd ever seen.

The service dragged on and on with hymns and psalms being sung with great fervour and I was extremely pleased with my kneeler, for I seemed to spend half the time on my knees. I can't remember too much about my father's part in all of this, because a lot of it came from the back of the church, but I do remember him having to lock and unlock the main door, and the funniest bit was when he tolled the bell. He did it three times and an old guy behind me turned to his mate and said, 'Oh well, that means the bugger'll only be here for three years, then.'

I turned and gave him an encouraging smile and he pretended not to notice me, but his mate laughed. Then on to the bishop's speech, welcoming us all to the parish on behalf of the village and, as it was last hymn, we were out of the door, with much smiling and shaking of hands.

Then it was down to the schoolroom, with yet more shaking of hands and proffered cups of tea, sandwiches and cakes. I, of course, was on my best behaviour following my parents as they appeared to be shaking hands with the whole county. Thankfully everyone must have thought I was small potatoes as I didn't have many hands to shake but they all welcomed me and showed an interest. I did however notice the local lads giving me scornful glances whenever they thought I wasn't looking. I knew the chips were down and all too soon I would have to prove myself.

Funnily enough, some forty-eight years later I was walking down the village with one of my dearest friends, who farms in the village. In front of us ambled an ancient gentleman en route to get his Sunday paper.

Calling out to him, my friend said, 'Hey, Bill, do you remember this chap? His father used to be the parson here in the fifties.'

Looking out from under the wide brim of his straw hat, he studied me from beneath bushy eyebrows.

'Remember him! I'll never forget him,' he replied. 'When he left here, half the village said Thank Christ for that, and the other half said he should never have been allowed here in the first place.'

My friend fell about, laughing uncontrollably. I never ever thought I'd left such a marvellous impression behind me.

However, I digress. The evening appeared to be going well and I saw His Lordship the Bishop heading my way.

'Well, John, the spotlight is very much on your parents tonight. But tell me, how are you liking your new environment? Do you like your new house? Are you settled into your new school?' He was a shrewd cookie, this bishop, but a truly genuine man, who most certainly had our welfare at heart. I assured him that I was fine on all counts and he wandered off towards my parents. A few minutes later I saw them both shaking hands with him and he was off home. I was now getting tired myself and my mother had also noticed this from afar.

'Off you go, John, you have to get up for school in the morning. Uncle and Auntie have got the key, they will make you a cup of cocoa and straight to bed.'

I walked with them through the village with my torch picking out the way. It was lovely and warm in the kitchen when we got in and, too tired to wait for a cocoa, I bade them a fond goodnight and climbed the stairs.

As sleep washed over me, I remembered the three year prediction in the church. I hope not, I thought dreamily. I really like it here. Sometime later I woke to hear voices outside and heard my father's deep laugh and my mother's whispered caution to be quiet. Lying there listening, I heard the front door open and relaxed deep in the bed. Trying hard to get back to sleep, my mind wandered through the events of that evening with its prediction of three years and I thought, sod three years; I hope we stay here for ever. As if in reply, an owl hooted its derision from the Larch tree opposite.

CHAPTER FOUR
Son of a Preacher Man
(Dusty Springfield)

The next morning was a struggle. I struggled out of bed, I struggled down to the bus and slumping in my seat, just grunted at my new found friend, the driver.

He quipped, 'By Christ, old chap, you look like me when I've been on the piss all night.'

'No, just tired,' I grunted in return. I managed to doze throughout the journey, between stops and starts and the constant racket from my fellow pupils. We finally got there and I scrambled out of my seat to meet the day.

After assembly I sat at my desk and thought, poetry . . . I can easily let this wash all over me. Imagine my horror, when through the door walked the headmaster. All around me I could sense everyone straightening in their desks, and I followed suit very quickly.

Sitting down at the desk he looked piercingly around the room.

'Miss Grant is away ill,' he snapped, 'so I have taken it upon myself to take this class today. Who is familiar with the poem by John Keats, 'Ode to Autumn?'

You could have heard a pin drop. I personally had never heard of it but, as always, the class swat held her hand in the air. He positively beamed at her.

'My father used to read it to us, sir,' she said.

I thought to myself, no guessing who will be head girl in a few years and wondered if she could recite seventy percent of the hymns in the English Hymnal, parrot fashion. That took skill, never mind John Keats. Two lines of that wonderful poem will always stand clear in my mind: Season of mists and mellow fruitfulness and, To bend with apples the mossed cottage trees. Well! Fair play; woe betide anyone sitting in the front row. He would have drowned them in spittle. To make matters worse, as he was trying to extol the wondrous use of the choice of words he kept repeating himself with such fervour I thought he'd rub straight through the top of the desk.

Thankfully, after ten minutes or so he was called away by a member of staff and, picking up his book he left, telling us to get on with whatever we were doing, bestowing the class swot with a beatific smile on the way out.

The rest of the day sped quietly by and it seemed no time at all before I was getting off the bus. On the way up the village I bumped straight into one of the lads who had been at the party last night. We warily eyed each other up and I finally asked him what there was to do in the village.

'Nothing much,' he replied, 'but we all meet up on the corner here on a Saturday morning.'

I agreed to be there. He said okay to this and we exchanged names. His name was Adrian and we still meet up and have a drink today.

Inside the house I made a fuss of Kim and was met by my mother and auntie. They were full of questions on how the day had gone and what did I think of everything last night? Telling them exactly what they either wanted or needed to hear, I went into the sitting room where the old man and my uncle were deep in conversation. This always happened when they got together, the most boring conversations I had ever heard. They broke off when I entered, both smiling at me and asking if I'd had a good day but I could see they both wanted to get back to it so I made my excuses and headed upstairs to get changed.

The weather was certainly getting colder and the mornings and nights seemed to be getting darker, also more quickly. Pulling on my sweater and an old pair of trousers, I removed the dreaded tie from my neck and slipped on my leather belt, adjusting the big sheath knife around my hip. I had been in the Scouts for two and a half years and was never without it, being invaluable when in the fields for whittling, making bows and arrows and all the things a boy could do in the early fifties. No one knew anything about assault, and wounding with a deadly weapon was practically unheard of in those far off days.

Having finished dressing, I sat in the chair by the window and contemplated my morning adventure. What would they think of me? I expected some stick about the old man but I was used to that and I was also keenly aware that I would have to prove myself in one way or another before being accepted.

Outside my window, across the drive, was a big old Larch tree which I decided I would climb at the weekend. I had learned my craft of tree climbing when living down in Hampshire and although a novice and also frightened to death, I soon forgot my fears and would climb both higher and more daringly than even the fifteen-year-olds after a while. I remember one morning my mother was giving the doctor some directions outside the gate and I was up this tree opposite. I was about fifty feet up on some very slender branches and showing off, I began to shout down to them. When they eventually spotted me I thought my mother was going to faint, but the doctor gave me a hell of a bollocking.

'Get down this minute!' he shouted. 'Do you think I haven't got enough to do without trying to patch up bloody idiots like you?'

When I got down, I got another off my mum, with a threat of telling my dad. Lesson learned: climb higher out of sight and don't show off.

A call to me from my mother to tell me that tea would be about an hour, stirred me from my reverie and I was down the stairs, collected Kim and out the back door in the blink of an eye. Walking around past the kitchen window towards the gate afforded me a good view of the old stone tithe barn opposite and I enjoyed standing there watching the cattle milling around the yard.

Tonight I heard a shout, 'How you settling in, then? You must be the Parson's son. Made any friends yet?'

I recognised him from the night at the school and asked him politely if he owned the land all around and if I could go on it. He replied that both he and his brother farmed it.

'Go where you like as long as you keep the gates closed and don't break any fences.'

I thanked him and he offered a word of advice.

'I should keep that dog up if I were you, though. This is sheep country and dogs get shot if they are seen chasing sheep.'

Assuring him that Kim never left the grounds, I thanked him and rushed in doors to tell my mother this information. She was horrified and said she would never take him out without his lead. Years later, I have seen the damage a wilful dog can do to a flock of sheep and would heartily endorse the actions they take, providing it's proven to be that dog.

There wasn't time to go back out so I returned to my room to read. I was always happy with a book and still am to this day. At this time my mother had loaned me some of her treasured books, written by an author called Jeffery Farnol and his tales of highwaymen, footpads, heroes and heroines were, and still are amongst my favourite books. However it was not long before the dulcet tones of my mother's voice wafted up the stairs with instructions to make sure I'd washed my hands and hurry up as tea was on the table and going cold.

Tea was a pleasant affair because with my uncle and auntie there, the emphasis was on them. I was only too pleased to sit and listen to the grown-ups chatter and tried to pick up any useful snippets of information I might be able to use to my advantage later. It seemed to go on for ever but at last the old man produced his pipe and packet of Digger flake and my uncle got out his Gold flake cigarettes. Within seconds a pall of blue-grey smoke hovered around our heads and asking to be excused, I hurriedly left the room with mutterings about getting my homework done.

There's marvellous homework is for an excuse. Adults can spot an untruth from miles away, but, just bring homework into the conversation and they're like putty in your hands. So off I go to while away a few hours until six forty-five light programme, when everything came to a stop in our house. The Archers, an everyday story of country folk. Mum and Dad used to sit there transfixed and I must admit I was a fan as well. Funny how at that age you can fall in love with a voice. I was head over heels with Christine Archer when she lived at Brookfields. I sulked for a week when she kissed John Tregorran and was quite chuffed when he got killed . . . in the series, I hasten to add! After it finished and left us hanging on a knife edge, I spent some time talking to our visitors and then, bidding all a fond goodnight I headed up to bed. To be honest the journey to school and back was killing me, but I knew I'd soon get used to it. Besides, tomorrow I was entering into uncharted territory.

Mum brought me up a cup of cocoa later on and I was still wrapped up in my book. 'Not still reading!' she exclaimed. 'Come on, son, you'll never get up in the morning . . . and don't forget to turn that light out or you'll burn the house down.'

I grinned to myself; in the first place I could have a lie in and as for the light, I knew they'd check it anyway.

It's a marvellous thing to be spoilt rotten when you are a young lad, growing fast and with the whole world stretching before you. I was awoken by my mother with a cheery smile and a hot cup of tea the next morning. Putting it down on the side table, she crossed over to the window and opened the curtains. The late autumn sunlight came flooding into the room and I closed my eyes for a second to accustom them to the sudden brightness.

Turning to me, she declared, 'It looks like being a lovely day, son. There was a frost last night so I expect winter is just around the corner. Still, we'd better make the most of this weather while it lasts. Now hurry up and drink your tea, breakfast will be ready in half an hour.'

After she'd gone I had a sip of tea and snuggled back down in the bedclothes to contemplate the day.

My first thought was, well, it was worth getting up at the crack of dawn for five days if I was going to be treated like a lord at weekends. Secondly, I loved the house and grounds and if I could make a few mates in the village, I thought this could be a pretty good place to be. The only shadow on the horizon was my school. Although I had made a few mates, I was not really enjoying myself. I had no intention of copying up all that work again, consequently I was struggling with the new work and deep down I knew it was only a matter of time before the roof came off . . . or as my new found friends who I was about to have the pleasure of meeting for the first time this morning would say, 'The shit would hit the fan'.

Throwing back the bedclothes, I jumped out of bed and into the bathroom for a quick wash, drying myself hurriedly, for it was freezing. I peered out of my bedroom window; although the sun was bright there was no strength in it and down on the tennis lawn I could see patches of white frost glistening on the patches of grass shaded by the overhanging fir trees. Rummaging through my drawer, I found a thick sweater and hastily pulled it over my head, then out through the door me, down the stairs and into the warmth of the kitchen. A few fond words with my auntie and I was tucking into my breakfast. Yes, I thought, life was running along very smoothly at this moment.

Draining the last drops from my second mug of tea, I gleaned some useful information from mother. Both the old man and my uncle had been picked up by the churchwarden of the second church he had been inducted into, and weren't expected back before lunch. This fitted in nicely with my grand entrance into the village. I suppose that people today think that I have the mind of a lunatic and are probably right. However, in my defence, being the son of the local sky pilot in the fifties had its problems, and years of experience taught me to take any advantage I could to avoid having to prove myself, or even worse, fight my way out of a situation. My mother's voice awoke me from my reverie.

'Well, son, what are you going to do with yourself today?'

'I thought I'd take Kim out first and then go exploring across the fields, Mum. There's a good stream along there and there may be some fish in it.'

'Well that sounds a lovely idea, son,' she replied, 'but take care and enjoy yourself.'

I smiled to myself for I'd learned long ago that a half truth was far better than no truth at all and I could always get lost and finish up in the village by accident. Washing down the remains of my toast with the last mouthful of tea, I left them both deep in conversation – sisters, eh? Crossing over to the sitting room, I was relieved to see it hadn't been cleaned yet. I looked around quickly and spotted what I was looking for; there in the ashtray amongst the stale butt ends lay two half-smoked cigarettes. I snatched them up and stored them in my shirt pocket, stealing furtively from the room, like a thief in the night. I thought, if pushed I can put plan B into action. There's nothing like shock tactics to get you recognised as an OK type of chap, and I intended to use every advantage I could to hasten my acceptance with the local youth.

Back in the kitchen, I called Kim and gathering up his lead we left by the back door and headed down through the paddock. Stopping on the way, I collected a pocket full of Hazel nuts, while Kim proceeded to pee everywhere. The nuts were now spilling out of their protective cases and were falling into the long grass, their dark brown shells gleaming amongst the frosted clumps of grass. It wouldn't be long now before they all disappeared, taken away by some small furry animal and stored in its larder or eaten with relish to add to its body fat in order to see it through the long winter months. Have you ever tasted anything as nice as a well harvested Hazel nut as it pops from the shell giving that sweet, milky, nutty flavour that you only get when fresh from the tree?

Down at the bottom of the paddock I called Kim and put his lead on and there in front of me lay the brook, large at this stage, meandering through the field, forming deep pools in its curves, ringed with tall alders, and all the while chuckling and bubbling over the pebbles as it wound its way along to who knows where. I looked furtively around for anyone but the coast was clear, so feeling like Livingstone on the banks of the Zambezi, I stole towards the first pool, with Kim pulling furiously on his lead, luckily avoiding going head first into its swirling depths. Hauling back on the lead and cursing him at the same time, I steadied myself and peered down into the water. Nothing. The pool was empty. I stared and stared but no matter how hard I stared, still nothing. Swallowing my disappointment I walked on farther along the bank, trying two more pools as I went. Still nothing. Kim had beaten me to the bank each time so I thought

I'd give it one last try. Retracing my steps, I came back to the first pool at the bottom of the paddock. Tying Kim to a tree just inside the paddock, I crept up to the Alders and easing around them, looked down. There, lazily swimming in the stream, were five of the biggest fish I had ever seen. They looked so close I felt that I could have just reached out and touched them. I stared, transfixed, as they seemed to float in the water surrounded by much smaller fish. I could see the spots across their sides and the yellow of their underbellies. I had not got a clue what they were but I knew I had never seen the like of them before. In my mind's eye I could see myself with bent rod, straining to land one on the bank, as I had seen the fishermen on the steps of the Trent in Nottingham do so long ago and a world away.

'Anything in there?'

I nearly fell in with fright. Looking up, I saw this little man grinning at me.

'There should be some good 'uns in there.'

I was stunned. Although coming fourteen, I was far taller than he was. He seemed to be sizing me up as his eyes twinkled from under the broad brim of his cap.

I managed a reply. 'There's a couple down there,' I lied, 'but not very big.' I found I was talking like an adult and my confidence was growing. 'Your land, is it?'

'Arr,' he replied.

I was about to ask him if it was alright to come on his ground when he asked, his eyes never leaving me, 'You'll be the new parson's son then. How do you like it here?'

I was about to reply when he spoke again.

'Well, I got to get going. See you around. Leave some of the trout for me; I uses a gaff, I do.' and with that he was gone, his tiny legs going like pistons as he rounded the corner and disappeared from view.

My mind was in a whirl. Had this really happened? Or had I had some ghostly experience? I ran up to the corner where he'd disappeared and gazed across the field. I could see for about a quarter of a mile but there was no sign of him. Kim was going frantic so I went back inside the gate to him. Two things stuck in my mind: firstly, the fish I'd seen must be trout, of which I'd only heard about and secondly, he'd mentioned a gaff. Well, whatever a gaff was, I would have to get myself one, come hell or high water. On reaching the back door I put Kim back inside and meandering down the side garden, I pushed my way down through the shrubbery, over the fence and into the churchyard. I hadn't been seen, so brushing myself down, I started forth to meet the village.

CHAPTER FIVE
With a Little Help from My Friends
(Jo Cocker)

As I walked down the path I could hear a tremendous row coming from what appeared to be the top of the village. The nearer I got, the louder it became and I must admit I felt a tightening in the chest and a slight feeling of nausea as I approached. However, I had one advantage; coming down the incline of path I could see them before they could see me. To the reader this might seem very melodramatic but, experience had told me – even at my tender age – that you cannot be too careful.

I could see several of the older lads were having a kick about with a football. This was where most of the noise was coming from and even to a seasoned swearer like me, the language was unbelievable. The rest of the gang were leaning against the wall of a cream painted house. There were about fifteen of them, both boys and girls, some of whom had bikes, and whose ages ranged from about ten to sixteen years.

As I appeared, there was a sudden deathly hush. I walked through the gate and, not quite sure what to do, leaned back against the churchyard wall and stood there waiting for someone to speak. I caught Adrian's eye but he looked away and I thought, you are on your own here, mate. They were weighing me up and I could see their eyes glancing over the big knife I had strapped to my waist. Except for the lad who was methodically kicking the ball against the wall, there was utter silence. I was just about to mutter, 'My name's John,' when all hell broke loose. They were taking no notice of me whatsoever, but shouting to each other:

'Shoot the liquor to me, Vicar,' while others were shouting, 'I'm a fucking parson's son,' over and over and falling about laughing.

My first thought was, what a bunch of morons, and I glanced over at Adrian, who winked. I stopped short of telling them all to piss off and began to realise this was some sort of bizarre test. Taking a deep breath, I thought, I'll test them now. Reaching into my top pocket I took out one of the butt ends and without taking my eyes off them I reached in again, took out a loose match, struck it on the wall, cupped my hands and blew out a long stream of smoke. The effect was magic. They looked from one to the other and most of them jumped onto their bikes and pedalled off furiously, looking as if they'd seen Frankenstein's monster. Even the dreaded football stopped. I took another drag and walked across to join the others who were grouped around Adrian, whispering.

'Anyone want a drag?' I asked, trying hard not to cough.

They all declined the offer, but the footballer came up and pushing his face into mine asked, 'Do you play football, mate?'

'A bit, but cricket is my favourite,' I replied.

He stared at me for a second then grinned and said, 'I'll have a drag, mate.'

I thankfully handed the dog end over.

Taking a long drag he told me his name was Clem and we still have contact to this day. He turned out to be a very good footballer which was his great love, that and motorbikes, and we used to tour round the local dances on our bikes checking out the skiffle groups and trying to make the birds.

He finished off the butt and went back to the football as if nothing had taken place and I turned back to the lads, who were full of questions regarding my past and we all chewed the fat for some time until Adrian's mum called him for lunch from the cottage opposite, so we broke up with promises to meet later.

Heading back up the path I was quite pleased with the way things had gone and I was soon over the hedge and back in my own grounds. Slipping down to the brook I took a handful of water and washed out my mouth and swilled my hands and headed back up the paddock and into the house, hoping that lunch would not be long. I spent half an hour in my room and heard the old man returning and at last my mother's voice calling me downstairs.

As the old man had been out, we were spared the usual Saturday fish or egg and chips, instead it was mashed potatoes and corned beef with lettuce and tomatoes. I hated salad of any kind so I stuck with the meat and spuds, thank you very much. Sitting down to a meal in our house always produced a conversation between the adults and I had been brought up to speak when spoken to at the table so I sat there, bored out of my skull, listening to the old man and my uncle going on and on about what happens in this parish and what happened in that parish and my mother and auntie equally as bad, rattling on about decorating and curtains. Finally they stopped and the old man turned to me.

'Well, Sunny Jim, what have you been up to this morning?' he asked.

All eyes turned on me as I related the story of the trout and the little man I had met in the fields. As usual the old man threw back his head and roared with laughter, pooh-poohing the whole thing, to which I just gave him the dead eye, but everyone else was enthralled and I chose this time to elaborate on my story.

'As I was coming back home I met a whole gang of lads from the village, who have invited me down for a game of football.' I finished.

My mother looked a little sad because she didn't want me to pick up bad habits and become a ruffian, but in fairness they had always allowed me to choose my own friends so I took it for granted I could go and everybody settled down to parishes and curtains again and didn't even notice me leave the room.

I spent the next half an hour in the hedgerow looking for a suitable forked stick with which to make a catapult. My last one had been confiscated by a miserable old get from the last parish who had caught me shooting at the sparrows in his garden and threatened to tell my old man if I didn't hand it over. I had bought some new cattylastic from a boy at school for sixpence and I had some leather from the tongue of an old shoe to make the bag with. At last I spotted a lovely piece of blackthorn. Taking great care, because the thorns are deadly, I managed to cut my stick out without any serious injury. I then became so engrossed in removing the bark, trimming it to size and splitting the tops of the two forks to take the elastic that I didn't hear my father shouting for me until he got closer. He came around the corner of the bush and right behind him was Adrian.

'John, this young gentleman wants to know if you fancy going for a walk,' he said.

I declared that it was fine by me so off he went, leaving us two men of the world to cement a friendship that is still shared today, some fifty-three years on.

That afternoon Adrian and myself set off across the fields and I told him about myself for a while and he told me about life in the village and who to watch out for and who could be trusted. I showed him the brook and the place where I had seen the trout, but he seemed in a hurry to get into the next field and finally said that the people who owned the land we were on didn't like anyone on it and played hell if they caught you. I explained about the little man and he told me he was one of the owners, so this made me wary. We got on really well and it was soon time for him to go home so we parted company and promised to meet up the next day. Heading for my house, I reflected that I was lucky to find a friend and was grateful for the advice he had given me. That night in my room I thought how fortunate I was to be living in such a marvellous place and my mind drifted back over the brief years of my life, the people that I had met and the experiences which I had crammed in to those few short years.

So now I had an edge on the locals and knew who to watch for; always good to have an edge. One thing I had learned from Adrian was not to split the catty stick, but to get a red hot poker and carefully bore a hole through each prong. This meant you could double the elastic through the hole and save all that binding. I couldn't wait for Sunday afternoon when the old man would be at his other church and Mum would be teaching Sunday school over at this church so I could stick a poker in the Rayburn. I spent the last hours of daylight searching for another catapult stick until I heard my mother calling me to come and wash my hands for tea.

Saturday night was when my father shut himself in his study and prepared his sermon for the next day, so after listening to the radio for a couple of hours and being rudely interrupted with the visitors and Mum talking, I went up and had a bath and read my book for an hour.

CHAPTER SIX
THE WANDERER
(Dion and the Belmonts)

My family came from a small village in the county of Gwent or Monmouthshire as it used to be called. My maternal grandmother lived in a village just up the road and met my grandfather when he moved up from Somerset as a young man, to follow the steel. They married and had a son and three daughters, of which my mother was the youngest. As with many families in the early nineteen hundreds the family attended the local church regularly, with the girls taking an active part as Sunday school teachers. After the First World War the oldest girls married local boys and settled down into married life, living about half a mile from each other for the whole of their lives. These two couples were my aunties and uncles with whom I spent many happy times as a child, and to whom I owe a tremendous debt of gratitude for the love and kindness they showed me throughout their lives.

My uncle, being my mother's brother, married some years later and moved away to a small seaside town where he sadly died at an early age. My mother, who was a Sunday school teacher, met my father who came to the village as a preacher in the mid-thirties; he fell in love with her and they married in 1939. My father took a parish in Norwich and my mother, who was expecting me, went with him, only to return to the village of Croesyceiliog because of the bombing raids on the east coast.

I first saw the light of day in a maternity home called the Coldra in a village called Caerleon in 1941, and went to live with my auntie and uncle at the highway in the Cross until my father got a parish in the dockland area of Newport. My first real memories of the Pill, as it was known, are somewhat hazy but some things stand out in my mind. We lived in a street called Bolt Street and just down the road lived an old drunk who used to call my father the Jesus man. Opposite was a pub called the Windsor Castle and there was a gas lamppost outside on which a boy had rigged a piece of rope and used to swing round and round. I used to watch him from the window, nose pressed to the glass and how I wanted to join him, but to no avail. One day a fight broke out between two women but I was quickly dragged away from the window.

I also vividly remember Dad wrapping me in a blanket and taking me outside on VE night to show me the celebrations. Everybody must have been pissed out of their skulls that night and good luck to them, if it had been today I would have been there with them. My poor old mum, bless her soul, was the most wonderful story teller and she used to keep me enthralled for hours with her stories of the Cross when she was a little girl. She told me of their Christmases in the snow and her memory was phenomenal, with so much detail it was almost as if you were there. My first school was a disaster, for my parents decided I should go to private school which they couldn't afford and which I hated. They were so proud, but I couldn't even get to read properly, never mind the rest.

I hadn't been there long, however, when my father was taken seriously ill and rushed into hospital. I wasn't told much at my age but I gathered he was on the danger list for some time and that his mitral valve had packed up. All this from listening to other people's conversations, So that was the end of private school and I was packed off to stay with my auntie and uncle in Croesyceiliog where I went to the local school and loved every minute of it. I settled in and the same teacher who taught my mum to read taught me as well. She had me reading in no time at all and after that I found it very easy and loved vocabulary and spelling. This opened up a whole new world to me and I will never forget the joy of reading Swallows and Amazons, Famous Five and Secret Seven books and anything else the school library had to offer.

My mum used to come out every weekend to give us the latest news, mostly in hushed tones when they thought I wasn't listening. Funny old things are parents, they play holy hell when they tell you to do something and you don't do it, with threats of taking you to the doctors to get your hearing checked, and then they talk amongst each other in loud whispers and gesticulating as if you were deaf anyway. However, I managed to glean from these weekly mutterings that Father was on the mend and I am ashamed to say that in my own little world, I hoped he wouldn't improve too quickly and I would be dragged away from my school and new friends that I had made. These friends were the first real genuine boys I had ever played with and they taught me many things, including how to swear. My folks would have been horrified at such rough behaviour, as they had done their level best to protect me from the local ruffians up to now.

But, alas, the best laid plans and all that, for one Monday there was a knock at the door and my mother was standing there with the news that Father was being sent to a clergy rest home to convalesce and she was going with him while I stayed with my auntie and uncle, if that was alright. It all sounded great to me; my only concern was for how long? Six weeks, I was told, which at my age could have been six years. So with this news ringing in my ears I sat back and pretended to read a book, while listening to the rest of the conversation of the adults. It appeared that my father had a major heart problem and that he could no longer take on the responsibilities of a busy town parish. The outcome of this was that we were going to be found a quiet country parish while he was recuperating at the rest home, which was in a town called Clevedon, somewhere in the West Country. They were going to be taken down by car on Wednesday and I was staying where I was for the time being. Grown-ups use some very strange phrases when it suits them. I pondered long and hard about how long the time being might be, before I was torn away from my lovely life and dragged halfway around the country.

All too soon it was time for Mum to catch the Jones bus back to Newport and I was given a big hug and kisses, made to promise to be a good boy and given a half crown for sweets and away went my mother as if she had never existed, with promises to write to me as soon as they got to the home.

After all the excitement had died down I must have seemed a bit quiet, for my auntie gave me a big squeeze and brought me a cup of tea with some milk chocolate fingers and I settled down to an episode of Dick Barton special agent on the wireless, then homework and then bed.

The weeks continued to fly by and I spent my spare time playing with the friends I had made. My reading skills increased as the more books I read, the more my vocabulary grew. My mother used to write on a regular basis to my auntie and she always enclosed a note for me saying that Dad sent his love and was getting stronger with every day that passed and that we would soon be all together again in our own home.

Before you could blink we had broken up for the last half term of the year. Bonfire Night loomed, just a couple of days away, and although I mentioned it on several occasions no one seemed at all interested, which even at my young age I found strange.

The day before Bonfire Night dawned clear and bright and after breakfast I went down on the lawn with a rake to gather up all the dead leaves, hinting to my auntie that they would burn well on a bonfire. This, however, seemed to fall on deaf ears. About twelve o'clock I was called up for tea and biscuits and kicking off my wellingtons by the back door, I burst into the kitchen. I stood stock still as I entered the room, for there sitting in the chair by the fire was my father.

He stood up as I came in and said, 'Hello, Sunny Jim, how are you?'

I felt strangely shy; he sounded the same as my dad but he looked so different. Also, he didn't attempt to pick me up as he always had in the past. Again, at six and a half years old I was far too young to comprehend the scale of the illness he'd survived.

'Good Lord, Gert, whatever have you been feeding him on?' he joked and turned back to me. 'Well, John, your mother and I have two weeks left at the rest home, and I'm taking you back to spend the time with us. After that you are coming back with Mum for a week, while I go ahead to my new parish to get the house ready for you, and I promise you that you will love it.'

It seemed we had just time for a bite to eat before a man called Mr Christopher from the local garage was taking us to the railway station. My case was already packed, which made me wonder how long this had been planned with no one telling me. However, a quick scrub and a change of clothes and we were off. I must confess at this time I felt as if I was being abducted by strangers. In no time at all we pulled in to the station approach and, carrying my small suitcase, we entered the station.

I will never forget how frightened I was when standing on the platform looking at these iron monsters hissing great clouds of steam and making the most horrendous noise as they pulled away, whistles piercing above the rest of the noise. Seeing my face, Father laughed and assured me that all this was perfectly normal and it was only the steam making the noise. Don't get me wrong, I had seen trains many times before from my auntie's house as they chugged along the floor of the valley from Ponty to Llantarnam, but these were miles away and their whistles seemed friendly. Dad suddenly exclaimed that the train was coming and I held onto his hand very tightly as it roared in with a tremendous racket, puffing steam from what appeared to be every orifice. It seemed to be never-ending as with a last hiss it came to a stop and all the carriage doors opened as far as you could see, with seemingly hundreds of people getting off, all rushing to some unknown point with looks of panic on their faces We entered the door into a long corridor and I followed Father, walking along until he found an empty carriage. Sitting down, I looked around. It had very nice, comfortable seats and two mirrors on the walls above them with GWR in gold written on them. Dad told me this meant Great Western Railway, but the thing which caught my eye most was a small cord up in the corner by the ceiling. It said communication cord and I supposed you could talk to people through it. My father saw me looking at it and explained that it was only to be pulled in an emergency and that if you pulled it for any other reason you would be fined very heavily. Not knowing what fined meant and not wishing to show my ignorance, I guessed it must be akin to being hung and vowed never to go anywhere near it.

Suddenly, all hell broke loose; there was much slamming of doors, men blowing whistles and I saw one man outside the window waving a green flag. The train gave a sudden jolt, then another and we slowly gathered speed and the gloom of the station was replaced with bright daylight as I looked out of the window to see the grey buildings of the town gradually being replaced with the different greens of the countryside. Dad settled back in his seat and lit his pipe. Taking out a paper from his coat pocket, he sank deeper into his seat, engrossed in the news of the day and I was left to gaze in wonder through the window as the different scenes flashed by. There was another world out there carrying on with its business, oblivious to me and my old man encased in our own little box like animals in a zoo, speeding through their world and leaving them far behind as we sped onwards towards the Bristol Channel.

The journey proved uneventful for the rest of the way with the exception of finding the toilet and being told never to flush it when stopped in a station. The other notable exception was passing through the Severn Tunnel which I found quite frightening the first time. As if on cue, my father finished reading his paper and folded it neatly away while the train slowed visibly and I could see the edges of the platform coming into view. The whistle blasted out and we slowed to a stop. A porter on the outside opened the carriage door and we got out and stood on the platform. Although the train was full, only a few people got off and it seemed to be a much quieter place than Newport. Following the signs marked 'Way Out' we walked passed the ticket office and out to the taxi rank. I noticed at this time how Father called everyone 'brother' and they mostly called him 'sir'. I was to realise later that the dog collar that he always wore prompted this, and that this small item of clothing was to cause me so much mental bullying whilst growing up. He gave the driver an address and within minutes we had pulled into the driveway of a huge stone and red brick house.

This, then, was to be my home for the next two weeks and as we walked into the large and imposing entrance hall, there with her arms held wide was my mother.

I honestly cannot remember much about the next two weeks except that it was right by the sea, but the beach was only pebbles and that Mum and I went on endless walks while Father was resting. Most of the people there were in their dotage and the most exciting thing was that they were all hatching a plot to get the owners sacked as the food was poor. Young as I was, I was amazed at all these Godbodies, all plotting to overthrow the managers. However, I added my threepennyworth by lying that my boiled eggs were never cooked properly. I was also bored stiff and missing my mates back in the Cross, so I was pleased when it all came to a close and saying another goodbye to Father, Mum and I boarded the train back to my auntie's for one last week.

CHAPTER SEVEN
Travellin' Man
(Ricky Nelson)

Here we go again, I thought. It was a Saturday morning and Mother and I were waiting for the train to pull out of the station. We were bound for Newport, Monmouthshire and straight through with no changes. Dad had left us early that morning, heading for some place called Reading, which I had never heard of. When he arrived, he had to go out in the country to his new parish and get the house set up for us mere mortals, who were joining him a week on the following Monday. Sitting in the carriage next to my mother, pretending to read my comic, I looked up from the pages every two minutes, frightened to miss something. The train gave its usual jerks as it slowly gained momentum and we pulled away from the station and into the surrounding countryside. This time we were not lucky enough to have the carriage to ourselves but had to share with two other people . . . a middle-aged business man who kept trying to chat to the other occupant, a very pretty and self-assured young lady who would have none of it. I can remember she had very long, stocking-clad legs and I was fascinated by them. I kept staring and staring at them, oblivious to all else until my mother spoke sharply to me and apologised to the lady. She just smiled and said it was alright and after all, we were only young once. I was quite sad when she got off at the next platform.

No such luck with the man who kept snapping his paper every time he read a piece. He got off in Bristol and we were finally left on our own as we headed up the home run. I felt as if I'd been travelling all my life as I recognised certain fields and little houses. I promised Mum that I wouldn't put my head out of the window, so she let me stand out in the corridor as long as I kept in view. Just a few feet up the train there was a window half open and I gradually crept towards it. Watching mum with one eye, I finally stuck my head out of the window. As I did, the down train came past at a great rate of knots and frightened me to death. I crept back in to my mother and buried my head in my comic and it was a long time before I stuck my head out of a train again.

It seemed no time at all before the message came through on the speaker: the next station we will be arriving at will be Newport, and I was helping Mum get the cases off the rack and out into the corridor by a door, as I had seen others do. In those days of manners and etiquette, the porter always lifted your cases off the train and assisted you down onto the platform, so as we stepped down, there was my uncle, all smiles and with a trolley to put the cases on, and it was no time at all before we were out of the station and back in the car heading for the Croesyceiliog and Auntie Gertie's home cooked.

It was nice to be back in what I thought of as home, because the place in Bolt Street was now finished with and the removal company had collected our goods and chattels and were on the long drive to Hampshire. I had been told by my mother that Dad would never be the same again, but he had mended well and had to have a country parish with no strain. Even at my tender age I thought he wouldn't stick that for long. He had always worked in the rough, mainly dockland, areas and thrived in that environment. Back in Auntie's front room with the fire burning in the black-leaded grate, it seemed as if I had never been away. After lunch, the adults were deep in conversation so, asking to be excused, I went down the garden and climbed up the Willow tree. I spent half my life in that tree. It must be long gone now but my name had been carved on just about every part of it. I would sit up there and whittle away and think my thoughts.

I had plenty to think about today. In a week I would be going into uncharted territory, leaving all my friends behind me and most important of all, leaving those near and dear to me, whom I had known since I was a baby. Not only my auntie and uncle with whom we were staying, but there was also my auntie and uncle down the road who had looked after me as well, during my early years. I had been told that I wouldn't be going back to school this coming week, but we would go up and say goodbye on the Friday.

I pondered what the new school would be like, what the teachers would be like and what the children would be like. It was too much for my small brain to take in at one go so I slid down out of the tree and back into the house. They were still at it, but my uncle had gone off to work at the local steel works. His shift this week started at two and finished at ten that night. I messed around up and down stairs, in and out of the different rooms; I was bored to tears, thinking about my friends and what they were doing up at the school, just up the road.

'Ida,' exclaimed my auntie, 'this child is bored to death in this house. He needs something to occupy his mind.' They went into a huddle, as all grown-ups did when they wanted to talk about you and after a few minutes of whispered conversation, my mother put on her hat and coat. Stating that she wouldn't be five minutes, she disappeared up the road.

True to her word, she was back in no time. There was another whispered conversation and she called me into the kitchen.

'I've a big surprise for you, John,' she said. 'I have been to see the headmistress up at the school and if you wish, you can go back to school until Friday.'

To say I was chuffed would be an understatement. Uttering my thanks, I tore up to my room and started to get my things together for the return to school. Never one to hang about, me, and as I lay in bed that night my head was full of the stories I would tell on Monday until, exhausted, sleep finally overcame me.

'Bloody hell, he's back!' shouted one of the boys as I walked through the school gates the next morning. Within minutes I had a crowd of kids around me, all clamouring to know where I'd been and what I'd been doing. Never short of a good story, me, and having all night to practise, I kept them going for breaks and lunchtimes with tales of derring do, in which I seemed to play a major part. Finally they drifted away and we got on with the task of enjoying ourselves as all children should.

The days flashed by and in no time at all it was Friday morning and a very subdued little boy walked through the gates of the school. I had been primed by my mother that she would be coming to fetch me at two thirty pm. The morning sped by and after we had our lunch I kept watching the door. Finally the door opened and in walked the headmistress followed by my mother. The headmistress was the lady who had taught me to read and I was extremely fond of her. Red-faced, I was summoned to the front of the class, whereupon she addressed the class.

'Children, you may or may not know that John is leaving us today to start a new life in Hampshire. John's mother tells us that in the short time he has been with us, he has been very happy. Well I must say that we have been happy to have him here. So I know you will all join with me to wish him every success in his new life.

I faced the class with my fists clenched hard to stop the tears and turned towards my mother. She was thanking the head for teaching me to read so well and as we left, the head turned to me.

'Keep up with that reading, John. You will never have to worry about your English if you keep it up.'

Back down the road to be spoilt rotten as my mother proudly recited word for word the speech from the headmistress. Later, when I was tucked up in bed, I got to wondering would I ever see any of them again? I didn't know it at the time, but the answer to my question was a very emphatic no!

CHAPTER EIGHT
Walk Don't Run
(The Ventures)

After all the goodbyes, promises to write, and soaking wet handkerchiefs, I found myself once more sitting on a train, pulling out of Newport station. My mother was sitting beside me with enough cases and bags between us to stock a clothes shop.

We had got up at the crack of dawn in order to catch the eight o'clock train and were due in Reading at twelve noon, where Father was going to meet us. So here we were, wide-eyed with the enormity of it all, off on our big adventure. My auntie had packed us sandwiches and cakes to eat in case we got hungry on the way, and we had comics for me and a magazine for Mum, so we were well prepared. It was by now familiar scenery to me and I was looking forward to getting past Bristol and a change of scenery. Luckily for us, it was a straight through train to Paddington, London so we had no changes to contend with.

Bored, I got out my copy of The Dandy and tried to get into the adventures of Korky the Cat but there was far too much going on around me to settle down, so I leaned back in the seat and studied the comings and goings of other passengers as they walked back and forth along the corridor. I must have been dead tired because I fell into a deep sleep and was woken by the carriage door sliding back and the monotonous voice of the ticket collector, requesting 'Tickets, please.' My mother fumbled in her purse and produced the tickets and I heard him reply, 'About twenty minutes, madam.' Jesus! I thought, I must have been asleep for ages.

Rushing along to the toilet, I locked the door behind me, did my business and splashed some water on my face. I tore back to Mum, half frightened that she would have disappeared, but she was getting the mountain of luggage down from the rack. I struggled to help her and together we dragged it out into the corridor ready for the porter. Mum left me while she went along the corridor to the toilet, I presumed to make herself look nice to greet father. Promising me she wouldn't be long, she left me with strict instructions not to let the luggage out of my sight for one second, so I stood there like I supposed Paul Temple might act, glaring at anyone who came near. I would imagine that anyone who saw me probably thought I was being taken out of a junior type Broadmoor for the day. Finally my mum came into view, and looking at her face, I knew I had been right. She was only just in time, however, because the boring voice came over the microphone announcing that the eight o'clock train from Newport, Mon would be arriving in Reading station within the next five minutes.

There was the usual shriek from the whistle as we entered the station slowly, then coming to a halt and immediately a porter appeared and lifted our luggage onto the platform. We heard a voice calling and here came Father down the platform complete with a porter pulling a trolley. I helped the porter lift the cases on to the trolley as my dad and mum were wrapped up in their own little world, for she told him he'd lost weight and he remarked she was wearing a lot of lipstick.

He greeted me with the words, 'Hello, Sunny Jim, I hope you've been looking after your mother. I've found you a lovely school and you should be very happy there.'

I thought to myself, thanks a bunch; I was quite happy where I was, but said nothing and away we went with the porter pulling the trolley, out of the station and into a waiting taxi. We sped across town to the bus station. On the way, Father pointed out the trams which intrigued me and those were the only working trams I've ever seen, except on Sunday school trips to the seaside. Getting to the bus station we boarded a number 9A bus marked Tadley and settled back in our seats while the taxi driver and the conductor loaded our belongings in the boot. Dad was in expansive mood, laughing and joking and calling everybody Brother and I caught several people giving him strange looks. Whatever they were thinking, I silently agreed, as this was a new man I was looking at and I thought it must be the tablets that everyone was talking about. Mile after mile we went and I could see that the countryside was very different to South Wales. The soil was sandy and everywhere was flat and covered with heather, gorse, broom and trees . . . mostly tall Fir trees and loads of smaller Birch. Dotted amongst these were large glades which were covered in bright green bracken.

The houses were different too, tucked away out of sight in the trees, with what appeared to be grass roofs. I heard my mother exclaim, 'Oh, Martyn, look at those thatched cottages!' and I realised that this was a thatch that I'd read about in my books. We trundled on, mile after mile, the engine of the bus lulling me into a trance-like state and if it hadn't been for the oh's and ah's from my mother as yet another beauty spot came into view, I would have fallen asleep. At last the bus started to slow down and the conductor shouted, 'Anybody for the Parsonage?' and my father and mother called to me that we had arrived.

We got off the bus and retrieved our luggage and I took a look at our new surroundings. We were standing on a long, straight road. Directly in front of us stood a very large, red brick house, standing back off the road, in its own grounds and surrounded by a high laurel hedge. I saw that to the right of the house stood an old village shop and a little lane ran down between them. On the opposite side of the road was the Heath, stretching as far as the eye could see. The cluster of houses that made up the village ran along from the large house into the distance, in a long line finishing up at the shop.

I saw my mother looking enquiringly at Father who smilingly pointed to the big house and with the words, 'We're home, my dear,' led us through the gate, up the path and in through the large front door. They both took their time looking around, as adults always do, but I did what children always do and raced from room to room and out of the back door, where the lawns stretched away into the distance. To my left was a small side gate and being the nosy little boy that I was, I opened it and found myself looking onto a large yard with a large building standing in it. I thought I must be in someone's property and beat a hasty retreat. Going back through the back door I heard my mother calling me and there, laid out on the kitchen table was a cold lunch and, in my father's favourite words, a nice hot cup of tea. I hadn't realised how hungry I was and demolished the lot in double quick time. I looked up to see them both looking at me and they asked how I liked it so far. I replied that it was super and Dad said he'd show us around the garden as soon as our dinner had gone down, so while he rested and my mother washed up, I sneaked out and relocked the back door. That accomplished, I wandered back in and went upstairs for another peek.

It really was the biggest house I had ever seen inside, with five bedrooms, a huge bathroom and separate toilet, which I was the first member of the Elias family to christen. For some obscure reason that fact will live with me until the day I die, and I can still see the powder blue walls and the big mahogany seat in that toilet. I walked from room to room upstairs, noting where my parents' room was and paying particular attention to mine. Dad had done a good job with my room; all my books had been put out and all my furniture was in place. I looked out of the window. It looked directly out onto the rear garden and below that I could see the church and another cluster of houses.

Father called me and I went back downstairs to find them both preparing for the tour of the garden. Walking around with them, my father pointing out this and that flower and telling us he was going to plant this and that soon became boring to a six-year-old, but I soon cheered up when he opened the little side door and pointed out that this was our backyard and that the big building was a long redundant stable block that was going to be turned into a church hall.

Looking around inside, it was really huge, with a large clock tower in the roof and a lot of outbuildings to the back of it. Walking down the cobbled back yard, he pointed out the back entrance which we always used from then on. The gate onto the road was a five barred gate with a small gate to the side. I thought, this yard alone is bigger than the whole of Auntie Gert's garden, both back and front. This started me thinking and melancholy set in as I wondered what everyone was doing back home in dear old Croesyceiliog. What would they think if they could only see us now, I thought to myself.

My mother must have noticed me getting quieter and putting her arm around my shoulders, talking to me, but addressing both of us, she said, 'Come on, son, I must get those beds made up, because someone I know is tired out and will sleep without rocking tonight.'

I must confess that after tea I sat in one of the big leather armchairs, listening to the steady drone of my parents as they discussed various things and soon I was far away, playing with my friends and sitting in that old Willow tree at the bottom of the garden.

Sitting on the sofa and looking around at my new surroundings I felt happy and hoped we would be staying here for ever. Father was puffing contentedly at his pipe and I was getting drowsier in this comfortable atmosphere.

At long last, my mother called me and after saying goodnight to my father, I went out into the large hallway and followed her up the stairs. I immediately noticed that there was no electric light upstairs but that candles were burning and casting shadows everywhere. Tonight I was too tired to complain and after a scrub with a flannel I was tucked up tight and promptly fell asleep.

CHAPTER NINE
With God on Our Side
(Manfred Mann)

Settling in the new house was easy, in fact we didn't have enough furniture to fill half the rooms but we managed to make ourselves comfortable. It was obvious from the start that most of the daytime would be spent in the kitchen. This in itself was huge and there was a very large stove built in to it. My father had found a large stock of cut logs in yet another outbuilding and this solved all our heating problems, We had three easy chairs around the stove and used to come in out of the cold and warm up in front of a glowing fire.

In the afternoons my father would light the fire in the sitting room and after tea we would go in and listen to the wireless. I used to listen to Children's Hour with Uncle Mac, then Dick Barton and later on either Paul Temple, PC 49 or Journey into Space. I remember Wilfred Pickles was another choice, not forgetting the nation's favourite, The Archers. When that started on the air the whole country must have ground to a halt at six forty-five pm. The one drawback for me, however was going to bed. At that age I was a little apprehensive of the dark and we had no electricity upstairs, so I was not a happy chick when, after reading for a bit my mother came and took away the oil lamp. I used to lie awake and listen to the noises of the house and wait for the goblins, gnomes and other such fiends to come and get me.

The week seemed to pass very quickly and thankfully I was considered too young to be involved in the rituals of the church with the new arrivals. However, I did attend the Saturday tea in the church and sallied forth with my mother and father to meet the congregation. After meeting all the adults I sped away to play with the other kids. At this time cowboys and Indians seemed to be the normal game, while the girls looked on in disgust. I was quite disappointed when it all came to an end, and my parents called for me to say goodbye, so with shouted promises to see each other soon, I followed my folks through the lych gate and up the garden path, home. At least I had made a few friends, but I couldn't understand how they spoke so differently to me, in fact everyone spoke the same. It sounded flat and burred slightly with no lilt or dragging some words out.

I remember some old codger saying to my mum, after hearing me speak, 'God, Missus, he vurry near sings when he got summat to say.'

My mother smiled back politely and I overheard her talking to my father about some elocution lessons, whatever that was, but it never happened and within twelve months I had almost lost my Welsh lilt and was talking like a local.

Sunday morning and I was called early by my parents and accompanied my mother to eight o'clock communion. This was followed by breakfast and I went off with my father for eleven o'clock Eucharist while my mum cooked the Sunday lunch. Then it was wash up the dinner things and into church for three o'clock Sunday school, back home for tea and back at it for six o'clock Evensong. This continued until I was fourteen and turned into a pagan, but more of that later. I was at that point possibly the most religious kid on the block and became a choirboy, having learned most of the hymns and psalms by heart. I followed everything with a blind faith and truly believing that the world in which I was about to grow up was a lovely place with no illness, no sin and no lies being told.

Monday morning and I was suitably washed, scrubbed and clothed. Breakfast eaten and with my new satchel slung over my shoulder, I climbed aboard the school bus with my father who, despite my protestations, told me he had to come today to enrol me. So, red with embarrassment, I listened to the covert whispers from the other kids as we proceeded along the road. The school was only a mile up the road so in a very short time we were rolling up to the entrance. The red brick building looked welcoming, surrounded by the ever present pine trees. Standing alone on the common, with its compliment of gorse and heather, it was a world away from the school I'd left behind, but I knew I could be happy here and I hoped they would like me We went in to enrol and my father asked the headmistress all about the school and if it had always been a Church of England school.

He then asked who looked after the spiritual needs of the pupils and was told quite sharply, that was the local vicar of the parish the school was in. I knew this needled him and in truth I didn't like the woman either, and resolved to keep well out of her way.

We said our goodbyes; he was going home to my mother and I was taken to the first form and introduced to my fellow pupils. Our class teacher seemed a very nice lady and her daughter, who was also in the same class, came to our Sunday school. I was told that I was in the higher part of Form One and would be moving up to Form Two after the summer holidays. It was soon playtime and I walked out into the playground. Horror of horrors . . . unknown to me, the school had not yet divided up with the older pupils going on to either secondary or grammar school, consequently the playground was taken up by lads and lasses of up to fifteen years of age. We smaller ones were confined to the common.

In fairness, this situation changed after Christmas and the school finally became strictly primary school only. With only two weeks to go to the holidays everyone was getting very excited as Christmas got closer. We looked forward, as all kids do, to presents and Father Christmas and the school party. The wonder of it all can only be seen through a child's eyes, before the onset of adolescence and the feeling that everything is a wind up, sets in.

My father and mother were also getting excited, but for very different reasons, the most important date in the Christian calendar. There were all the services to organise, the church to decorate and the Sunday school party to sort out. On top of that, my father had to go to a meeting in Winchester so he would be staying away for one night. With all this going on I was left pretty much to my own devices and as it was dark early, spent most of my time reading, as we had a school library and also a mobile library visited fortnightly. One great improvement was that we had electric light upstairs which my father had rigged up. God alone knows how, but if it had been today they'd have locked him up and thrown the key away. Still I was so happy I could go to bed and read to my heart's contentment. The weekends were the best of all and I had teamed up with a boy from school called Alan. He lived not far from me and we became inseparable He used to call for me and we used to go across the heath opposite and wander for miles, despite stern warnings from our parents.

It was a wonderful place to be and full of ponds varying from small to quite large. I was strictly forbidden to play near these ponds; however, boys will be boys and the Saturday before school broke up on the following Friday I fell in up to my waist. My friend and I had the bright idea that if I ran around for a bit my clothes would dry and no one would be any the wiser. So I stayed out for perhaps an hour in December in soaking clothes until I panicked and ran home. I remember my little legs were red raw where my short trousers were chafing me. Needless to say, my mother went ballistic. Luckily my father was out and I was put into a hot bath, but alas it was too late and by early evening I was sneezing and feeling ill. By the next morning I was no better and had a tight chest so the doctor was called. He diagnosed bronchitis and told me in no uncertain tones I would be lucky if I didn't get pneumonia. He gave me some vile concoction and said he'd return the next afternoon. Well, I was lucky but I had a fortnight in bed and missed the school party, the church services and all the excitement of the festive season. Eventually I was allowed to come downstairs after the fire was lit and the house warmed up and a young lady from the village came and sat with me when my folks had to go to church. All that fuss, I thought but when I got better my mum sat me down and explained that as a baby, I'd had pneumonia and nearly died so I had to be extra specially careful in future. If only she had known what lay in store.

Back into school for the new term, as good as new and raring to go. These were the biting cold January days of deep winter.

The crystalline white covering of last night's frost turned the heath into a wonderland, with myriad spiders' webs sparkling against the weak, watery sunshine. Blowing on your fingertips as you had seen the adults do, with the resulting tingle as the blood returned, all made you feel alive and ready to take on anything.

I certainly did later that day, for at afternoon playtime I was approached by a gang of the older girls. They teased me about my father for a little while and I totally denied any part of his belief.

The trap was set, for the next words were, 'Prove it then.'

Totally nonplussed I asked, 'How?'

Thinking for a minute, the ringleader asked, 'Can you swear?'

Like a babe in arms I took the bait. Could I swear? Of course I could swear, try me.

'Tonight,' they replied, 'on the bus, on the way home.'

The bus duly arrived and I clambered aboard. They were all over me like a rash and cried, 'Go on then!'

I proudly recited 'bloody' as many times as I could, followed by 'bugger.'

With this, they all moved down to the front of the bus, grinning broadly. We stopped outside my house and there was my father standing in the gateway. They couldn't get to him fast enough.

'Vicar, vicar!' they cried, 'Your son has been swearing on the bus. He said "bloody" one hundred times and "bugger" fifty times!' I stood there like a sheep nailed to a board, watching his expression change.

'Is this true, son?' he asked.

I answered truthfully that it was, and was led into the house. Looking behind me, I could see the look of pure satisfaction on the face of the leader.

My father wanted to know exactly what had happened and for some strange reason I only told him that I had been dared to swear by some pupil unknown to me. He appeared to accept this and after a long lecture on the sin of using profanities, I was sent straight to bed with no tea and no wireless programmes. As my mother brought me up a sandwich and a drink, plus another lecture on swearing, I thought I had not done too badly and that was the end of the matter. Little did I know what was in store for me at school. On arriving, I was sent to the headmistress's study. My friends from the village had been telling tales. I was told in no uncertain tones that behaviour like that deserved its own punishment. I was taken to the cloakrooms and there, in front of the whole school, was given an enamel mug filled with salt and water and told to wash my mouth out until it was all gone. After completing this task I was sent back to my class in disgrace. When I got home I told my parents what had happened and my father went up to the school that evening and played holy hell. On reflection and after having taught myself for a number of years, I just wonder would that woman be allowed anywhere near children today?

The village, its people and the surroundings were fantastic. I spent hours outdoors and teamed up with one boy who was a lot older than I, but very clever with his hands. He taught me how to make bows, arrows, catapults and dens very like igloos out of bracken. I had four wonderful years growing up. Unfortunately all this was to come to an end, but that is for later.

During my time there I had learned to make both a bow and arrows, a catapult and learned how to fire both with a small degree of accuracy; I was a proficient tree climber, beating many boys a lot older than I was and I had come to realise that I had a very good right arm and could throw a stone further than anyone in the school. So as you can see, I was well on the way to becoming a doctor or solicitor. I was also very good at getting my own back on anyone who deliberately dropped me in the mire. In all, I had become a devious little sod and needed a very rude awakening.

CHAPTER TEN
Going Up the Country
(Canned Heat)

I was settled in well in Hampshire and loving every minute of it. To make things even better the old crone who had made me drink the salt water had left, rather hurriedly, and been replaced by a very nice lady who was kind, but stern so we all respected her and knew how far we could go. The only thing left for me to achieve from the salt water episode was to get my own back on the little cow who had purposely dropped me in it, firstly with my father and secondly, with the ex-headmistress. One winter's evening I saw my chance coming as clear as daylight. We could either cross about two hundred yards of heath and catch the bus on the village green or walk about half a mile along a path through the heath and catch the bus further on down the road. The latter passed several gravel pits, some deep and others not so deep and it gave us a wonderful place to play on the way home, for even if we missed the bus we only had about another half a mile to walk home.

It was only a few months later that this way was strictly forbidden as some lunatic had broken out of Broadmoor and killed a couple of children, so this route was strictly banned. I, along with three other boys, had to stand up in front of the class and have three strokes of the cane for breaking this rule. This in its turn brought the dire consequence of no wireless programmes that night. Before this, however, I hatched a plan with my mate to tell the older girls that I was going for a swim in the last gravel pit along the path, on the way home the next night. This was a ridiculous statement to make, for in the first place that pit was deep, in the second place I couldn't swim and in the third place, it was late March and although mellow for that time of year, it was certainly not swimming weather.

That afternoon on the way home we hung about till the main gang had run on and sure enough, along came my friends, the girls. Fully clothed, I stood on the edge of the bank while they shouted, 'He's frightened!' or some such rubbish. My mate had a long stick and holding onto this I lowered myself into the water. Apart from it being freezing cold I was also frightened to death, but I needn't have worried for the stick broke and I was only up to my waist. Clambering out of the water we both ran for home as fast as we could. Running into the house, I was screaming blue murder that the girls had pushed me in. My mate backed me to the hilt and it worked like a charm, for who would deliberately throw themselves into a gravel pit in March? My father went up to the school the next morning and played hell with the head with the result that the girls were threatened with expulsion should they bully any more juniors. All square and they left to go to senior school that summer so I never saw them again, which was probably just as well, for me, anyway.

We lived about a mile from the forest and I used to go down there to look at all the dead animals hanging on the gamekeeper's gibbet. I know that it's not the best way to study wildlife but we were able to identify many species from these gruesome visits. Snakes, birds and animals all in various stages of decomposition hung there. Just on the edge of the forest was a water meadow with a beautiful little stream running through it where we used to try to catch minnows in jam jars with very limited success.

One morning I was playing outside my house when I saw two kids studying me. They had nice suits on and told me they had come to visit their granny who lived next door to us. Innocently, I asked them if they would like to go and catch some minnows to which they replied yes, so I collected my jam jar and off we went. We had a wonderful time and must have spent hours down there until finally we headed back for home. This again must have taken a long time for they were much younger than me and were tired.

When we finally got to the top of the road all hell broke loose. One man on a bike spotted us and rode off. Shouting, 'I've found them!' at the top of his voice. The next thing, this woman ran up crying and saying she was going to kill me. Apparently, I'd ruined their new clothes, they had missed their bus and consequently the train in Reading. She also told me her husband would bloody well kill me as well. Luckily for me, my parents arrived and calmed her down a little, offering to pay for a taxi and contribute towards the ruined clothes.

Once more I was sent to bed in disgrace, I think to pacify the people next door, but laying there that evening I puzzled how it was that someone could be killed twice and concluded that there must be some pretty clever grown-ups about. Needless to say, I gave next door a pretty wide berth for some time to come.

I had graduated from being a choir boy to the man who pumped the organ during my final years in Hampshire, with strict warnings of what would happen if the bellows ran out of air. However, I must say I did a pretty good job, and only saw panic register on the organist's face a few times. I got paid for it as well and enjoyed it thoroughly. I became a member of the Wolf Cubs and went to camp with them three times. I'm not quite sure but I think we went to a place called Maiden Early twice and another place called Chalfont St Giles. These were special camps set up for Scouts and Guides from all over the country and we had a marvellous time with songs around the campfire on the last night.

One Sunday night I was kept up late; this was a great treat for me and at last I was wrapped up warm and my father took me down the garden to see an eclipse of the moon. It didn't seem much to me at the time but I remember my father's words that moonlit night as if it was yesterday, 'Well, Sunny Jim, you will see another but your old dad won't. By the next time it comes around I'll be pushing up the daisies. I wondered what this meant and asked my mother, who told me he was having a joke and to take no notice.

It was about this time that my father went away a couple of times and left my mother and me at home on our own. I thought nothing of this at the time and the adults would have told me a load of rubbish anyway. That year we had a lovely Christmas and it snowed and froze very hard, so during the holidays we went across the heath and had tremendous fun skating on the frozen ponds.

If only I had been a little older, I would have realised that my glorious days in Hampshire were running out.

I was now in the big class at the school and everyone was talking about the eleven plus exam. This was still some fifteen months away but my father went on and on about it, asking, 'How was school today?' and 'what have you learned?' on a more than regular basis. To be honest, I don't think I was doing that well except for English, at which I was running away from the rest of the class. I came home one February afternoon extremely excited and rushed into the house with the news that I was going to be in the Easter concert. Both my parents were home and I thought took my news very quietly. I sat down at the kitchen table in readiness for my tea when my mother spoke to me.

'John, we've got some news to tell you. Your father's feeling a good deal better lately and wants to try a busier parish, so we are going to live in Warwickshire.'

There it was, just like that. I was speechless. Four years, which to be fair was a record for me. My father then spoke.

'I've been up to the school this morning and told them you will be leaving next Friday. I have found you a nice new school which you will really enjoy.'

I now have a saying which goes: There is no answer to that, which just about summed up my feelings. Looking back, I realise that although I was very young I had no option and I went back some years later and the only thing I was remembered for was trying to knock off PC Perfect the policeman's helmet off with my catapult. So I must have made a huge impression on Hampshire!

Looking back into my memory, it was a beautiful place to live and we used to make dens out of bracken, miles out on the heath. It was on this heathland I smoked my first cigarette and coughed for an hour. Here I made my first bow and arrows which, although clumsy and ill-made, served their purpose. Here I became a boy and enjoyed boyish pursuits, including becoming a proficient tree climber. As far as my education was concerned, I was top at all English subjects, Religious studies good, with everything else total rubbish, but being fair I was not pushed in these other areas. However, a few weeks down the line I was in for a dreadful shock and would have to pull myself up by the bootstraps.

CHAPTER ELEVEN
Blue Monday
(Fats Domino)

Sitting on an upturned tea chest that Monday morning in March, I was pissed right off. We were waiting for the delivery men to arrive to load the last few items on the small van. The main furniture had been loaded on the Saturday and was leaving or had already left that morning. It was seven-thirty and we had breakfasted and packed the last things away. We had said our goodbyes over the weekend and I knew my mother was upset although she didn't show a thing.

Neither of us knew what it was like in our new parish, except from my father's garbled conversations as to how wonderful it would be. I was not given to swearing a lot since the girls on the bus episode, but that morning I could quite easily have given anyone I met, including my father, a mouthful of my vocabulary. Making the excuse of using the toilet, I ran upstairs to have a final look around. Going into my bedroom only made matters worse. It was bare and looked like nobody had ever lived in it. Crossing to the window, I had one last look down the garden and hearing the roar of the removal van pulling in outside the front gate, I pulled the shutters over and put the bar across. I thought ruefully this was the first time they had been used since we opened them four years ago.

It didn't take long before everything was loaded and we piled into the long bench seat in the front of the van and, with a roar from the engine, the heath slipped away behind us and was soon lost from sight. The driver must have noticed that we were unusually quiet, except for my father, who was in a buoyant mood, for he started explaining how long the journey would be and the different places and counties we would pass through. There were no motorways in those days and very few dual carriageways so we were all stuck together in the van for a very long time, like it or lump it. After about twenty miles my bad mood slipped away and I started to enjoy the scenery as we wound our way up towards the Midland Shires of England, the driver pointing out different landmarks and county boundaries. I cannot remember a whole lot about the journey except that we went through Wiltshire, Oxfordshire and Leicestershire and into Warwickshire and with a short break for lunch and the toilet, the whole journey must have taken about five hours.

After the lunch stop I must have dozed for a while, because I woke with a start to hear the driver saying to my parents, 'We can't be far away now look, there are some coal tips.'

I took one look at my mother and her face said it all as we looked across to where he was pointing, to see the stark black mountains of slag in the distance and the pithead wheel standing like a dark skeleton close by. The countryside was completely different with no open heath land and all hedges and fences, with far less trees. The soil was a different colour, too; more black, and my mother said, 'Well, we might as well be back in the valleys of home, it looks exactly the same except for the mountains.'

I looked across at my father and thought, get out of that then, but he seemed oblivious to everything and carried on talking to the driver. We drove through a large town . . . no quaint little market towns here, I thought, as we followed the road through to the outskirts. Although the houses lined the road here, they thinned out dramatically. We then entered another built-up area, passed under a low railway bridge and entered a tree-lined road with semi-detached houses on each side and pavements. I hadn't seen a pavement for four years except for my infrequent visits to town and I hated them.

The driver could see his mate parked up just in front and pulled up behind him. Jumping out, I had a quick look at my surroundings. I can only describe it as town, with a capital T. I thought if this was my father's idea of a little busier parish, then God help him. I looked at the new house and thought to myself, how the hell is all our furniture going to fit into that?

Most of the furniture had been offloaded from the big van and I followed it through the front door. Taking a quick look around upstairs and down, I finally entered the kitchen which was tiny and I couldn't believe my eyes, for there under a table was hidden a bath; a white enamelled bath. I shot out of the back door and into the garden, which was all of forty foot square. Two men were digging it and stopped to shake hands with me, making me feel very important.

Gradually, more people arrived and were all shaking hands with my mother and father so it was obviously a welcoming committee. They took over the kitchen and made us cups of tea and gave us cakes and then as fast as they had arrived they disappeared again.

The removal men had by now unloaded all the furniture and even put the beds up, and were now ready for the off. As they left, my mother's last words were, 'Well, I suppose it will be dark by the time you get home and the heath will look beautiful in the moonlight.'

Reading her thoughts and the wistful look on her face, the driver replied, 'Don't worry, Mrs Elias, you'll soon settle in and if the people are anything to go by you'll never want to leave after a while.'

Being a cynic even at that age, I wondered how often he was faced with that sort of situation and had to lie his way out of it.

To set the record straight, I am in no way a snob and have no doubt been very unfair in my initial comments about my new abode. The only excuse I can give for this is that we had just come from a large five bedroom house standing in its own grounds of about three quarters of an acre, surrounded on three sides by heathland stretching away as far as the eye could see, which in turn was bordered by forest. Suddenly I found myself in a totally different environment with houses all around me and was completely out of my depth. The other thing I noticed was that they all talked differently and I missed the broad Hampshire burr. Once I'd settled down, however, I found them to be some of the kindest people that I'd ever met, the schooldays were the happiest of my life, and bordering the village was glorious open countryside with fields and coppices where you could walk for miles.

Back to reality and fortified by the tea and cakes, we started to make inroads on moving things around to my parents' liking, so we could at least sit down and have a rest and meanwhile, my mother made the beds up. It was now turned five o'clock and I was starting to feel really tired and I knew they must be as well. Switching the wireless on, the first good thing was the reception and we all sat down and listened to the six o'clock news. This made me laugh, for the local news contained nothing of interest to me as I didn't have a clue as to where anywhere was they were talking about. After the news I got up and put the lead on Kim and took him out for a turn around the garden, but spotting a gate in the corner, we found it led to a lane which ran along the back of the houses. It was still fairly light so we crept along the lane, with Kim tremendously excited, peeing on every blade of grass he could find.

Back in the house, I noticed how warm the house was compared to Hampshire. This was down to the stove in the kitchen which threw out a colossal heat, not only warming the house but also giving us gallons of hot water. My father had told us the coalhouse was full, and as this was a mining village, we would never go short of coal. He disappeared on some pretext and my mum was unpacking china, but I could see her heart wasn't in it and guessed she was homesick for the Heath, so I wandered up to my room and sorted some of my books out. Fair play, the removal men had done a good job and although there were no floor coverings down, all my furniture was in the room and even better, we had electricity in all the rooms.

I heard the back door go and my father calling me. On going into the kitchen, a most wonderful aroma pervaded my nostrils. It was the smell of fish and chips, a smell I remembered from my days in Wales when my father occasionally brought some home, but a treat I hadn't had for at least four years. I hadn't realised just how hungry I was and we all sat at the table in our new house and devoured the lot. The Elias family had arrived; look out Warwickshire!

Later that evening I needed no second bidding to go to bed and saying a very tired goodnight, retreated to my room. Although I had put my book out in readiness I must have fallen asleep as soon as my head hit the pillow. My final thoughts as I drifted off were, it is a nice warm house, fish and chips for supper and electricity in every room . . . this might not have been such a bad move after all. How fickle are the young at heart? What happened to all that loyalty? Never mind, I was sleeping the sleep of the just.

CHAPTER TWELVE
A Whiter Shade of Pale
(Procol Harum)

I awoke next morning in very strange surroundings and rubbing my eyes, looked for the clock on my side table. The clock wasn't there and come to that, neither was the side table. I jumped up in bed in a panic and then realisation of where I was suddenly dawned on me. Surveying the clutter of furniture around me, I groaned inwardly. No prizes for guessing what I'd be helping to do for the next few days. No wonder I wasn't starting at my new school until the following Monday.

Getting quietly out of bed, I crossed to the curtainless window and peered out. Across the small garden I could see the lane and immediately behind that I could see fields and woods stretching away into the distance. Both to my left and right stretched the gardens of the adjacent houses. Looking for a sign of any human being I drew a blank; the whole place was deserted and concluding that it was very early I decided to get back into bed, but a sudden urge for the bathroom changed my mind, so opening the door as quietly as I could, I tiptoed across the landing and into the bathroom.

Everywhere was warm and cosy, unlike the parsonage, where you had to jump around for ten minutes to get your blood to circulate. Retracing my steps, I saw my father coming up the stairs with a cup of tea.

'Oh, you're up,' he said. 'I was just bringing you a nice cup of tea.'

That clinched it. I knew I was in for a hard day. Asking the time, I found it was 7.45 so hurriedly drinking my tea, I got dressed and went downstairs. I could immediately hear a loud buzzing sound and looking through the front room window, could see the traffic piling up outside as it inched its way in both directions past the house. The pavements were also filling up and I could see people queuing up at a bus stop further down the road. This is a little different to Hampshire, I thought as I crossed to the kitchen. Dad was making toast and I asked him where Mum was. It appeared she had a bad migraine and would be staying in bed for a couple of days. This came as no surprise to me as she did suffer with bad migraines and after yesterday, I could understand her not being very well. Together we ate our toast and I took Kim down the lane while Dad did the washing up.

We started on the front room and I looked for the carpet square in the spare bedroom, making a noise, but being unable to help it. We finally got the front room done, laying the carpet and tacking the linoleum surround around the edge and putting all the furniture back as we thought Mum would want it. The trouble was that the house was so small and we had to move everything about four times to enable us to do anything. Next we moved to my room and finished that and then it was dinner time. Heinz baked beans on toast was the order of the day and we were getting on famously, my Dad and I. I really don't know if I was much help at my age, but I was a willing gopher and he seemed to appreciate my help. After lunch I helped him with the stair carpet. This being a straight flight, I only had to push the rods in as they had been left behind by the previous tenant.

Dad was in a jovial mood as he could see what we had achieved in a day, leaving only their bedroom to do as soon as Mum got up. I'm ashamed to say we had fish and chips again that night as my father had to go out to a PCC meeting that evening. I listened to my programmes, took Kim out and my father left, promising to be as quick as he could. He also said Mum was feeling better and would like me to go upstairs and talk to her.

Going quietly upstairs, I knocked softly on the bedroom door and entered the room. I was surprised that although there were no curtains up at the window yet, the room was quite well lit and then I realised that the light was coming from the electric light standards placed at regular intervals up and down the street. I instantly wished that I had a room in the front as well.

My mother was sitting up in bed and motioned me to sit on the bedside chair. She looked very pale and wan and I noticed her voice sounded weak as well. She asked me was I alright and if my father had been feeding me. I confirmed this and explained that it wasn't as bad here as I had originally thought. I told her that there was countryside all around us and miles of places to go for a walk. She listened to everything I had to say but I could see she was still thinking of Hampshire and understood in my childlike way. She asked me was Kim all right and getting his exercise and told me my father had said I had been a great help and he couldn't have managed without me. This was a great boost to my ego. All the time we'd been talking, I was itching to get to the window to see what was going on outside. Noticing me squirming in the chair, Mum told me to go and satisfy my curiosity but to mind no one saw me as there were no curtains. Crossing over to the window like a secret agent, I peered up and down the road. There were several gangs of kids playing outside in various places up and down the road, some talking in groups, some playing ball under the lights. There were both girls and boys and I thought I should find some friends here. My mother was interested as to what was going on, so dragging myself away from the window I sat down again and told her. I don't think she was much impressed with any of it and after some more small talk I gave her a kiss goodnight and went back downstairs to listen to the wireless.

I let Kim out in the garden about nine o'clock and about half an hour later, my father returned. After a quick cup of cocoa and some biscuits, I said goodnight and went to bed, knackered but full of joy when he said, 'Goodnight, Sunny Jim, and thank you for all your help today. I couldn't have managed without you.' At that moment I felt ten feet tall and would have swum the Channel for him. I climbed into bed and read a couple of chapters of my book imagining myself with the Famous Five on Kirrin Island before sleep claimed me.

Next morning I woke at seven o'clock to hear the rain pattering on my bedroom window panes and I got out of bed to have a look outside, but it was too dark to see anything much. However, next door had an outside light which was switched on and I could see a man unchaining his dog from the kennel. I love all dogs but had never seen a dog like this before. It was brown, stocky and very agile as it was continuously jumping up past his waist. Even in the lamplight I could see his muscles and noted his bullet head. Having put him on a lead, he disappeared out of his garden gate and I made a mental note to look at him in daylight. Having had a wash, I dressed and hurried downstairs and on opening the kitchen door, there stood my mother making a cup of tea. Nothing against my father, but it was wonderful to see my mother back to normal. It felt like she had been gone for weeks. Still, all was well with the world again.

Kim was giving me a welcoming lick and I told my mother about the dog I had seen next door. She paled visibly as I described it, saying it sounded like a bull terrier and we'd have to be very careful of Kim for they were killers. Having owned five bull terriers in my life, three English and two Staffordshire, I have to say in their defence that if brought up properly, they are the best dogs you could wish for and I have never had any trouble with mine.

The door opened and my father walked in, clutching the Church Times and smiling. It was obvious that he had missed my mother too and was pleased to see her back in the land of the living, which was one of his favourite expressions.

After breakfast I took Kim up the lane, checking first that the dog next door was back on his chain. Then it was business as usual as we set about the main bedroom, while Mother tackled the mountain of washing up that seemed to have strangely accumulated.

We had finished the room by lunchtime and my parents left me to my own devices afterwards while they argued which picture should hang where and what piece of furniture should be placed where. So, bored to tears with all this, I decided to go exploring on my own Leaving by the back door, I went around the side of the house to find myself on the pavement in front of the house.

I made a mental note of the number, one hundred and seventy five . . . at least I wouldn't get lost. I decided to turn left and walked along the pavement, noting the houses on each side of the road. After a short while they stopped and there was a patch of tarmac with a strange looking building at the far end and a large notice board telling me that this was Saint David's church.

I stopped dead in my tracks never having seen a church anything like it. There was no churchyard, no gravestones and no grass surrounding it. Puzzled, I thought this can't be our church, but deep in my memory I remembered the dockland church in Newport. That, as far as my memory served me, was the same except that one was red brick. Looking back at the sign again I saw I had missed something in my haste. It actually said St David's Mission Church and that told me this was the same as the Newport one. My heart sank because I knew instantly the work which my father had taken on, and I also knew my mother would go mad when she found out.

After studying it for a few minutes I moved on up a steep hill and at the top stood my new school, completely different to the school in Hampshire. It stood surrounded by tarmac playgrounds, a lot bigger than my last school but somehow I wasn't at all worried standing there, taking in the scene and knowing that come Monday morning I would be walking through the gates.

Finally, I retraced my steps back down the hill, pausing for a minute to take in the view from this elevation. Although the houses on my side of the road had the fields behind them, further on down I could see they developed into a large estate, while to my left the houses had rows and rows of other houses behind them and I realised just how big the village was.

Entering the back door of our house I could smell polish and food; a strange mixture, but it told me that things were getting back to normal and I had a good feeling about everything, happy in the knowledge that no matter where night fell on us, we would be okay as long as we were all together.

CHAPTER THIRTEEN
Johnny Be Good
(Chuck Berry)

The rest of the week passed quickly by with Mother getting better as time went on, and by Friday she was even up to coming up the lane with Kim and myself and around the big field at the top of the lane. She had been talking to our neighbour next door about the dog and even went round to pat him. His name was Bruce and he was perfectly alright with other dogs but was never let off the lead until he was in a field on his own.

Word had soon got around, however, about yours truly. One night I went out through the back gate to find about twenty kids there of all ages and sexes. They were very friendly and wanted to know all about me and where I'd come from, so I had centre stage for a while. They then told me about their own lives, and ninety percent of them had fathers who worked down the pit at the top of the road. More information to digest, but when I told my mother, tongue in cheek, she already knew, so that was another potential storm weathered.

Sunday was amazing with the church packed out to see the latest Godbotherer. The choir stalls were packed and all the ladies wore mortar boards on their heads. The Sunday afternoon classes were huge and I met a lot more acquaintances who were at my school.

Cometh the hour, cometh the man and sure enough, on Monday morning, accompanied by my father, I climbed the hill again. This time to be enrolled at my new school, which took all of two minutes and I was ushered around a maze of corridors by the school secretary and introduced into my new class. All eyes were upon me as I shook hands with the form master, a very severe looking man called Mr Green. Introducing me to the rest of the class, I was placed in the front row with another lad who introduced himself to me as Len. The lesson had already started and I sat back and listened to the master as he was showing a sum on the board and how to solve it. I had never seen a sum like that before and was completely bemused when he wrote down ten similar sums on the board and told us all to have a go to see how many we could get right. After what seemed an age to me, he walked around the class and finally looked over my shoulder. At this stage I was sweating blood and was expecting, at the very least, a clip round the ear, but he said nothing and carried on around the class. Meanwhile, I continued to struggle hopelessly until the end of the lesson.

During the milk break, I walked out into the playground and was met by a huge gang of boys and girls who showed great interest in me, where I came from and some of them asked me to meet up after school. At my age I found all this attention very flattering and my confidence was growing minute by minute. On returning to class we sat down to a double lesson of English and I was in heaven. I found myself streets ahead and loved every minute of the lesson. This finished, we had a lesson on spelling before lunch, where again I found no difficulty and was enjoying every bit of it.

Lunchtime and I ran down the road for lunch at home, to be met by endless queries from my parents as to how everything had gone that morning and what sort of people were they and was it as nice as Hampshire. Replying as best as I could through a mouthful of sandwich, I wondered what had happened to 'children should be seen and not heard at meal times'. It appeared to me that parents could change the rules whenever it suited, but we mere mortals just had to sit and take it. Gulping down my cup of tea I prepared for the return trip, not wanting to be late back on my first day, but I had plenty of time before the bell rang and we made our way back to the classroom.

Monday afternoon was craft day, a lesson I was not familiar

with and when we were each given a sheet of paper, a ruler and a rubber, I was completely mystified. Worse was to come when we were told to draw two straight lines at the top of the paper and to mark the top line off in half inches and the second one off in quarter inches. The only time I'd seen a ruler close to was when I was given six strokes across the hand for misbehaving in class at Hampshire. Today, however, was different. I drew the lines alright but had no idea how to read the ruler, and guess who was standing right behind me? Mr Green, who looked down at me and asked what I was doing. Seeing my embarrassment, he simply said to Len, 'Show him what to do, lad and stick with him this afternoon.'

Although grateful I was also red with shame as Len, looking pityingly at me, showed me what the graded marks were on the ruler and watched me like a mother hen as I carried out my simple task. As the afternoon wore on I found I was picking it up quite easily and was soon drawing diagonals and circles and thoroughly enjoying myself, when all too soon the bell rang for the end of school. Clearing up our mess and handing our papers in, Mr Green asked me to stay behind as he wished to speak with me. What followed was probably the finest thing that had happened to me in my school life, and made the difference in my transformation from a dunderhead into a reasonably intelligent human being. This form master was the finest teacher I have ever known; he knew how to get the best out of someone without ever raising his voice.

Once everyone had gone he told me to bring a chair up to his desk and we . . . or rather he, got down to it.

'Well lad, what have you been doing during your school life so far? Without putting too fine a point on it you've got Eleven Plus exams coming up next year and as it stands you haven't got a snowball's chance in Hell. Your maths are non-existent, you don't know what a ruler is for, or how it works. On the good side, your English is amazing and you are quick to learn.' All this with hardly a breath taken. 'Now lad, I think you've got it in you to do well, so if you will help me by doing some homework every night, I will help you to achieve what I think you are capable of. Have we got a deal?'

Nodding in agreement, I muttered a very quiet, 'Yes, sir.'

He grinned at me. 'Well give us your hand, then; we'll shake on it.'

This done, he told me gruffly to get on home and that he would talk to me on Friday evening when he'd had a chance to assess me further.

I headed out of the door and down the hill for home, wondering what it was about this man that could get the most out of his class without raising his voice, and could get you on his side with a wink and a smile.

The week passed quickly, for I had never enjoyed myself in school so much. Each lesson was a fact-finding mission and made me realise how little I knew, and how much I had to learn to bring me up to the standard of the rest of the class. The difference here was, I wanted to do well and prove myself to Mr Green, who in my eyes could do no wrong. Another bonus was that every Thursday afternoon, the last lesson of the day was library day, and I was in seventh heaven as the choice of books was enormous, with many titles I had never seen before. This class was taken by the headmaster and we had to make our choice of books very quickly as the rest of the time was spent on exercises, such as making up and cracking codes, or finding how the hot water system worked in your house. This was, of course, all good stuff for a nosy youngster to get his teeth into.

Friday afternoon came around and we sat in the last lesson listening to Mr Green reading a couple of chapters of Five Go Off in a Caravan. Being an ardent fan of this series, I was spellbound listening to the teacher reading to us and wished it could go on forever, but all good things have to come to an end and our last exercise of the week was to copy down the list of questions concerning the two chapters we had just listened to. The bell rang and everyone rushed out with their homework and their plans for the weekend uppermost in their minds, while I waited by the desk for my extra work. Watching the last of my fellow pupils disappearing through the door I glanced round to see the teacher watching me. Laughing, he asked me had I ever heard of the Famous Five. I replied that I had about six books at home.

'Well lad,' he said, 'I expect you can do that bit of homework standing on your head, but this is what I want you to concentrate on this weekend. We have a few months to get you up to scratch before the build up to your exams and then it will be too late, so have a look at this.'

I gazed down in dismay to see a sum headed Long Multiplication and another one headed Long Division at the top of the page. Underneath was an example of how to do them and below again a list of ten sums of each type.

'Now lad, I want you to study these and have a go at them on your own and we'll have a look together on Monday.'

Thanking him profusely, I left the room and clutching my two assignments, headed out through the playground and down the hill.

Halfway down the hill I spotted two girls who were hanging around a bend in the school wall and to my dismay were obviously waiting for me. I must have been as red as a beetroot as I approached them and recognised them from the playground. We walked down the road together and they told me they lived opposite my house and asked me if I was coming out after tea, to which I replied that I might. This seemed to satisfy them as they wished me goodbye and disappeared into their houses. After they had gone, I realised that although they seemed to know my name I didn't have a clue as to either of theirs.

Sitting down to tea later, I asked, 'Can I go out for an hour after tea, please? Some friends from school have asked me to spend some time with them and I will only be outside the gate.'

Parents always seem to take forever in answering a question, especially when they know you're hanging on your every word. Finally, my mother replied that as long as they were nice boys she had no objection and with a final warning to be 'Back in the house by seven thirty' I hurriedly left the table before she could change her mind. I didn't know it at the time, but I was about to embark on the first long time romance of my life. If I had known then what I know now in my Autumn years, I would have probably stayed in the house and never gone out again. But there are many if only's in life and believe me when I say I've had my share of them; I most certainly have.

CHAPTER FOURTEEN
Let the Four Winds Blow
(Fats Domino)

Despite my outward calm I was churning up inside and having second thoughts as I sat in my bedroom filling in the questionnaire on the Famous Five. The man was bang on when he said I could do it standing on my head, and I thought I would leave the arithmetic until the morning. It's not that I was anxious or anything (not much I wasn't), but I kept going across to the bedroom window to see if the girls had come out yet.

Kim had been for his walk earlier with Mum so I was just killing time and unable to concentrate on anything. Going downstairs and into the front room, I found both my parents reading. The light was on as it was just getting dusk but the evenings were drawing out quickly now and before long the clocks would be going on and spring would be here.

Looking up from her magazine, my mother questioned me. 'I thought you were going out for a while, John?'

I replied that I was in a minute and glanced outside again. There, sitting on our wall were the girls, waving to me as bold as brass. I quickly drew the curtains across and in answer to my parent's startled look, explained that anyone could look in while passing on the road. This seemed to suffice for they thanked me and settled back down to their reading, while I made a quick exit out of the back door. The street lights were on as I walked down the front path and everything looked an orangey colour. The girls looked as if they were suffering from a bout of jaundice and I must have looked the same to them.

The lights had only been changed a week ago and were a different colour to the old ones which gave off a brilliant white light, while the new ones were supposed to be better for motorists, or so my father had told me, and he was supposed to know everything.

The girls chorused, 'Hello, John,' and made room for me on the wall.

The one thing about these lights, I thought, was it didn't matter if I was red, blue or green; no one would notice. Tactfully not sitting down, I made the excuse that I had to check the church notice board, so together we walked down to the church. After pretending to study the notice board I sat down on the wall accompanied by the girls, who by now had introduced themselves as Alice and Belinda. Alice was blonde with a long plait in her hair and very pretty, while Bell, as she liked to be called was the opposite, with long, dark hair. They asked me where I had come from and what it was like, which by now I could recite parrot fashion, but now I had lost my shyness and told them stirring tales of derring do carried out by my gang in the forests of Hampshire. This must have greatly impressed them for they both edged closer and I felt like the King of the May sitting on that wall. Funny how time flies when you're enjoying yourself, and it seemed no time at all when they told me, reluctantly, that they must go. Alice said her mother was coming down the next day, while Bell had to go shopping so we promised to meet in the back lane on Sunday in the late afternoon. Feeling a giant amongst men, I walked the few yards home with them and stepped up my garden path with my chest expanding fit to burst. My parents were listening to the wireless when I got in and so I went into the kitchen and sat by the fire with my book, trying hard to concentrate, but it was Alice's face that was on my pillow when I fell asleep that night.

The next morning, it was pouring with rain when I got up and went down for my breakfast. That finished, I struggled into my old coat and put Kim on his lead. We went for a quick walk around the field and were both glad to get back in the house. I took off my wet clothes and while mother was drying Kim, off I went up to the toilet and emerging, crossed on impulse to my parents' room. Looking through their window I could see the house across the road and who should be looking across at me from the upstairs window, but Alice. Taking a deep breath I looked across at her, not sure if she could see me, and sure enough she waved. Feeling like the hero in one of my books I waved back and nearly fell over when she waved again, blew me a kiss and disappeared from view. I must have waited there for at least half an hour but she did not appear again so with my heart beating wildly in my chest, I went back downstairs to see if my comic had been delivered.

My father had gone out on church business and my mother was too busy with her polishing to talk to me, so feeling somewhat at a loss I got my maths homework out and sat at the kitchen table deep in concentration. After studying the methods shown I had a go at the first sum on a scrap piece of paper, and after a few attempts managed what I hoped was the right solution. It must have taken me a long time, for the next thing I knew Mother was asking me to clear away my stuff because my father would be home soon and she wanted to set the table for lunch.

Taking my papers back upstairs, I had a quick look through the front window but there was no sign of anyone about across the road. After lunch, my father always had a nap in the chair and I took the opportunity of showing him what I had done towards my homework. He studied it and got out his pen, showing me where I had gone wrong on some of them. I could see my mistakes and understood them but he then wanted to show me his way of doing them. Flatly refusing his kind offer, he got the hump and I stalked off in high dudgeon to my room to correct my mistakes

Looking out of my bedroom window, I saw the weather had cleared and went downstairs, pulled on my wellingtons and went out through the back gate. Wandering across the back lane, I ran into a couple of lads from school and we got chatting. They were going across the fields to a wood to look for nests and I joined them. We seemed to trudge for miles across field and scrub, past pools and small plantations until we finally came to the wood.

This wood was totally different from Hampshire and full of deciduous trees standing in a square, almost as if it had been grown there to order. It was also fenced all around and looked strangely foreboding with its bare branches reaching towards the sky, reminding me of the wild wood in The Wind in the Willows. Climbing the fence, we entered the wood, trudging through last year's leaves and Beech mast lying deep on the floor. The drips from the morning's heavy rain ran down our necks and looking up, I could see a faint smudge of green as the new buds of spring were breaking through. Except for the noise we were making underfoot there was complete silence. My companions must have felt the same as they suggested it was too early yet and it was with some relief that we climbed back over the fence into the safety of the open country. I spotted a rabbit burrow on the way back and noticed that the soil scrape was a completely different colour to Hampshire and was almost black.

All the way home it was boys' talk and I asked where I could get some catapult elastic. This got them going and they asked if I could make one. Having assured them that I could, they left me by my gate with promises to find some elastic. That little statement got me a lot of respect and a lot of bad press with some of the parents, forbidding their offspring to have anything to do with me. When I got to school on Monday morning there were several boys asking me to make them a catapult. Word must have got around or somebody had complained, for in assembly on Wednesday morning we got a lecture from the headmaster on the dangers of using such weapons with a further threat that if anyone brought one into school there would be very serious action taken. Amazing how, from one innocent remark, you can be seen one minute as a nice little boy and the next as the devil incarnate.

However, I am getting ahead of myself, for after Sunday school I hung around the back lane waiting for the girls and finally they appeared. Once again we talked for ages but I kept stealing surreptitious glances at Alice. After a while they both had to go for tea so we said goodbye. Back in the house, it was shoes off and straight upstairs to the loo, back to the bedroom window and there was Alice, waving. I got another kiss blown and she was gone again, leaving me to my boyish dreams, only to be rudely interrupted by my mother calling me to wash my hands as tea was on the table.

Sunday being Sunday, I might just as well not have existed for most of the day and apart from the routine of the services, I was left completely to my own devices. At a loss of what to do, I managed to get my bike out of the clutter of the shed and took it out to the back lane. Up and down I pedalled, slowly at first and gradually speeding up until, sure enough, I hit a patch of black mud and straight over the handle bars I went. I lay there for a couple of minutes wondering what the hell had happened to me, and then the pain kicked in from my right ankle and also my right knee. Looking down, I was horrified to see my Sunday suit was covered in black mud and green algae from the post I had hit on the way down. Scrambling to my feet in a panic, I felt the pain in my left leg as I straightened up and put some weight on it. I picked up the bike but couldn't push it as the front wheel was buckled, so lifting it off the ground I headed for home as best as I could, all the time wondering what the folks would have to say. I got through the gate somehow and threw the bike against the hedge, limping in through the back door.

Mum was in the kitchen and taking one look at me, cried, 'John! Whatever have you been doing?'

I must have looked a pretty sight because, unknown to me, I had grazed my forehead and my hand in the fall so I had blood everywhere. Replying that I had skidded on some mud and fallen off my bike, she was all over me, checking for serious injuries of which I'm happy to say there were none.

Iodine seemed to be the order of the day in those far off times, designed to give maximum discomfort when applied, as if you weren't suffering enough anyway. But Iodine it was, like it or lump it, and when she saw my suit I thought she would throw a fit, but she took it away before my father saw it, muttering that she would clean it somehow. In my dressing gown, I limped into the front room where my father was smoking his pipe.

'Good Lord, Sunny Jim!' he exclaimed. 'What the devil have you been up to?'

Tongue in cheek, I told him and if looks could kill I would have dropped dead on the spot. I wondered tentatively if tonight's sermon would be, 'If you do as much to these my little ones, even so you do it unto me,' but he suddenly calmed down and I thought, wait until you see the bike. Needless to say, I was in the doghouse no matter how grave my injuries might be, and all because my mother couldn't go to church that evening but had to stay home and look after me. For my part, I thought it best if I sat quietly and said nothing, but in the end my resolve broke and I stood up and took a few steps to see what the damage was. Fortunately, although stiff, it was not too bad and I limped upstairs to the toilet, checking the bedroom window on the way. Coming back downstairs I saw that my mother had made me a sandwich and a cup of tea. Having eaten and drunk my fill, I decided to have an early night but in truth, decided to get out of the way before my father came home. Finishing off my homework, I put the light out and was soon fast asleep.

The next morning my mother woke me to see if I was well enough to go to school, and apart from my knee and ankle being stiff I was fine and dandy and would milk it to the end with my new-found girlfriends. Looking in the mirror I had quite a shock, however, for I had a big bruise on my forehead and a nasty scrape. Being the devious little shit that I was, my brain was already working out what mileage I could get from these injuries.

The girls were waiting for me and were obviously concerned, but I passed it off with the dubious tale of how if it hadn't been for my avoiding action, some mysterious child would have been badly hurt. This got around in a matter of minutes and I became the hero of the day, limping around the place like some demented Douglas Bader.

During the second lesson, which was writing, I was called up to Mr Green's desk and he produced the homework I had handed in earlier. Grinning at me, he told me to learn to duck in future and pointed out where I'd made a few mistakes. He told me well done and he would give me some more later on in the week. I was really pleased and for once in my life wished school would go on for ever, but also realised that we would be breaking up the following Friday for the Easter holidays.

After school finished, the girls were waiting down the road and we walked home together. Bell reached home first and shouting, 'See you later!' disappeared around the corner of her house.

Alice and I walked the few yards further on and as I left to cross the road, she pressed a piece of paper into my hand and with a hurried 'Bye!' ran up the path to her door.

Stuffing the paper hurriedly into my trouser pocket I walked, whistling, up to my back door. Mother was standing by the stove as I entered, making a cup of tea.

'Who were those two girls you walked home with, John?' she asked me and followed up with, 'Do they come to our church?'

Muttering that they were just two girls from school and that they went to Chapel didn't seem to go down that well, but it seemed better than saying they were not practising.

'Well you seem to be spending a lot of time with them,' she replied and I noticed a twinkle in her eyes.

I said nothing but went upstairs to wash my hands and change out of my school clothes. Hurrying into my bedroom, I pulled the piece of paper from my pocket and scanned it quickly. Written in a large, bold script were the words, Will you be my boyfriend? And underneath, I love you, with a load of kisses. Heart beating wildly, I stuffed it back in my pocket and crossed to my parents' window and there she was. I could even see her smiling from that distance. Blowing her a kiss, I hurried downstairs, completely hooked, head over heels . . . whatever. As I sat down my mother smiled sweetly.

'Your young lady across the road has been waving to you,' she laughed. 'You should ask her over to tea one evening.

God! There often were times when I hated supercilious, know-all grown-ups with a vengeance. But come what may, nothing could mar my mood for I was in love, me, and nothing but nothing would be allowed to come between Alice and me. There is a wonderful feeling of being in love at the tender age of ten and a half. I must have already been planning the wedding and how many children we would have. Oh, the innocence of youth, so soon to be swept away, followed by a torrent of lust and lies and jealousy, matrimonial disasters and whatever else, but the time was now and I was in love, me, and nothing but nothing would be allowed to come between Alice and me.

CHAPTER FIFTEEN
HERE COMES SUMMER
(Jerry Keller)

That evening I was in a quandary as to how to play it when I met the girls. Not wanting to upset Belinda and also ruin a good friendship, which they had obviously shared for a long time before I came on the scene, I decided to play it cool and say nothing and see what happened.

However, it was a very nervous young chap who walked down the path to meet them both that evening. Bell was full of bounce but Alice was quieter than usual as we sat on the church wall and discussed the day's happenings.

This continued for about half an hour until Belinda finally said, 'My friend here tells me she really likes you and wants to know will you be her boyfriend?'

I went bright red and wished the earth would open up and swallow me, but found them both gazing at me intently. There was obviously no escape from this situation so, clearing my throat, I replied that I would love to be her boyfriend as I thought she was beautiful, but not at the risk of losing Bell's friendship.

Bell replied instantly to this with, 'Well go on, give her a kiss, then.'

Oh, the innocence of youth! Screwing up my courage and with my eyes tightly shut, she was in my arms and I tried hard to remember how they did it in the few films I had been fortunate enough to see, and gave her my interpretation of a full-blown Hollywood forties-style kiss. This operation took quite some time and we finally broke apart, breathless, and with Bell clapping delightedly by our side. This kiss seemed to seal the bargain as from then on, Alice always held my hand which in turn made me feel a prince among men, with most of the boys in our class becoming extremely jealous.

I well remember those far off days with the evenings lengthening and the gardens echoing to the sound of the lawnmower. The lime trees that lined our side of the road were full of the noisy chirping of the tree sparrows nesting in their uppermost branches and everything seemed to be wearing its new spring coat. Alice and I were inseparable and wandered for miles over the fields, wrapped up in each other with the innocence of first love. As her mother came to visit every other weekend, I spent these times with my friends, bird nesting and making various weapons of one sort or another, or talking about sex which none of us knew anything about.

School was also going well and thanks to Mr Green I had caught up by the summer holidays and was really enjoying my class work. There was one small cloud on the horizon, however, for when I took my school report home that summer, despite glowing reports from my beloved form master, the headmaster in his summing up had written: John needs to concentrate and pay more attention if he wishes to succeed in his eleven plus exams.

I really owed him one; after all the work I had done, all I heard that summer was, 'If you don't pass, you are going to boarding school', or 'Don't think I'm having you in that secondary modern up the road!' Talk about snobbery and class distinction, I was ashamed to hear them carrying on.

Before we knew it, the corn harvest arrived and the fields were a rich golden brown, seeming as if the whole field was moving as the ears of corn swayed with the breeze. Alice and I used to walk around the edges of the field and watch the binder as the corn fell like so many soldiers beneath its blades. No combine harvesters in those days, with the men of the village gathering around the perimeter of the field with every gun imaginable, to watch for the rabbits as the last square of corn was cut. No myxomatosis either to invade the fields with its sickening symptoms.

That summer was a marvellous time for me, as a boy growing

up. Although we were only kids, we had that innocence and really enjoyed each other's company, going to the matinee performance on the occasional Saturday afternoon and generally sharing each other's company as often as possible. I remember when the Coronation was taking place, Alice had gone to stay with her mother in Coventry and although there was plenty going on with parades and parties, I felt completely lost and went home early, much to my parents' amazement.

There is a saying that all good things must come to an end and the person who wrote it must have had me in mind, for all too soon the holiday came to an end and it was back to school on Monday morning. Not that I minded this, mark you, but had I known what lay in store I think I would have done a runner, entered a monastery or whatever.

The pressure started to build on the Sunday night as I was going to bed, when my father, bidding me goodnight, finished with, 'Don't forget, son, these next few months you will have to really buckle down, nose to the grindstone, for we all want you to pass your exam.' This with my mother standing in the background, nodding in assent.

Climbing the stairs that night, I really thought, Bollocks to this; I've worked my guts out for months through no fault of my own and not one word of praise, and I went to bed extremely angry with both of them. Little did I know that this was only the beginning for they were on to me at every chance, asking to see what homework I had brought home, making me stay in and finish it before I went out and in general, making my life a misery.

As time went by, Alice and I started to grow apart as I was spending too much time at my studies, but around the Christmas period I had some respite for they were far too busy with the seasonal services to bother about the more mundane things. This didn't matter as by now Alice and I had split up; no tears, no recriminations, just goodbye. So I had my mates and was already looking around for someone new. Oh, the falsehoods and fickleness of youth!

Back after the holiday, I loved the lessons and was doing really well, but kept having that nagging worry that I wouldn't pass. At home, the bribery started, with promises of a new bike, etcetera. Was there nothing grown-ups wouldn't sink to?

Well, finally the big day arrived and we were locked away out of sight and sound and given our papers. I don't remember much of this tremendously important occasion, except some of it I found easy and some not so easy, but stepping out of the classroom after it was all over, I breathed a sigh of relief. No more inquisitions for you, son, I thought to myself. Getting home that day, I found both my parents waiting for me in the front room. There was an air of expectancy about them as I walked in, but if they expected me to go through the whole of the exam piece by piece, they were disappointed. To all their questions I just gave a monosyllabic, 'It was all right' which in fairness must have infuriated them, but in all fairness to me I was only telling the truth.

Mother had made me a special tea, which I thought was a bit previous and I wondered idly how I would give it back, should I fail dismally. The questioning went on through tea with an exasperated, 'Well, how do you think you did, then?'

My answer was that I really didn't know, but here I craftily threw out the lifeline, saying that I thought I had done well but that was only what I thought. This seemed to mollify them but my father couldn't help but throw in the boarding school threat. I wondered what his reaction would be if he only knew that at that precise minute I was thinking, What a bloody good idea . . . I would go anywhere to get away from this constant barrage of questions.

We had the next day off, but I was bored at home and glad to get back to school the following day. Doing a rerun with Mr Green on the exam papers made me sweat and I began to wonder if it was going to be boarding school after all. The weeks passed and the summer holidays loomed closer. One morning as we sat in our desks for the first lesson, the headmaster came in with a sheaf of papers and told us that he had the results of the exam and that he would give them to us and tell us what new school we would be starting at after the summer holidays.

As alphabetically I was close to the top of the list, he quickly came to my name. Sitting there, he seemed to me to be taking forever to read it out, but finally announced 'John Elias, you had a pass mark and have to go for a day to Atherstone Grammar School to meet the staff and be shown around the wonderful facilities that will be available to you as a pupil. Good luck and well done.'

Actually, the correct name for this hallowed seat of learning was The Queen Elizabeth's Grammar School and on the day I visited I was completely overwhelmed by the grandeur of it. No pupils were allowed to wear their shoes inside the school because of the oak floorboards. We listened to the choir singing the school song which began with the words: Whatsoever in this life you have to do, play the game, and were shown around the school by the headmaster, a very grand gentleman who was called Doctor. We met our new form teacher and had a very nice day and then it was back home for yours truly, to face another inquisition as to whether I had managed to behave myself.

All too soon, it was end of term and I suddenly found myself shaking hands with my mentor and bidding him a tearful goodbye.

'You'll do alright, lad,' he said, 'and don't forget to come back and see me and tell me how you're going on.' Laughing, his parting shot was, 'And leave the girls alone for a bit; I noticed you were having a serious liaison a bit ago.'

Blushing, I beat a hasty retreat and made my way down the hill realising that a part of my life had gone forever and I was leaving a school where I had never been so happy.

That summer was alright as summers go, but if I tell the truth, I missed Alice and although only living opposite, I never saw her again to speak to. I was forced to go with my parents to get my new school uniform which, although all sold in the same shop, seemed to take forever. I then spent a fortnight down in dear old Croesyceiliog with my aunties and uncles, who made a tremendous fuss of me and finally, I returned home for the new term at my new school.

Setting off that first morning with the good wishes of my parents ringing in my ears, I would have sold my soul in that instant to be going back up that hill. However, I boarded the bus, looking around in vain for another uniform but there was no sign of anyone, so I settled down in my seat keeping a watchful eye out for my stop in case I should miss it. There was no school bus to my new school so we had to catch a service bus and show our pass. That morning I found I was half an hour early thanks to my over zestful parents, but I soon got into the swing of things. I found the first few weeks very strange, but as time went on I settled down and was starting to enjoy myself. I made some good friends and by half-term was really looking forward to the rest of the year.

I arrived at home on the last Friday with a week's holiday in front of me. I thought whimsically as I put my satchel in the hall that it would take me the whole of the holiday to do all this homework. I went into the front room to have my usual cup of tea before changing out of my uniform and there sat my folks, for once strangely silent. Guessing there was something up, I looked enquiringly at them. Finally my father broke the silence.

'We have got a bit of news, Sunny Jim. I have been offered a parish in Nottingham and have accepted it, so you won't be going back to Atherstone after the holidays as we're moving in three weeks.' So there it was. No consultation; no, 'How do you feel about it?' Just 'We're going and that's it' or 'Bugger you, Jack, I'm all right.' I did get my own way though, and went back to school for a week to say my goodbyes, and wondered if my father had ever heard the words of the school song, which went, second line: 'Always try to keep above board straight and true.'

Many years later, I heard a saying which fitted my feelings of the time. 'We operate a mushroom management system. Keep them in the dark and throw plenty of shit at them.' However, it didn't make one scrap of difference as yours truly was about to find out.

CHAPTER SIXTEEN
Confusion
(The Electric Light Orchestra)

Can you believe it? October 1952, just broken up for half-term and I'm sitting in our lounge looking at my parents, who have had the gall to sit there and tell me that the new school that I'd worked so hard to get to, the school that I was gradually getting accustomed to, was now completely defunct as far as I was concerned and I wasn't even going to say goodbye to any of my teachers and classmates.

I looked across at them in disbelief and Father was grinning from ear to ear at this wonderful news. At least my mother did look somewhat shame-faced as my father launched into his speech as to how it was going to be marvellous, how I would be going to a far better school and so forth. Not waiting for him to finish, I interrupted, saying flatly that I didn't want to go and that this was the first I'd heard about it. That took the smile off his face and my mother quickly jumped to his defence by saying they didn't tell me before in case it didn't work out and I would get upset for nothing.

Upset, I thought, as I climbed the stairs to my room. It's obviously mind over matter: they don't mind and I don't fucking well matter. Throwing my satchel across my bedroom floor, I jumped on the bed and lay there, contemplating leaving home . . . anything to get my own back. It wasn't long before there was a gentle knock on the door and my mother appeared, carrying a cup of tea. Always the peace keeper, my mother. She stole into the room and sat on the side of my bed.

'I know you are very upset, son, but it is your father's work and he wants to try a town parish again, so try not to be too hard on him and I'm sure things will work out.'

There spoke the eternal optimist and loyal wife

'What about me?' I asked. 'I haven't even had time to settle in to my new school. I had to work like a lunatic to catch up and even get in there. So far, I've been to five different schools, made five different sets of friends—'

'I know, son, and so does your father and we appreciate all the work you have put in, but just think about it and give it one last try.'

So there it was; no problem, just phone the removal men and goodbye Warwickshire.

I drank my tea and went back downstairs. There was no sign of my father and Mum was in the kitchen, getting tea.

'I have told your dad that although you are very upset you will give it a try,' she said.

That's nice of you, I thought to myself, but said nothing. She then said that my father was writing to the headmaster that week to explain, and he was also off to Nottingham to meet some elders from the new parish. I was tempted to ask was he taking the pony and caravan, but instead demanded that I be allowed to go back and say goodbye to my form teacher and class on my own. This she agreed to, as long as she came along and waited outside the school for me. So there we had it, no more to be said. The waiting time went by quite quickly. I didn't see a sign of Alice but said goodbye to all the rest of my friends. I had packed all my school books in my satchel and duly took them over to the school on the Friday before we left. My mother accompanied me and true to her word, waited outside the gates as I hastened in. I really don't know what I expected, but the whole thing was a damp squib and I wished afterwards that I hadn't bothered.

Monday morning came and with it the removal men and once more the place I had grown to like was so empty and bare, with all its memories wiped out in a matter of hours. I should have been used to it by now and I am sure I would have made a brilliant removal man. Finally, everything was loaded and we set off with a flourish, packed into the seats like so many sardines, my father beaming to everyone as we set off for another big adventure.

Unlike the move from Hampshire, it seemed to take no time at all before the driver exclaimed, 'There we are, Vicar; we have just arrived in the City of Nottingham,' and to me, 'Well, John, this was the home of Robin Hood.'

To be honest, I think Robin would have been horrified if he had seen the area through which we were travelling through my eyes that gloomy Monday afternoon. There were certainly no forested areas, no babbling brooks . . . in fact, just what seemed to me to be miles and miles of cobbled streets. However, I was always prone to exaggeration. But in truth, we seemed to bump along cobbled streets forever. The area we were heading for was known as the Meadows and the street was apparently known as 'Wilford' something or other, my memory fails me. We finally entered the right street and pulled up outside a three storey semi-detached house, which had a small garden in the front and was separated from the neighbours by iron railings. The house had bow windows in the front with stained glass in the top lights and a matching front door and looked very pleasant from the street.

My father was the first out, followed by the removal men, with my mother, Kim and myself following on. My father had already opened the front door and proceeded to show my mother around while I stood at the rear of the van to help unload. As I said previously, I was quite an old hand at this now and knew there wouldn't be that much to see, anyway. In truth, I was still smarting from my hasty removal from my last home and couldn't give a shit about any of it, really.

Apparently, my father was taking on two back street mission churches, also filling in where needed at the parish church, all of which were extremely busy, allegedly, and he would be directly responsible to a head vicar who was the priest at the rather grand parish church, which stood some streets away on the way into the city centre.

My mother had busied herself in the kitchen making tea and my father was puffing away on his pipe, lost in some private world, while we menials were moving the furniture in to its designated rooms when I saw a car pull up and a silver-haired man get out and knock on the open front door. One look at the dog collar he was sporting told me he was one of the chosen and I put my head down and hid myself behind whatever I was carrying. He must have been the head man, for my mother was smiling and shaking hands and my father was guffawing and calling everyone brother to make a good impression.

Suddenly my father spotted me and called, 'This is our son, John,' and as if in apology, 'He does like to help out the workmen.'

I found myself shaking hands with this tall silver-haired man who had staring eyes and who I took an instant dislike to. 'Good afternoon, sir,' I said. 'I'm very pleased to meet you.'

'So you are John,' he answered. 'You must come along to the parish church and we can find a place in our choir, that is until your father gets one started of his own.'

With that, he dismissed me without another glance and I couldn't get back to the job in hand fast enough. I just hoped upon hope that this was going to work out for my father, because I don't know what it was but I just didn't like his boss and all my life I have never been far out with my estimation of people in general. Little did I know, however, that I was to get to like his daughter a whole lot more . . .

My mother's rock cakes, washed down with tea, went down a treat and now the men were saying goodbye and we stood, the three of us, like lost sheep staring at our unfamiliar surroundings. The house, to be fair, was very nice with a sitting room, dining room and kitchen, pantry and cloakroom on the ground floor. There were three bedrooms and a bathroom on the first floor and two more large bedrooms on the second floor. I immediately asked for a bedroom on the second floor, but this request was turned down by my mother, for what reason I never found out, so I chose a big room on the first floor and to be honest, it suited me just fine. I looked out of the front window and saw that there was a school opposite which got me to wondering what my school would be like and if I would get on alright.

We had a late tea or early supper and my father, who was in a jovial mood, told me that a few streets further down from our house there were miles and miles of recreation grounds leading down to the river, which I was told was called the Trent, and it was very deep and wide so I must not get too close to it. This instantly intrigued me and I thought to myself, I'll have a look down there in the week.

I then asked how far it was to my new school and he told me about a quarter of a mile, that it was a lovely big school and that he had been and signed me on the register and I would be starting there next Monday. Bloody Hell, I thought, that's three weeks down the pan, I'll never catch up all this missed time.

Little did I know what lay in store for me as for the next few days I helped my father getting the house ship-shape and to my mother's liking. That Sunday I went with my parents to the evening service at the mission church and wondered why it was supposed to be such a busy place. Where were all the Christians? For it wasn't even half full and as we walked home along the cobbled streets, I seemed to detect a note of despondency in my parents' attitude. Off to bed, duly scrubbed and told not to read for too long as I had a very important day in front of me tomorrow, I lay there wondering if everything was as it should be downstairs. Lying there in my new bedroom, I looked across at my new uniform hanging on the wardrobe door and wondered what the next morning would bring.

Monday morning at precisely eight-forty found my father and yours truly entering the school gates. Clad in my new clothes and with shoes polished to perfection, I surveyed the school and the hundreds of blazer-clad pupils of all ages, shapes and sizes. Although, as mentioned previously, I could be prone to some exaggeration, this place was huge compared to my prior places of learning. My father seemed to know his way and under the curious glances of others, led me down a long corridor to a door marked 'School Secretaries' and waiting for one to become free, we stood there. Everyone, it seemed, needed a school secretary and the sheer volume of people coming and going did nothing for my confidence. Finally, a lady with her hair in a bun, wearing a very tight sweater and displaying a very large bosom, stepped forward and greeted us.

'Good morning, sir, and this must be John? Welcome to our school; the head is waiting so follow me, please.'

We were ushered into a large study, in which sat several people and I thought that there must have been a meeting taking place. Everyone stood up as we entered and a tall, thin individual introduced himself as Doctor Greene, the head. He then introduced the rest of his colleagues as head of this department and head of that.

Finally, looking down at me, he said, 'Well, John, we looked at your report sent to us from your last school and feel that you will do well here. Our team has decided that you will fit into form One Alpha and Mr Jones will take you there now.'

With that, I was whisked away, trying vainly to get another look at the lady with the big tits, but to no avail. Mr Jones set a cracking pace, his gown billowing behind him and I had to jog at times to keep up. After what seemed several miles down corridors and across quadrangles, we finally came to some glass and wooden fronted buildings. At the one with One Alpha on the door he knocked and we entered to be met by a middle-aged lady who introduced herself as Mrs Black, the form teacher.

Mrs Black then introduced me to the form, saying, 'This is John Elias, everyone. John has come to us from a grammar school in the Midlands. I know you will all make him welcome and help him to settle in.' She then put me to share a desk with a boy named Colin and the morning began.

As the morning progressed, with each subject came a different teacher and by lunch time I was fed up with introducing myself and was glad to hear the bell ringing to signify the end of the morning's lessons and set off home for lunch. I found that I could walk it quickly in around five minutes. Getting through my front door, I was bombarded with questions, which I did my best to answer between mouthfuls of food. Five minutes to play with Kim in the back yard and it was back up the road to my seat of learning. By the end of the day I had a satchel full of homework and a pile of copying up to do, in order to catch up with the rest of the class. By the end of the week it became abundantly clear that I never would be able to copy up three months' work in every subject and also complete the current homework I had been set. The syllabus they were working to was completely different to the one I'd been working to at the last school and to cap it all, there were some lessons I'd never taken at all, for example, Latin, which was complete double Dutch to me. The net result of all this was that I sat up every night until gone ten o'clock copying from other pupils' books whilst the new work I was set was not being done.

Outside of school I had developed two interests. The boy that I was sitting next to in class, whose name was Colin, was very friendly towards me and I found out that he was a member of the parish church choir. When I told him who my father was, he invited me to join the choir if I passed a voice test. He also advised me to go along to some services so that I would be noticed and this would stand me in good stead. I duly asked my parents, who in fairness could hardly refuse, as it was their boss who was in charge of the parish church. However, my father insisted that I attend eleven o'clock Eucharist at the same time as he was officiating. This turned out to be a blessing in disguise, for I was sitting in the rear pews the first morning when a vision of loveliness walked past me and smiled sweetly at me. I couldn't believe my luck, especially when, at the end of the service, she did the same thing again. My heart was beating fit to burst and as I didn't know anyone I couldn't ask who she was, but I made a silent vow that come hell or high water, I would find out.

The following week my mother came home from a meeting at the parish church full of praise for the lovely vicar's wife and daughter and, giving me a packet of liquorish root, told me the daughter, whose name was Josie, had sent them for me. I wasn't much interested as I had taken my vision of the previous Sunday onto my pillow every night that week and couldn't wait for Sunday morning.

Sunday morning came along and I was sitting in my seat, rigid with anticipation, but to my utter devastation she didn't come. I walked home with my father that Sunday very down in the dumps and wishing I was back in Warwickshire amongst my friends. Sitting down to dinner and listening to my parents' idle chatter over the table, I heard something that lightened my mood no end.

Apparently, the vicar's wife and daughter had gone down with heavy colds and wouldn't be leaving the house that weekend. My mind clicked up a gear on hearing this. Could it be that my vision was the head man's daughter? And could it be that it was she who had sent me the liquorish root? If this was the case, then it offered up all sorts of permutations and I would have to be patient, a characteristic I had not been endowed with. Monday morning and back at school, I was informed by my classmate, Colin, that the choir master wished to see me that evening after school to give me a voice test, so we dutifully called at my house on the way home to ask my parents' permission. My father was out but my mother agreed, so off we trundled to the parish church and thence to a hall around the back where Colin introduced me to the choirmaster, whose name was Mr Gravelle. I think my voice had started to break at this time so I struggled a bit with the top end of the scales, but he gave me a smile and told me I was in.

Back home to a nice tea and to break this exciting news to my folks, who didn't seem that impressed, to be honest. Next day it was back to school and get my head down, but I was floundering and Latin, especially, was a nightmare. By now I had copied up weeks of work but none of the teachers seemed to be in the slightest bit interested. Still, I consoled myself that it was only another three weeks until the Christmas holidays.

Back at the church we were at choir practice three nights a week getting our carols into shape, and on the following Sunday my vision was back in church again and gave me a lovely smile on both entering and leaving the service. Apart from school, things were not working out too badly for yours truly at the moment.

CHAPTER SEVENTEEN
I'm in Love Again
(Fats Domino)

Now anyone reading this will think I'm some sort of sex maniac, but I was only thirteen and very lonely and I felt that Josie must like me as she had sent me some liquorice root, so like it or lump it, I went to sleep every night with her on my pillow. At choir practice and every Saturday morning, I would meet Carol and her friends and we would chat outside the library for ages. Carol was a close friend of Josie and I was told I could trust her. She kept asking me about a boy at our school and knowing she fancied him, I told her I would let him know when I had a chance. She reciprocated by telling me she would pass my letters on to Josie and they would be safe with her. This cemented a firm friendship and she really was a super girl.

Monday night at choir, she passed a note to me. Hiding it in my pocket, I couldn't wait to read it back at home. These days when I get a Dear John letter it can only be bad news, but this one sent me whistling down the street. It said she would like to go out the following Saturday afternoon and would I reply via her friend, Carol. I couldn't wait to put pen to paper and hung around the library building the next afternoon and passed over the letter as if it was my life, agreeing to meet by the suspension bridge. I bought a packet of Robin cigarettes from a little shop in the back streets and smoked one for pure devilment. I was so pleased and wondered what the old folks would say if they knew, but resolved to tell them nothing. My big problem at the time was the school. I bloody well hated the place and the whole of the work was totally different. However hard I tried, I was getting nowhere and I think I about gave up at that point.

The next Saturday, face and hands scrubbed I headed for the suspension bridge, dragging on a ciggy as I marched along. In all honesty, it was a great wonder that someone didn't report me for smoking and I seriously thought I was out in the Hampshire heath or the Warwickshire countryside, instead of bumping into hundreds of people along the pavements of a big city. I still believe to this day that had I stayed in the city I would have been locked up sooner or later, but thank you, whoever; it didn't happen. Waiting was never my strongpoint and after ten minutes or so I was bored and looking for Josie to arrive. At last I saw her swinging along the pavement. Giving me a bright smile, she apologised for being late, but said her father kept asking where she was going. I did not like the sound of this one little bit and felt a bit uneasy with the situation, but faint heart never won fair lady – I knew this was true as I had heard it said on the wireless.

To get away from the crowds, we cut across onto an area where the Grantham canal ran. A friend of mine had shown me this area a few weeks ago and there was a cheese factory a little further up on the opposite side of the canal. It was very quiet here and we sat on a large boulder and smoked a cigarette. Watching the canal and lost in ourselves, just two kids enjoying each other's company. Some fifty-nine years later, I managed to find her again and we had some fascinating conversations about our lives. She is a happily married lady with two grandsons and lives in another beautiful county which I know quite well called West Sussex and is enjoying life to the full, I am very happy to say.

What it is to be in love? On reflection and reading this, I think our parents would have been worried sick at us children going into these deserted places, never mind the dangers of who or what lurked around the next corner. All things considered, we had a really nice afternoon and we got on very well together. I eventually saw her back onto the main Trent Bridge and we promised to meet as soon as possible. Walking home that afternoon I felt ten feet tall and was already working out plans for the future in my devious little mind.

Back at school, it would appear that no one wanted to know me and time was getting short to the build up to Christmas. I presumed this was all because of my terrible results, but by now I just couldn't give a flying fuck about any of them, especially God's gift to teaching, Mrs Black. There was one lad who had been on my case since I had arrived and I really owed him one, but I thought I was in the mire enough. Anyway, on the last day of term he pushed by me in the doorway and the buckle on his satchel caught me across the back of the hand. One look at his face told me, here we go, and I caught him a beauty on the side of his head. He went down with a crash and started to gasp very loudly. Mrs Black was down on her knees and another master from the next classroom rushed to help him and he gradually settled down to normal. All I heard was, 'Please Miss, please Miss, John Elias hit him, Miss.'

God's gift to teaching told me she was going to the headmaster with this, but time was running out and I didn't care, although I was sorry . . . sorry that I hadn't missed him and caught her.

Reaching home, I thought it best to break the news to the folks in case they were sent for by the head. They were suitably horrified but saw my side of it for once. I need not have worried as I never heard any more about it.

Nottingham – what a huge place I found myself living in. Gone the Heath and gone the Common, just miles of houses to the right spreading away to the city centre with its huge shops, cinemas and cafes, while to the left were miles of recreation grounds and memorial gardens, stretching down to the mighty Trent. I knew in my heart of hearts that I could never settle down there and everything was wrong, even to the point where we spoke differently. But being a seasoned campaigner by now, I resolved to get the best out of my experiences. My main problem was the school which, apart from anything else, was truly frightening in both size and people. I still managed to get lost on its campus and could not name three quarters of the staff. It had its compensations though and I was learning the violin and several different hobbies. It was here that I read The Odyssey by Homer from cover to cover and enjoyed every page of it.

CHAPTER EIGHTEEN
Rocking Goose
(Johnny and the Hurricanes)

Christmas time in any big city is wonderful, and my Christmas in Nottingham was no exception. Travelling to and from the parish church gave me a chance to see the wonders of a big city's attractions and after a practice or a service, I would walk up into the city centre with my friends to look at the lights and the shop windows which were a marvellous sight for a country bumpkin such as myself. I took my mother up town one night before Christmas and she was overwhelmed with the grandeur of the city centre shop displays and also with the knowledge I acquired of the different streets and areas of the city. All the flower shops had bundles of holly and mistletoe. This was the first time I had ever seen the latter and asked my father about it but got a short and sharp answer that it was a pagan symbol from years ago and had no place in a Christian church. It wasn't until many years later that I actually saw it growing in the orchards of Herefordshire. The one thing I never saw during my stay in Nottingham was the Goose Fair and I always wonder if it is still held.

By now, everything was happening at a frantic pace as the festival loomed closer and we were starting to get into the services with nine lessons and carols being the first. I had become quite friendly with a girl several years older than I was, who sang in the women's section of the choir and she told me that the vicar's daughter would like to go out with me again after Christmas and she would arrange it. Obviously I was extremely chuffed with this information and could hardly contain myself. There was, however, a small fly buzzing around, which would shortly be landing in a very large tub of ointment, and of which at that moment in time I was blissfully unaware. I was so caught up in my own daydreams that I failed to notice the faintest of undercurrents from my parents, and the comings and goings of several of the senior members of my father's congregation. Then the whispering and sometimes raised voices coupled with the guilt ridden silences and innocent expressions when I entered the room unexpectedly. Oh John, lad! With all your past experience you should have had your ear to the ground.

Christmas came and went with a flurry and at the first choir practice after this I was bored and decided to liven things up. My voice was now in the last stages of breaking and I could sing quite deeply, and finally turned into a double bass. However, at the end of one hymn I decided to drop deep at the end as low as I could. Suddenly everyone stopped and I was left on my own, making this hideous moan.

The choir master jumped up and asked, 'Who did that?'

With a stupid grin I replied that it was me. He went berserk and told me to get out and to tell my father he had sent me home and why. Fearing the worst, I headed for home and broke the news . . . I have to say, not completely as it happened, and to my amazement my parents were very understanding, both agreeing that they weren't a bit surprised.

Again, I should have picked up the vibes, but I was completely shocked by their acquiescence and sat down with a cup of cocoa thinking I'd come out of it very well. Needless to say, I didn't go back to the parish church but went to the mission with my parents. Once more I got into trouble and once more it was all my own stupid fault.

Every Sunday night, while I was in the choir, my father used to give me threepence for the collection. This could get me a packet of fruit gums from the shop on the way to the service. When the collection plate came around I used to pretend to put something in and bang the coins for effect. I saw no reason for this to discontinue when I went to the mission, but gradually got braver and one night put a button in. After the service I went into the vestry to find my father and the two sidesmen fuming over this button. Later, on the way home I was asked the question and admitted it was me. I was always a sucker for the George Washington story but telling the truth got me nowhere and I got a hell of a bollocking, no supper and was persona non grata in our house for a week.

Back at school, things weren't much better as my mate who had got me to join the choir had disowned me and I found myself very much on my own.

Gradually things got back to normal at home but I had started to eavesdrop on conversations, especially between my parents and some of the elders of the parish. They all treated me as if I was deaf anyway, so I managed to pick up some useful titbits and I was stunned when I overheard my father holding forth about how wrong it was to be closing down the Mission churches and he, whoever he was, would never get away with it. These conversations were getting quite regular now and I knew from the serious tone of the voices that there was trouble ahead.

I, however, had my own worries to contend with at school as the school exams were approaching and try as I might, I had no idea of what I was going to do. My parents were far too busy with their own affairs for me to add to their worries, so I decided to sit back and let it all wash over me. The day finally arrived and the whole school went into exam mode with people in corridors immersed in books or wandering around muttering to themselves, totally unaware of what was going on around them. I had been told that we were one of four first forms. Alpha, Beta, Gamma and Delta and supposed that as we were the highest, I would at best get relegated to Delta and at worst get kicked out altogether. As I sat there going from paper to paper, I knew it was goodnight nurse, especially when it got to the Latin paper and all I did was write my name and form on top of the paper. Anyhow, it was all over now and I sat back and waited for the inevitable.

Back at the ranch, my folks were now so wrapped up in their forthcoming battle with whoever, I don't think they even understood I had taken any exams. I was going into the library on the Saturday morning when I bumped into Carol from the choir. I was very pleased to see her and we had a long conversation in which she said that the vicar's daughter now went for a walk every Saturday afternoon so I arranged to meet her again by the suspension bridge across the Trent that afternoon. I spent the morning in the Library which I loved, for it was huge with an enormous amount of books, both lending and reference, and also had a rule of silence. I used to sit there for hours looking at various reference books and choosing other books to take home, but that morning I sat there in a trance, wondering what I would say and if her parents knew she was meeting up with me, whereas I didn't mention it to mine.

That afternoon, both suited and booted, I must admit I dragged my feet but finally arrived at the suspension bridge and looked up and down the embankment but could see no sign of her. I waited for some ten minutes but there was still no sign and I was kicking stones and vowing to never trust another woman when I looked up and could see her walking along in the distance.

There was no shyness in this one for as she approached, she said, 'Hello John,' with a lovely smile and kissed me on the cheek. I caught the sweetness of her breath and felt my colour go up as we stood there, two strangers, but we were only kids and soon forgot our shyness. I took her across the fields to a place they called the pans where there were little lakes filled with wild birds and I showed her the various breeds. We talked and she climbed a tree as I watched and we had so much in common. I had bought a packet of ten Robin cigarettes again, purely to show off, but she had one and we coughed our way through them. She told me the reason she was late was that her mother wouldn't let her come without knowing where she was going and who she was meeting. She then said I seemed a nice lad but she was not to tell her father. I knew we were doomed but also I wanted to make the most of it. I also found out that my name was mud over the choir episode and she told me her father was raving over it, but that she hated the choirmaster and thought it was funny. All too soon it was time to say goodbye and with promises to meet up in two weeks we parted, shyly giving each other a light brush of lips. I was hooked; completely and utterly hooked as she turned and waved before disappearing from sight and I walked home, my heart pumping inside my chest.

Back home and I could sense the atmosphere with my parents and wondered what the hell was going on but I still couldn't get to the bottom of it and was too frightened to ask. Sunday was the usual boring round of services and notwithstanding the worry of the looming exam results, I was quite glad to get back to school. The day passed alright as days go and on the way home I met up with my friend, Carol, from the choir, who was obviously waiting for me.

She was smiling and said, 'My word, John, what did you get up to on Saturday? Whatever it was, you certainly made a good impression.' She handed me a letter and told me to let her have any reply on Saturday at the library.

Nodding my assent, we parted and I headed for home and the privacy of my bedroom. It was a very nice letter from Josie, telling me how much she had enjoyed our time together and how she looked forward to the next time and hoped I felt the same. It also told me that her mother had quizzed her when she got home, as to what I was like and that she had told her I was very nice and that she really liked me. She finished it 'with all my love,' which to someone of my tender years meant we were together for life. At the back of my mind I thought, if her old man finds out about this lot we are all going to get some grief, not the least yours truly. I spent the rest of that day composing a long and much involved script confessing my undying love and signed it with a flourish. I did think of writing BURMA on the bottom or some other coded message, but common sense prevailed.

That Wednesday morning, the shit hit the fan big time in the form of the exam results. Straight after the morning assembly we went back to our form room and were sitting there when a strange master came in. Introducing himself, he told us it was his job to tell us the results of the mid-term exams and that they would be sent home to our parents together with our reports within the week. Needless to say I was overjoyed with this and thought I might spew all over the floor at any minute. Luckily, he read them out in alphabetical order so I was spared the ignominy of mine being read out last. He soon came to my name and asked John Elias? I put my hand up and gave him a sickly smile. They were terrible, except for English language and literature. Maths, sciences, geography, history – all suffered the same ghastly fate, finishing up with Latin at which I got a big zero. I could hear the hushed silence around me, broken by the sniggers of some of my class mates, as he looked at me and then passed on to the next name on the list. I went home that dinner time, feigned a bad stomach and didn't return until the Friday.

Friday afternoon, just before the bell rang for the end of school, I was called out to the desk of our form teacher, Mrs Black. Dear Mrs Black, who I will always remember with such devotion, called me out and in front of the whole class waved my report at me. She asked if any of the class had a biro she could borrow as she had never written a bad report with her own pen that some far distant pupils had given her back in time, and as mine was the worst report she had ever had to sign, she would not sign it with her own wonderful pen. My heart went out to her as a model of the teaching profession and as I have taught O level pupils with some degree of success, I wonder how in hell she ever got to be in charge of children, fervently hoping they buried her pen with her when she went to that big classroom in the sky.

Feeling somewhat pensive, I trudged home that Friday afternoon and it wasn't just my satchel that weighed heavy as my feet rang out along the dusty pavements. Over the last few weeks my parents had seemed wrapped up in their own little world and didn't bombard me with the usual barrage of questions which I suppose should have rung a bell, but they were not the only ones who were on another planet, so I was not in the least bit surprised to find several elders from the church in the lounge, devouring our biscuits and spilling the crumbs all over the carpet. For this heinous crime I would have been chastised for a week, but it didn't seem to matter a jot to my parents. However, all conversation stopped as soon as I entered the room and my mother was quick to usher me out into the kitchen where I was somewhat mollified with a nice cup of tea and some chocolate biscuits.

CHAPTER NINETEEN
It's Over
(Roy Orbison)

Saturday morning came and after spending a sleepless night trying to figure out just what was going on with my folks and the members of the splinter group who seemed to have become part of our furniture, I got up from my bed feeling none too clever. Bleary-eyed, I retrieved my letter from its hiding place, put it inside the books that I was taking back to the library that morning and went downstairs for my breakfast. My mother gave me a bright smile and told me my father was out in the parish. Doing God's work, I thought sarcastically, well there's nothing strange there. After breakfast I went upstairs to the bathroom and had a good scrub, cleaned my teeth and felt ready to meet whatever the world had to throw at me. If I'd had the faintest inkling of what that was to be, I would have returned straight to bed and stayed there until Sunday, but not being a psychic, I set off up the road with my library books clutched under my arm, blithely ignorant of the fact that my little life was to be turned upside down once more before nightfall.

There was no sign of Carol, the choir girl, as I approached the library, so I walked in and handed my books in at the desk, almost forgetting to take out the letter in the process. Crossing to the reference area, I got out the books which I wanted and finding a table, I was soon immersed in the world of the dinosaur in the silence of the room. After what seemed like ages, something made me look up and I could see Carol, the choir girl smiling at me. Quickly replacing my book, I walked to the outside room where you could talk and sat down beside her. She gave me another letter and I handed mine over and she told me that Josie was afraid there was something going on with her father and that she thought it affected my family and would try to find out what it was and let me know. With that we said our goodbyes and knowing she was sweet on a fifth former at my school I promised to do my best for her if I could get close to him. I then returned to my beloved books, but try as I might I couldn't concentrate... not after reading the letter which confirmed what I had already been told.

A couple of hours later, I walked through my front door and straight into my mother and father who were sitting in the lounge, apparently waiting for me. I say apparently as my father was holding up a copy of my exam results and my mother was clutching my report, and they didn't look happy.

My father kicked off with, 'Well, Sunny Jim, doesn't look too good, does it?'

Then my mother, with a shocked voice, 'John! Your report's terrible.'

As if I didn't know. I waited for the next barrage and was surprised there was nothing more forthcoming as they were both gazing at me expectantly so I went into my side of it and if I do say so myself, I did a good job of it. I got straight into my stride, kicking off with my being dragged away from every school I had settled in to, especially the last one, followed by the bullshit I'd been given about it being a far better school I was coming to. Then I got into the eight full exercise books that I had filled up with a term's work, which not one of the staff had even bothered to look at and which had resulted in me getting so far behind I could never catch up. So on I went to exams, finishing up with my form teacher's kind remarks and refusal to use her marvellous pen.

A deathly hush fell on the room.

At last my father spoke, and in fairness it was an honest answer.

'Sunny Jim,' he replied, 'I know we have not been fair to you and we know how hard you have worked since you have been here. It would have been fairer to you if you had gone to boarding school; however, your mother did not want that. From our part, things have not worked out as we had hoped, causing these moves to happen and uprooting you just as you were getting settled. For all this I apologise, but there is something else I would like to say. Things haven't been going as well as I had hoped and I have found I need to get back into a country parish for health reasons. I am going to be away for a few days next week, firstly to have a meeting with the bishop and secondly to look at a new parish in the country far, far away from here, so I need you to look after your mother for me and to go to school next week as if nothing has happened. When I return, I will come to the school and talk to the head and the woman who signed your report, who in my opinion is not fit to be around children.'

I was totally flabbergasted and also full of questions but I was told that he couldn't tell me any more and I was to repeat what I had been told under fear of death.

All this time, my mother had been smiling and now gave me a cuddle and went out to make lunch while I, still in a daze, went up to my room and sat on the bed, trying hard to contemplate how this information was going to affect me both in the short and long term. The most important thing, short term, was that I was getting out from this school, which by now I loathed with an all-encompassing hatred, and common sense told me that it was the best thing for me, or else, even at that tender age I would have done something really stupid. Long term, I was going to have to go through all the processes again, but on the bright side, perhaps it would be easier than where I was at the moment. The only problem I faced was telling the new love of my life and I was not too pleased about that as I had taken quite a shine to her and had high hopes for the future. I needed to get in touch, so I would have to find the girls that afternoon. But then again, I was sworn to secrecy and if my father found out I was meeting up with her, I would be up shits creek without a paddle, so to speak.

My mother called me and feeling a bit like Dick Barton, I descended the stairs and sat down to lunch. Amazing how a bit of straight talking clears the air and we were all buddy-buddy over lunch with my father winking at me across the table and reminding me that my information was strictly between us. I must have been in favour because he gave me an extra shilling pocket money that afternoon. The rest of the weekend passed by and I didn't go to church on the Sunday, feigning headaches. I got up for school on Monday thinking, well old mate, this could be your last week in this place, so keep your head down and keep out of trouble.

When I got home for dinner, my father had left for God knew where and my mother remained tight-lipped about the whole thing. The week was going very slowly and we were breaking up for half-term on the Friday. However, on the Wednesday I was walking home that afternoon when I bumped into my choir-girl friend, or rather she was waiting for me with a message from Josie to say that she couldn't make it on Saturday, but would meet me on the Friday after school in the same place. I agreed to this and my friend told me that it was urgent so I had to come up with a plan to get home late on Friday. No problem . . . my devious little mind sprang into action I had joined the violin class some weeks ago and been loaned a violin, so it would be only right to hand it back, especially as I was leaving in the next couple of weeks, hush, hush, and let some other pupil have the joy of using it. Great, I thought and proceeded to explain that I would be late home on Friday as I had decided to hand in my violin and would probably be a couple of hours late so there was no need to worry. End of story. I was home and dry and my father wouldn't be home until later that evening so I was well pleased with my alibi.

Friday afternoon found me by the suspension bridge waiting for Josie, and feeling a right lemon in my school uniform. She was apparently always late but I finally spotted her, swinging her satchel and striding along towards me. Once again she gave me a bright smile and a gentle kiss on the cheek and I was lost forever as we smiled at one another. People passing were giving us some strange looks so I suggested we cross the river and go and sit in the memorial gardens. Sitting down, I asked her what was wrong. She swore me to secrecy and told me that there had been a hell of a row between my father and her father, coupled with the fact that he had managed to winkle it out of her mother about us meeting on the Saturday. He had gone ballistic, ordering her to have nothing more to do with me. I was suitably dumbfounded, but kept my head and said nothing about the things my folks had told me.

She was obviously frightened of her father and kept looking around as if she expected him to rise up out of the ground at any moment. Being the hero of the day, I told her not to worry as it would soon blow over and meantime we could keep in touch by letter. I also made a promise that I wouldn't look at another girl and we shared a passionate kiss and went our separate ways, waving until we lost sight of each other. I walked home in a very black mood, thinking that not only had Father cocked up my schooling, he had also cocked up my love life as well. To describe my feelings that Friday afternoon is hard for me to explain. Firstly, although only kids, in our little world Josie and I were as fond of each other as you can be at that age and out of loyalty to my parents, I hadn't said a thing about their conversation with me. On the other hand, they had not told me the whole truth, and whereas I was thinking it was all to do with health reasons it was really the fact that Father had fallen out with the boss man, so regardless of anyone's feelings, we were off again to God knows where and I couldn't mention it to anybody. I thought to myself as I trudged along the endless pavements, Well old mate, it's obviously a question of mind over matter; they don't mind and you don't fucking well matter.

I eventually got to our gate and on opening the front door heard the sound of people talking. Going into the lounge, I found my parents sitting there, both their faces wreathed in smiles as I entered the room.

'Well, Sunny Jim, I've got some marvellous news,' my father said. 'I have been to see the bishop and he has given me a beautiful parish in the heart of Wales. I have been to see it and it's all mountains and woods in a lovely little village. Of course you'll love it there and I am sure we will all be very happy as I think my days of town parishes are over.'

Well, what do you say to that, I ask you? I suppose the truth is there is no answer when you're that age, but given time, I thought to myself, one day I will have my say. During the course of the evening I was told that we would be going in just over two weeks and that my father would come up to the school with me on the Monday we started back to tell them I would not be going back. This I refused, saying I wanted to do it alone, so we settled on the option that he would write a letter for me to take to school with the instruction that I was to come straight home.

That week flew by with no message from Josie, and I guessed that she was keeping a low profile. In a way, I was glad because I would only have been telling her a pack of lies anyway, knowing my departure was imminent. The only thing that gave me any pleasure was that I was allowed to ride my bike, providing I kept away from the main roads and went carefully, so I had endless fun rocketing around the back streets of the meadows.

Monday morning found me clad in my uniform, this being due to my mother's view that I should go properly dressed. I would have to preferred to go out in a blaze of glory, something like James Cagney: Hey, Mama! I'm on top of the world, but never mind, I went anyway. On reaching the school gates I headed up the corridor towards the secretaries' offices, hoping fervently to see the woman with the big tits again. No such luck; I was confronted by some old harridan, who read my letter and growled at me to wait as she disappeared through a doorway behind her. After what seemed like an eternity she came out again followed by the master who had read out the exam results. He was holding my letter and came around into the corridor.

'So you're leaving us, John,' he said. 'I am sorry that I haven't had a chance to speak to you since the exam results, but I do realise that things haven't been as straight forward as they should have been and had you stayed I would have sorted them out. However, you are leaving us and on behalf of the school, I wish you well and every success in your new school.' With that, he shook my hand and I felt one hundred times better as I walked home with a spring in my step. Climbing out of my uniform, I was mentally preparing myself for a week of packing, stacking and all the tasks which I could help my father with.

Still being sworn to secrecy, I kept to the house as much as

I could in case I bumped into Carol, the choir girl, and was asked some awkward questions, but there was no sign of her or her friends and I took my library books back early one afternoon when I knew they would be in school. That last weekend, I went down for a last look at the Trent with my mother and father on the Sunday evening. The weather was fine and the nights were getting lighter with each passing day. As we walked through the long stretches of recreation grounds, there were hundreds of people either walking or sitting on the benches with some brave souls sitting on the grass, and horror of horrors I saw one couple who looked about fifty to me, actually making out, and I quickly looked away hoping to God my parents hadn't spotted them. Then it was back home for supper and off to bed. One more night to go and it was bye bye Nottingham.

There was nothing much to do the following day as everything was packed and ready for the removal men who were arriving mid-morning to load everything on the one van, except for the bare essentials which were to be loaded at seven o'clock the next morning in order for us to get off early, for it was a very long journey that lay ahead. Lying in bed that night, I reflected on my time here and thought that apart from my school, I had a good life here, a totally different life, in a big city and my last thoughts as sleep overcame me were, perhaps I was born to be a country boy, after all.

CHAPTER TWENTY
On the Road Again
(Canned Heat)

It's six o'clock on Tuesday morning and I'm sitting on an upturned bucket in the kitchen, surveying the empty ruin that had been my home. Everything had been loaded and I was listening to my parents clattering around the upstairs rooms, checking that nothing had been left behind. At last we were ready and climbed aboard the van, complete with sandwiches, a couple of flasks and our beloved dog, Kim, who was more than happy to leave the city for the countryside. The other van had gone ahead and our driver was starting to get impatient so as we slammed the door, he asked if everything was alright and, getting the nod, started the engine, checked his mirrors and we were away.

Talk about a journey! Mile after mile we drove, right down through the Midlands, bypassing Birmingham with two stops along the way for toilets and food. Gradually the built-up areas lessened and the countryside changed. After a long time, we saw a sign for Hereford. I had never heard of the place before but everyone else seemed to know it and the mood in the lorry brightened considerably. I remember we were driving up a long and straight hill with houses on each side, and the pavements were full of school children, some in uniform and others not, but all walking up the hill, in the same direction that we were driving. Knowing the city for many years now, I can only think it must have been up the Ross road in the Redhill area, but what we were doing in that part of the city I can't figure out. All I do know is that I was completely knackered and as the children were going home I can only conclude it was around half past three.

'We won't be long now,' commented the driver. 'It's only another couple of hours at the most.'

I could have cried. It had been the longest journey of my little life.

On and on we trundled, down leafy lanes, along the sides of river banks, past little cottages with the monotonous roar of the engine lulling me into a trance-like state somewhere between sleep and consciousness. I must have nodded off for a short while but my mother's voice broke into my sleep and I woke with a start, to find that the scenery had changed dramatically. Gone were the pastoral lowlands of the shires with the rich, red brown soil, the herds of white faced cattle and the large undulating fields with their regimental hedges dividing everything into neat fields.

Gone were the hedgerows, to be replaced by fences with pig netting and a barbed wire strand across the top, the lush green grass of the lowland was replaced by a lighter variety, mixed with clumps of stunted bracken and here and there clumps of rushes sprouted. The trees were smaller, with their branches all leaning one way as if blown that way by the wind, which of course was the case. Above all this, the ground rose into grassy hillocks, getting bigger and higher the further we travelled, while in the distance, looming ever nearer were the heather and gorse covered slopes of the hills and mountains of Wales.

There is something about mountains or very high hills, which to be fair, most of them are in my part of the country, but it really doesn't matter; everyone calls them mountains anyway. They rise majestically with their peaks seemingly reaching into the sky. Their flanks covered in scrub trees, gorse, heather and bracken, sometimes hiding the delicious whimberries which give so much mouth-watering joy in August, when busy mothers turn them into scrumptious tarts. Yes, there is something awesome about the mountain that makes you want to explore his hidden valleys and scale his lofty heights. My earliest memories were of sitting in my aunties' houses in Croesyceiliog and looking out of the windows at the mountain towering over Upper Cwmbran with the railway line winding its way along the bottom, heading for Newport or Cardiff. I remember gazing at his highest peak, Twm Barlwm, I think they called it, standing there full of mystery and secrets of a thousand years past. I always vowed to climb him but never did and alas the old bones would not be a challenge for him now.

On and on we climbed in very low gear until we levelled out and entered a wide and open pass, the road twisting its way between the grass-covered slopes of the surrounding hills.

My mother cried, 'Oh! Just look at that!' for with the sun setting towards him, walked an old shepherd, his dog and his flock of sheep. It was my first view of a large flock and I was transfixed with the sight of the ewes and their lambs running along beside them, all making a tremendous din and leaving their droppings all over the road. It seemed to take forever to get past them, and I can still see my mother's face and the glow of pleasure that she got from the experience. On and on, through little villages which seemed deserted until we finally saw a lady wearing a shawl and carrying a basket. We pulled in to ask how far we had to go. She seemed to take a long time to consider the question and was also overawed by a situation where a large lorry full of complete strangers should descend on her in the middle of nowhere, all speaking with funny accents. Finally, she answered that we had to keep following the road for about five miles and we would come to the village we were looking for. I noticed she appeared to have quite a job speaking English and her pronunciation seemed almost German but my mother laughed and said we were in real Wales now. Shouting our thanks, we waved goodbye and headed off along the road. All weariness had left us as we knew we had nearly reached our goal.

After what seemed like an hour, the driver remarked that a Welsh five miles would seem to be ten times as long as an English one. The road had narrowed considerably now and the gradients had also become very steep when the driver finally found a place to pull in and look at his map. After studying it, he said that we were very close now, which was just as well for it would be getting dusk in a couple of hours. At last, we crested the top of a hill and there beside a church stood the other furniture van.

The mood of the two drivers was ecstatic and you would think they were long lost brothers returning from some far off war as they hugged and laughed and lit up their cigarettes, obviously recounting details of the journey. At last our driver returned and told my father that the first lorry had been unloaded and that the driver and his mate would follow us down to the house, which was only half a mile away and unload the second van. This statement puzzled me as there was nowhere to unload the lorry except in the church, but I glanced at my parents' faces and they seemed perfectly happy, so I concluded that all was well.

Away we went, with much tooting of horns as the other lorry followed us down the leafy byway, past a school, along a straight stretch and we were entering the village which comprised of about eight houses, including a delightful shop and post office. Up the hill and we finally pulled in outside a little primrose coloured cottage with a huge bush-like tree at the side of it.

I remember thinking that this must be where we pick the key up from but to my utter amazement, my father, all smiles said, 'Well, everybody, here we are.'

As I sat there, dumbfounded, he descended from the lorry and bent down to pick up a key from under a stone outside the front door. I say front door, but as I was to find out very shortly, it was the only door and believe it or not it was painted green.

CHAPTER TWENTY-ONE
Green Door
(Jim Lowe)

The song went something like this: 'There's an old piano and they play it hot behind the green door,' which in this case was complete rubbish because if you put our piano behind the green door in our new abode, there definitely wouldn't be room for anything else. I had been through a few front doors in my short life and climbed a few stairs and looked through a few windows, but nothing would ever compare with this. The cottage consisted of a front room and a kitchen downstairs, both with stone slab floors. In one corner of the front room an open tread staircase ran straight into an open bedroom which I just knew would have to be mine, while to the left, another door opened into the main bedroom, which I just knew had to be theirs. There was no toilet or bathroom and the whole place was no bigger than the sitting room at our house in Hampshire.

I hoped in vain that this was just a stopover point and we would be going on tomorrow, but alas this was not the case. I thought to myself that my father had really lost it this time and that my mother would give him hell for dragging us all the way to this, but I could hear them talking downstairs and she didn't seem in the least bit upset, quite the contrary in fact. I realised then that they had only told me half a story and I couldn't wait to hear what the other half was going to be. My thoughts were interrupted by a knock on the door and I could hear a lady with a lovely Welsh voice talking to my mother and father and I went downstairs to be introduced and be nosy.

My parents were talking to a lady whom I can only describe as motherly. She had a kindly face with eyes that twinkled when she smiled, which seemed to be all the time. She was white haired and quite plump. Looking at me, she asked my parents if I was their son. My father answered that I was and that my name was John. Stepping forward I shook hands with her.

'Well, John bach, I'm Mrs Lewis. It's lovely to meet you, so it is and I'm sure you will love it here,' and bending down, gently pinched my cheek. With that, she said she would be over later when the men had gone, and disappeared through the door.

My mother was handing out cups of tea from a huge white enamel teapot, together with piles of buttered scones which the lady had kindly brought round, and we weren't long demolishing the lot. Looking around me, I could see that the men had finished downstairs and wouldn't be very long now. Still puzzled, I asked my mother where all the rest of our furniture was.

'It's all being stored at the church, John,' she answered.

Suddenly, it started to fit into place and I thought, why didn't they tell me all this in the first place? Why all the secrecy? However, I was too tired to argue and looked outside. It was beginning to get dark and for once, I was longing for my bed.

I must have dozed off in this new and odd environment, which was very strange with all the racket going on all around me, but I awoke from a heavy sleep to find the removal men had gone and the room was lit up with an eerie light. I could hear someone bumping about upstairs and climbed up in the flickering shadows to find my parents making up the beds. The strange light came from lighted candles which were placed around in Wee Willie Winkie candlesticks and gave everything a strange, ghostly aura. My room was made up so I stumbled back down the stairs to find Kim, our dog, had stolen my spot on the sofa and was wagging his tail as if to say, 'Well at least we're still all together.' I suddenly realised that I was bursting for a pee and opened the front door to find it was pitch black outside. Not being the bravest of souls at that age, I counted to ten and walked along the side of the house to the corner of the gable and looking furtively around, unbuttoned my trousers and directed a stream onto whatever happened to be in front of me. I swear that if something had touched me on the shoulder at that moment, I would have messed my pants and no problem. It's always the same when you're in a rush and my operation seemed to last forever, but I finally finished and found my way back into the house. A sudden thought struck me: what and where was the toilet and how the hell were we supposed to find it in the dark?

As I sat there contemplating this and other things, there was a thunderous knocking on the door. The dog jumped off the sofa, snarling and spitting blood and I jumped up so quickly I thought I was going through the ceiling. My father came rushing down the stairs, calling me to hold the dog tight while he opened the door. It was the little lady from across the road again, who had brought us another giant pot of hot tea and a large steaming casserole of something she called cawl, which I found out much later was lamb stew but which smelt delicious. She had also brought across a Tilley lamp, which she said had been freshly filled. Then, wishing us a nice evening, she was gone. She truly must have been an angel of mercy, for we had no means of cooking anything that first night. So there we were, thanks to the kindness of others, sitting around a table in the kitchen of our new home tucking in to large helpings of cawl and washing it down with hot, sweet tea. I am not a lover of onions, or stew of any kind for that matter, but I can truly say that nothing ever tasted better than that candlelit meal on our first night in Wales.

By the time we had finished, I was about dead on my feet or in this case, my arse, and everybody agreed it was high time I went up the wooden hill, so with goodnights all round and clutching my candle, I left them, with promises to be careful with the candle. Sitting on the side of the bed, almost too tired to take my clothes off, I struggled with my socks and put my feet on the bare floorboards. This soon woke me up as the boards were very hot from downstairs where my father had hung the Tilley lamp on a beam in the front room. Staggering back down the stairs, I warned them of the problem and fell asleep thinking how I had saved us all from being roasted on our first night.

I was awakened next morning by the sun shining through my

curtainless bedroom window and lay there in a dream, wondering about yesterday's happenings and what the hell we were doing in this tiny cottage with no bathroom. Hearing footsteps on the stairs, I looked up to see my mother's head poking around the opening that served as a doorway.

'Brought you up a nice cup of tea, son. Did you sleep well?' she asked.

Replying that I had, I asked what time it was.

'Seven-thirty,' came the reply and she told me that breakfast would be about half an hour and that my father was off to the local town to get some much needed supplies as well as some groceries.

I lay there wondering how he would get there, probably horse and cart, I thought sarcastically. My mother's voice broke in on my thoughts, calling me with the words that I had precisely five minutes. Looking around, I spotted a fresh set of underwear she must have put out last night, and I quickly struggled into my clothes and walked over to look out through the bedroom window. Outside was a small path running the length of the back of the house, with an old stone wall separating it from the woodland which rose up steeply from the top of the wall and stretched upwards and lengthways as far as I could see. Going down the rickety stairs, everything looked different in the daylight; in fact it looked even smaller than it did last night. My mother was spooning some hot porridge into a bowl, which she had heated up on the range in the front room, and she motioned me to sit down at the table.

'How has Dad gone into town?' I asked.

'With Mr Lewis in his van.' She explained that Mr Lewis was the husband of the angel of mercy last night. 'Your father's got a lot of things to get and Mr Lewis kindly offered to take him and bring him back with them.'

I wondered to myself if it was Mr or Mrs Lewis who had kindly offered. Next question, I thought and sure enough, here it came.

'Well, son, do you think you will like it here?' she asked.

'Depends how long we're going to be here,' I replied, 'because I can't see us sticking living like this for long.'

She then explained that it wouldn't be for long, that there was a big house coming along that was going to be the vicarage. I nearly added: and they all lived happily ever after, but didn't, out of respect. She then told me that they'd had hardly any sleep that night as Kim had diarrhoea and when they had let him out he'd bolted, so they had spent half the night creeping around trying to find him and frightened to death because of the sheep, which were everywhere. But worse was to come, for when they finally found him and got him inside they had lit some candles and found the floor was alive with cockroaches. The net result of this was my mother refusing to stay another night unless my father did something about it, hence his trip to town. We both had a good laugh about this and I promised not to let on that I knew about the cockroaches.

I asked where I had to wash and was told at the old brown sink in the corner, and be sure to wash behind my ears. Mum fetched me a kettle of hot water from the range and I added some cold from the nearly empty bucket in the corner. Washing accomplished, Mother asked me to fetch another bucket of water, which I thought would be from a pump, but she told me it was coming from the stream across the road, but that it was only for washing. The drinking water was to be fetched from the spring down by the post office, about a quarter of a mile away. Having done this, she gave me a toilet roll and asked me to put it in the toilet outside in the garden. This was quite handy for I was feeling the need myself and so I rounded the corner of the house and proceeded to lift the wooden latch on the toilet door. Apart from the fact that it stunk to high heaven, I crept forward and looked down into what was just a very deep hole in the ground. The place was also full of the most evil looking spiders I have ever seen and I vowed never to enter the dump again, whatever the weather. Now being quite desperate, I ripped off some paper and headed up into the wood where, unseen to prying eyes, I completed my morning ablutions, and felt no end the better for it. I then did some exploring for a while until I heard the noise of a van pulling up down below so, descending through the trees, I made my way back to where Mr Lewis and my father were busily unloading the van.

My father was in jubilant mood, showing us the things that he had bought which, apart from groceries, included a generous supply of DDT and a metal pump gun to spray the powder, assuring my mother that this would destroy every cockroach in Wales, and I now think while writing this by today's standards, every human being as well. To complete his journey he had bought a chemical toilet, complete with chemicals, plus three Tilley lamps and three gallons of paraffin with some methylated spirits to start them up with. Needless to say we were very impressed with all of this, to varying degrees. With regard to the chemical toilet, I had already selected my own, natural, one.

After setting up the paraffin stove, we had some lunch and I accompanied him down to the spring with two buckets and the yoke to get some drinking water and at only twelve years old, managed to stagger back for most of the way with the water, while he managed to get his breath back after the first fifty yards. Later on that afternoon, Mr Lewis took us up to the church in his van to collect various things that had been forgotten, including my father's and my bikes and the most important thing in the world, my father's primus stove which although old and battered, cooked a mean fish and chips if you'll pardon the pun.

Well, we were in residence with no electricity or gas, in a little Welsh cottage surrounded by mountains, woodland and sheep with everyone in the village speaking Welsh except us. I wouldn't have changed a thing about it lying in bed that night, reading my book and listening to the bleating of the sheep and the continuous bubbling of the stream opposite as it wound its way over the lichen covered pebbles past my bedroom window. Tomorrow would indeed be another day. The last thing I remembered was Kim giving a contented snore as he had his box in my room because of the DDT that was scattered around downstairs.

CHAPTER TWENTY-TWO
When I Grow Up to Be a Man
(The Beach Boys)

For the rest of that week the sun shone down on us and I had a wonderful time exploring the countryside on my bike. There were some fearfully steep hills around the area and I took some dreadful risks tearing down them. One morning I was hurtling down this pitch, as everyone called them around there, the sun was shining and everything was well with the world when this large fly or bee hit me straight in the eye. The pain was terrific and I swerved all over the road, narrowly missing the banks on either side, but finally managed to pull to a stop with tears running down my face from my injured eye. I sat down on a moss covered bank with my grubby hand pressed over it until the pain gradually subsided and thanked my lucky stars that I hadn't crashed, but it certainly steadied me up which was no bad thing. I remember thinking at the time, now why did that happen, I haven't done anything wrong? and then thinking, don't be such a prat, nobody cares a fig about you, especially nature. Looking back, I suppose I was growing up, but nature had taught me a lesson that day by being cruel and in another sense, saved me from far worse.

The hedgerows were a sight, filled with foxgloves, dog roses and a myriad other wild flowers that I didn't know by name. There were lizards sitting on rocks and if you picked one up by its tail, the tail would drop off in your hand as a defence mechanism. If you stood still you could hear the millions of insects droning as they went about their daily business. I remember when I found my first stinkhorn; wondering what the smell was, I found it growing in a hedge covered by a mass of flies. I was quickly learning the ways of nature in a totally different part of the country and I found this very exciting and was, and still am totally devoted to the ways of the countryside.

The rest of the week passed by swiftly and although I watched for the school bus as it stopped in the village, I could only see younger children getting off, which led me to believe that I would be spending most of my time studying nature. Sunday did little to change my mind, for after attending church three times most of the children seemed to be much younger and the few that were not, seemed to have their own agenda. My mother must have picked up on this and on the Sunday night she said, 'Never mind, son, I expect you'll soon find some nice friends at school tomorrow.'

Monday morning at eight-fifteen precisely found me waiting for the school bus outside the door, albeit rather self-consciously, as I had no uniform as yet and felt at a disadvantage. The bus arrived bang on time and was packed to the gills, all staring at me, while I was trying hard to ignore my parents who were waving like mad. Talk about showing you up; I wished the earth would open up and swallow me. There was nowhere to sit until a girl much older than I was pointed to the seat in front of her and told me to, 'Sit here, lovely.'

I gratefully accepted her kind offer, whereupon she quizzed me all the way to school. On arriving she told the boy in the seat by me to keep the place for me on the way home and promptly told me to follow her, saying, 'Don't you worry, lovely, I'll take you to where you need to go. She told me her name was Megan and she must have been very senior because everyone gave her respect, but she had obviously taken a shine to me and I wasn't about to look a gift horse in the mouth.

My new found friend escorted me off the bus and led me down a corridor with a door at the far end marked headmaster. Telling me that she would wait for me, she knocked the door which was opened by a silver haired plump individual, who told me to come in. He motioned me to a chair and after welcoming me to the school, told me that my father had been to see him and explained that I would probably settle in a lot better here than I had in Nottingham. He also informed me that he ran a tight ship, this with a glint in his eye, and hoped I would be an asset to his school. Telling me that Megan was waiting outside and would take me to assembly and thereafter to my form room, I was promptly dismissed . . . and there was I thinking she fancied me. Anyway, we set off to a church across the road where I was ushered into her row and subjected myself to the rituals of school assembly which was all the same throughout the country.

Megan then dutifully took me back across the road and introduced me to my form teacher, telling me that she was always on hand should I need anything or should I get lost. I nearly burst out laughing but managed to control myself. Get lost indeed! This place was tiny compared with my last school, and so I settled in to my first day at my new school. I was pleasantly surprised and began to get my confidence back as I found the work covered stuff that I had done some time before and it wasn't very long before I was taking an active part in the lessons. No one can imagine how great a weight had been lifted from my shoulders when I found there was no Latin and the only inclusion was metalwork. After dinner we could go where we wished and I followed some of the class down onto the local park, where I used to dig up ground nuts with the other boys. My mentor came along and asked me if everything was alright and one of the wits asked me if I was giving her one. I gave him a grin which meant everything and nothing, but improved my credibility no end.

After school I walked down the path to find about six buses pulled in but I need not have worried as there was my friend Megan, waving frantically from the window and beckoning me into the bus. When we reached my stop I was praying that my parents would not be out on the road to welcome me. I leaned over the seat and said a big thank you to Megan for looking after me so well.

She blushed a bright red and said, 'You're welcome, lovely, and I'll see you tomorrow.' No one else got off with me and thank the good lord, my parents were inside the house.

Our little cottage looked very neat and tidy when I got in

and when I went upstairs to change out of my school clothes, my bedroom looked more like my bedroom should look. I had even got some bookshelves put up and a carpet on the floor and curtains at the window, so it was in a very jovial mood that I went back downstairs and thanked them both for making everything happen. As we sat down to tea that night they were full of questions about my day and the new school and for once in my life I was able to truthfully say I had enjoyed myself and the work was well within my capabilities. I must admit that it was a great feeling to be comfortable with my surroundings and my life in general. That night as I switched the lamp off and snuggled down, I felt I was really going to get somewhere at last.

The weeks passed by quickly and before I knew it we were into half-term. I had made a friend down the bottom of the village and we got on well and spent a lot of time on our bikes, touring around the various lanes and visiting his relations who were farmers and I was learning all I could about the countryside around me. I even learned the names of the mountains whose peaks stood up, blue black in the distance. Then it was back to school for the last half of the term before the summer holidays. My mentor and I had become firm friends by now and talked together on the bus. It seemed she was a farmer's daughter, and she invited me to her house during the summer holidays. At school, we were preparing for the end of term exams, and I did have a hollow feeling in the pit of my stomach, remembering the last debacle in Nottingham.

Well, exam week came and I hoped I had done well for I felt quite comfortable with it all with the exception of French. After an interminable wait, I sat in my desk one morning and the results were read out to us. May the saints be praised, I had done really well in most things and was middle of the road in the rest with the exception of French, which I will not dwell upon. That afternoon we were given our reports and my form teacher said, 'Well done, John, you've worked hard for this,' and I came away clutching my report and feeling a million dollars.

On the bus home I confided in Megan who answered, 'Well done, lovely,' and gave me a peck on the cheek, at which the bus erupted and I, red as a turkey cock, sank down in my seat.

I was so excited, I couldn't wait to get in the house and show my parents, who were delighted with my results and I remember thinking, I could go to this school forever. We only had a week left in the term and the whole school had an air of expectancy about it. We had our sports day and various other events and at last I was on the bus and on the way home for the summer holiday, planning what I would do with myself. Saying goodbye to everyone, some of whom would not be returning, finally it was my stop. Promising to go and see Megan over the holiday we said goodbye and she was gone, disappearing from view in a haze of smoke and dust. When I got in I asked where my father was, to be told that he wouldn't be back until late as he had had to go and see the bishop.

He got back much later, arriving in a taxi, and was full of good humour, telling us he was very pleased and his day had been wonderful. I drank my cocoa and bidding them goodnight, went up to read my book and to dwell upon the happiest days I had had since leaving Warwickshire. Later as I lay there waiting for sleep to come, I could hear them talking downstairs and wondered drowsily what the meeting with the bishop was all about.

The next morning, I dressed and went downstairs to find them both sitting in the front room.

'Good morning, Sunny Jim,' said my father, all smiles. 'Did you sleep well?' Replying that I had, he motioned me to sit down and my mother made room for me on the sofa. I suddenly felt queasy and had a horrible feeling that that there was bad news on the way.

My father started off by telling me that the house we had been promised had fallen through and that was why he had been to see the bishop, who had offered him another parish in a village some miles away in a different county and he had accepted. Not waiting for the rest, I went ballistic and threatened them with everything I had in my arsenal, but what could I do at my age? I gradually calmed down, but made a promise to myself that when I grew up I would make my own decisions and they could all go to hell. Going up to the back garden which was in reality the lower slope of the mountain, I just stood there in absolute amazement.

My thoughts that day were centering on madness and I swear I was not responsible for my actions, but thankfully nobody came out to find me. Looking back now, I realise that this was the final piece of the jigsaw and I had somehow subconsciously written off my school destiny, and whatever path I was to choose in life was my choice, one way or another.

CHAPTER TWENTY-THREE
Young Emotions
(Ricky Nelson)

So there it was, no matter how you looked at it, just as school was going well and I was making friends, the ground was being ripped from under me and I had no option but to go. I had thrown everything into the pot but all to no avail and it was a very sad lad that climbed the stairs that night. As I lay in bed I vowed vengeance on everything but didn't realise that I was plotting my own downfall, and in the frame of mind I was in I would probably cause myself more problems than anyone else, but I felt the necessity to kick out and hurt someone, no matter if it was me.

However, this was only part of the story and as soon as I had got over the initial shock, they told me the rest. My father had agreed to go on a sabbatical to a theological college somewhere in Wales and would be gone for a month, so my mother and I were going to stay with my auntie and uncle in Croesyceiliog while he was away. When he returned, we had one night to spend in our cottage before we moved to the new parish. The rest of the day would be spent packing everything away in readiness for the removal men who were coming to load up everything on the day of our return and all that would be left were the beds to go on the following morning. All the rest of the furniture was being picked up from the church in advance. But this was all in the future. I believe today it is called logistics; be that as it may, my thoughts were, if this lot works out, the moon is made of green cheese. Best of all, the magical Mrs Lewis had surpassed everything by having a nephew who was going down to Newport the following day and would give us a lift down to Croesyceiliog, so I felt as if some unseen hand was pushing me from behind. The following afternoon we loaded our cases, ourselves and the dog into this benefactor's car and were on our way to the Cross.

Arriving at about five o'clock, we had a lovely meal and the folks settled down to have a good chat, while I went outside to see if anyone was about that I knew. I had clean forgotten it was a Sunday and the place was like the grave, so I spent an hour amusing myself throwing a ball against the wall and catching it, finally giving up and going back in to eavesdrop on the boring conversation of the adults. It wasn't long before my mother caught me yawning and I was packed off to bed with my book and a mug of cocoa. Looking out across the fields at the lights twinkling up on the mountain, was a sight I had not seen since I was a baby and I watched as a train caught my eye as it rattled along in the valley, heading for Newport and God knew where else.

The next morning I could hear everybody about, for my uncle was on six till two at the Avondale works and my father had to catch the bus to Newport and get the train to his sabbatical, wherever that was. I struggled downstairs just in time to get a lecture from my father about behaving myself in his absence, and then he was gone with a wave of his hand.

Back in the house, Mum was getting ready to visit other relations and as I did not want to go, I was left to my own devices so my first port of call was a sweet shop up the road where I bought ten Woodbines. Since we had been living in the cottage I hadn't bought any or even thought about it, but here I had to show off when the need arose and felt ten feet tall lighting up. Back down the road and through the gate, I saw the lad I knew from next door. His name was Reg and his dad was a postman and they were a nice family, who had known my mum for years. We got to talking and I asked what the crack was and apart from the local lads and a friend from Griffithstown coming down occasionally, nothing much was going on. I had met the boy from Griffithstown before and he was a good scout, so after a chinwag we headed off up the village for a walk and then went down on the field below for a game of stick knife, which involved throwing your knife at selected targets such as trees or clumps of grass. The morning passed quite quickly and before we knew it lunch time had come around so we headed back home and would see each other later.

That evening, I walked around to the patch of ground that separated our place from next door. There were about five lads sitting around on the dividing garden walls. Some I knew and those I didn't soon got talking and we spent the evening trying to best each other with experiences and I felt better than I had done for a week. During those weeks that followed, I also met up with a girl called Jessica who, although a little older than I, was very pretty. We spent a lot of time together, much to the dismay of my friends, but it also earned me a lot of respect as they had all tried to go out with her and failed dismally.

Time flew by that summer and in no time at all I was told that my father would be coming home the following weekend. I started to feel insecure again, wondering what the hell our new place would be like and how long we would be staying this time. I also felt the anger coming back from the feeling of having to leave my last school. I had acquired a large sheath knife and wore it constantly on my belt, feeling like a back woodsman when I was down the fields, and became quite proficient at throwing it from a distance into tree trunks. As my mother was mostly busy I could spend my time out and about without too many questions being asked. That week I spent most of my time with Jessica and we practised our snogging techniques down the fields, promising to be true to each other and I found myself saying I would come down and stay at my auntie's at every holiday.

Saturday came along and the house was alive with expectation with my mother in the front room window, watching for every Western Welsh or Jones's bus that pulled in at the bus stop opposite. Sure enough, she gave a shriek of joy at last and ran out to meet him. In he came, face wreathed in smiles, making a grab at me as I ducked out of his way.

'Well, Sunny Jim, are you too old to give your old dad a hug?' And in the next breath, 'I hope you've been behaving yourself while I've been away?'

Assuring him that I had and feeling totally embarrassed by all this affection going on, I made myself scarce down the garden, thinking that time was indeed running out for yours truly.

The next day, being Sunday, it was decided, horror of horrors, that we would all attend evensong at St Mary's church that night and I was made to scrub up and put on my best suit to accompany them all to the service. This I did with very bad grace and to make matters worse, I could feel the scornful looks of my friends as we passed them on the way. Service over and I thought we would never get home as they reminisced and shook hands with every bugger and his brother, trying to involve me, but I pretended not to hear and looked on from a safe distance. At long last we headed for home and after cocoa and biscuits, I was packed off to bed with the words that it would be a long day tomorrow.

Laying there, looking across the mountain to the lights of Upper Cwmbran, I wondered what fate would be bestowed on me before I lay in this bed again.

The following morning, after saying goodbye and thank yous by the bucket load, we were on the bus heading for Newport station and the long train journey back to the cottage. After many changes, waiting rooms and footbridges, I finally found myself in the back of a taxi heading along the country lanes to the cottage.

Mrs Lewis had got the place spick and span and the following morning I found myself sitting in the back of a furniture van, complete with dog and goldfish en route and, although I didn't know it at the time, my destiny and my village.

CHAPTER TWENTY-FOUR
I'm a Boy
(The Who)

That late autumn day when Adrian came round I realised that I had crossed the threshold and managed to get myself accepted by the village lads. We got on famously and he showed me many different things, told me who to watch out for and in general gave me a good grounding into village life. Through him I was accepted by the rest, even the older lads, who I think saw me as a strange kind of oddity and liked to show me off, forever saying, 'You'd never think he was a parson's son, would you?' At that time I didn't mind this in the least and backed all this up with a few Fs and blinds when I saw the need arise. Looking back, they must have thought that I was a little bit odd, but the skills I had learned in my previous homes also gave me a lot of respect. Once I had settled in, I spent every bit of time I could tramping around the surrounding countryside, exploring brooks, woods and hillsides. We made catapults, bows and arrows and throwing arrows . . . the latter went for miles but with no accuracy whatsoever.

The weeks had simply flown away and half-term had come and gone. With bonfire night a few nights away, I was looking forward to the village bonfire. The days now were bitterly cold, with a sharp frost every night, and looking down on everything was my mountain. Clad in his winter coat of rust covered bracken, he seemed to look down in icy splendour. No matter where you went around the village, there was no escaping him as he stood like a sentinel, his many crests fading away into the distance. I knew the time was fast approaching when I would scale his flanks and look down upon the village.

It was about this time that Adrian said to me, 'Reg is coming home this week.'

Not having a clue as to who Reg was, I asked the obvious questions: who was Reg? Where did he live and where had he been in the last two months?

He explained to me that Reg lived just out of the village, that he was a bit older than us, had been in hospital for some time and, most importantly, he was very clever with his hands and was always making catapults, bows, knives and all things pertaining to being a great lad. I obviously couldn't wait to meet him, but Adrian had no idea exactly when he was arriving. This had to do for now, and with the village bonfire fast approaching on Saturday night, I had other things to occupy my devious little mind.

The first week back at school was the normal humdrum of getting up early, getting home late and the usual cycle of lessons, some of which I'd grown to hate. Even my favourites did not give me the buzz of past years. To be truthful, looking back, I was sinking further into my shell. I seemed to have developed the ability to move my mind away from the lesson in hand and dwell upon any subject I chose, far away from my surroundings. Whatever the situation, the week passed quickly enough and I soon found myself back at home on Friday evening with the weekend to look forward to.

Saturday dawned clear and chillingly cold, with a biting east wind that seemed to drive right through you. I looked out of my bedroom window while getting dressed and all the trees at the rear of the tennis lawn, with the exception of the conifers, had shed all their leaves so I could clearly see through them the grey stone walls of the church and the regimented lines of the gravestones in front of them. Breakfast finished, I could hear my parents talking in the hall. Apparently my father had got up with the onset of a heavy cold, which usually meant that we'd all be walking on eggshells for a few days. As I walked in on them, he was in the process of telling my mother that he wouldn't be going to the bonfire that night. To me this news was, to say the least, catastrophic as he was supposed to be taking me with him. Worse was to come, for my mother then said that I shouldn't go either, as, believe it or not, she thought I was too young to go out in the dark on my own. I had a heck of a lot of grovelling to do before she finally relented. In truth, I had to promise the world to gain permission, but hey ho, another small gain in my downward spiral.

Having taken Kim for his morning walk, I headed off down the village to tell Adrian the good news The usual gang were on the corner as I opened the gate, some on bikes and some on foot, but as normal a few of us broke away and walked down to the bridge at the bottom of the village, behind which was a builders' yard housing an old tractor and various bits of redundant machinery. We spent many hours in there in the winter months, sheltering from the cold and smoking the occasional ciggy that we'd either cadged or nicked. After an hour or so we made our way back up to the top of the village, calling on the way to check the progress of the bonfire.

Adrian had several sisters and one brother, all younger than himself, and they were all going to see the fireworks that night. As I was going on my own I was invited to join them, which I thought was very good of them. But being the strange character that I was, I hated to have my style cramped, for who knew what possibilities might present themselves?

It wasn't long before my stomach told me it was nearing lunch time so I left them, promising to see them later and arriving back home, took solace in the warmth of the Rayburn. That afternoon the local football team was playing at home so we all met up on the field. Managing to scrounge some fags from the older lads, we took shelter in the lee of an old stone wall and watched the match with satisfaction, shouting obscenities at the opposition and cheering like mad when our team scored. At last it was all over with the final whistle being blown. Our team had won easily.

It was the custom of everyone to follow the teams down to the local pub where they got changed and had a few beers together, so all the younger element hung around the pub, hoping to scrounge a mouthful of beer. I had been strictly forbidden to go anywhere near the place, so I was very wary of getting caught, but it was a Saturday afternoon and I knew father would be hidden away in his study, compiling his Sunday sermons. With one eye on the road leading home, I joined in with the rest of the gang. It was bad news anyway and there was no beer forthcoming, so after a while I headed for home and the warmth of the house. Dusk was falling as I walked up the road and I wondered should I go up the path through the churchyard or go around the road. The path won, but I felt really uneasy as I passed the rows of ancient gravestones. Too much reading and too powerful an imagination did my mind no favours and I'm not ashamed to say I broke into a run as I passed the yawning black cavity of the church porch. Once around the corner of the wall, I could see the light from the kitchen window and I slowed to a dawdle, looking behind to make sure no one was following me.

As I came in, Mother was making tea and looked up from her cooking.

'Have you had a nice afternoon, son? How was the football match?'

Replying that everything was fine I carried on upstairs to wash my hands ready for tea. There is something very strange about growing up and teenage years. I notice the same behaviour in my own grandson and laugh to myself. One minute I was a normal, garrulous teenager; the next I was answering everything in monosyllables and wouldn't speak at all if I could get away with it.

Tea finished, I got up from the table to get ready and was stopped by a few choice words from my father.

'We want you back in this house by a quarter to ten tonight my son, and mind you behave yourself. Remember whose son you are, and it's me who has to stand in the pulpit and face these people.'

The sermon on the mount. I could have recited it parrot fashion, I'd heard it so many times before. I felt like saying, 'How could I ever forget, as I get the piss taken out of me twelve hours a day because of your pulpit, and wouldn't it be nice to be treated like a normal person for once instead of having to prove myself every day of my life?' However, I simply said, 'Fine,' left the room and headed for my bedroom. Once inside I calmed down and checked the clock It was only five-thirty and I had an hour to kill before I needed to get ready.

Picking up a book, I found my place and started to immerse

myself into the story. I was only disturbed by a gentle knock on the door and my mother crept softly into the room.

'Don't take too much notice of your father, son. He's not at all well and is only worried about you,' she said.

I replied that I was fine, she left the room and I crossed to the bathroom to get myself ready.

I was rugged up really well to go out that night; my mother saw to that and clad in my new duffle coat, holding a torch in one hand and a handful of penny bangers clutched tightly in the other, I stepped out into the darkness. This was the first time I had been out in the dark on my own and I felt more afraid than I had ever felt. My torch was jumping about like crazy as it finally picked out the gate at the end of the drive. Pulling myself together I thought, steady on mate, you're not even off your own ground yet. There was no way I was going down the church path so I stuck to the middle of the road with my eyes trying to pierce the darkness and my ears straining to catch any noises that I could not identify. My heart was beating like a trip hammer inside my chest and I swear to God and all his Saints that if anything had touched me that night I'd have dropped dead on the spot. After what seemed an age, I rounded the corner of the churchyard wall and there shone the lights from the village houses. I was safe.

The village was hushed as I waited on the corner opposite Adrian's house but I didn't mind, I had won a victory with myself. Not a big one, but a victory all the same. I was at least ten minutes early and my eyes were getting accustomed to the gloom. Reaching inside my duffle coat pocket, I took out a half cigarette and cupping my hands to shield my eyes from the glare, struck a match and blew out a long stream of smoke. I didn't realise it at the time but I was well down the path of becoming a habitual smoker, which was to cost me thousands of pounds and very nearly my life in later years. But on that cold November night in 1955, who knew these things and who gave a shit anyway?

A quiet cough roused me from my thoughts and I looked back up the road which I had come down to see the orange glow of a lit cigarette coming towards me. A figure loomed up out of the gloom and as it entered the light from the windows I could see it was a stranger to me. A young lad, a bit older than me, looked across at me and asked if I lived around here or was just visiting. I answered his questions and told him I lived at the vicarage and had been here for quite a while. He laughed at this and said he guessed who I might be, also saying that I was quite famous in the village, mainly down to my big knife and mixing with the village lads.

He was very quietly spoken and didn't give much away, but I guessed he must be the famous Reg I'd heard so much about from Adrian. He confirmed this and we became firm friends. He married a village lass and I still visit them regularly. Adrian was right, he was very clever and there was nothing he couldn't do if he put his mind to it. We waited for Adrian and his family and all walked down to the fireworks together. The fire had just been lit when we got there and there were loads of families coming in through the gate. The whole evening appeared to be a huge success. Adrian stayed with his family, while Reg and I drifted among various groups, occasionally drifting into the darkness of the perimeters for a quick fag. The more we talked the more we got on; he had left school last summer, but had got some battery acid in his eyes and been away to hospital to have them treated. He was going away soon to start an apprenticeship in engineering and would be home every other weekend. The one thing he couldn't understand and in fairness, neither could any of the other boys, was why I went to a different school to the rest of the village. I had found that by far the easiest way to explain this was to say it was my folks' idea and that I had no choice in the matter. This seemed to be good enough for now, anyway. The one thing that I did notice that evening, indeed I had noticed it before, was that when I looked around quickly or covertly at groups of people, I would find them staring in my direction and whispering. When I walked towards them they would then look away and start talking about something else.

I managed to pick up on one conversation and heard one man say, 'Hell, boy, 'e's a nice un, smokes and curses; boy 'is old man must 'ave a game with 'im.'

I grinned to myself. So I'm wrong when I become a goody-

goody and I'm wrong when I become normal. Well, Mr Whatever-your-name-is, I don't curse half as much as your boy, but that's for me to know and you to find out. I was to make a much bigger mistake before the night was ended, which in fairness probably sealed my fate as an all-round bad egg.

I was walking around the perimeter of the firelight, threading my way through the various groups of people, when I slipped into a bloody great cowpat that I didn't see. Apart from doing the splits, I also wrenched my back, but managed to save my new school duffle coat. I was really hurting and came out with, 'Fucking hell, Reg! I nearly split my trousers in half then.' As soon as I said it, I realised my mistake and saw one group of choir girls turn away quickly. Someone else said, 'Did you hear that?' But it was too late, the damage was done and I would have to wait for tomorrow to find out if anyone would tell the old man.

I said goodnight to Adrian's gang and walked up to the bend in the road with Reg, who was still killing himself over my little faux pas.

'Don't worry,' he said, 'half of them come from the next village and the girls in the choir won't say anything.'

This appeased me somewhat and we shouted cheerio and I headed up to the house as fast as I could in case the bogey man might get me.

Mother was still up, but thankfully the old man had gone to bed, apparently feeling much the worse for his cold. I drank a hot cup of cocoa whilst being bombarded with questions, but I had slipped into my monosyllabic state again so she finally gave up and wishing each other a fond goodnight, we headed up the wooden hill to Bedfordshire.

As sleep began to wash over me I thought, I'm going to start that cold in the morning. There will be no eight o'clock service for me. Waking with a start, I remembered vividly my outburst when I slipped over and I lay there sweating, thinking to myself, Johnny boy are you ever going to be in the shit if your folks find out about this? I must have lain there for about an hour, trying to think up some pack of lies to get me off the hook before sleep overtook me at last.

CHAPTER TWENTY-FIVE
Footprints in the Snow
(Johnny Duncan)

Amazing as it may sound, I awoke the next morning with the start of a heavy cold. Mother came in and called me early but she could see at a glance that I was far too ill to go out into the cold morning air and sit in an even colder church. So as they went off to do their Godly duties, I relaxed with a nice hot cup of tea and a few more chapters of my latest book. I heard them returning with the crunch of their feet on the gravel outside and the noise of the front door opening and, snuggling down in the bedclothes, feigned instant sleep. It wasn't long before my mother popped in to see me with some hot buttered toast and another mug of tea. Drawing back the curtains, she told me it was bitterly cold outside and to stay where I was until dinner time and then see how I felt. I thought to myself that how I felt would depend on whether I would be expected to go to Sunday school, but thankfully I was let off the hook. I got dressed and went downstairs at twelve o'clock; Mum was surprised to see me and fussed around a bit, as all mothers tend to do. She told me that my father was feeling a lot better than yesterday and he had not returned from the morning service yet. She also told me that she was staying at home that night and wouldn't be going to evensong. I felt really guilty about this, for I knew just how much she loved the evening service, but no matter how much I protested, she was adamant. I heard the back door opening and the old man appeared.

'Well, Sunny Jim, how are you feeling this morning?'

Muttering that I still felt a little weak, I left them to talk about the morning's service. So far, so good, I thought; my previous night's debacle hadn't reached his ears yet.

Lunch over, I was left to my own devices as the old man set off for the afternoon service in his other parish, and my mother took the short walk across to the church to take Sunday school. Kim and I settled down in front of the fire and enjoyed the peace of each other's company. For my part, I seemed to be dividing down the middle. On the one hand I enjoyed the company of different people, understanding their lives and habits, and sharing stories with them. On the other hand I loved solitude, walking on my own and I never felt lonely for my mind was constantly taking me to different scenarios, so vivid that I would find myself living the part.

That Sunday afternoon it was the latter. As the coals shifted in the grate and the logs spat and sizzled, I went back in time. Back to faces I had known, back to Breconshire to its beautiful undulating countryside and its winding lanes with the high hedgerows and grass growing in the middle of the road. Back to Nottingham's busy streets, some still cobbled where it seemed to take forever to cross the road in safety. Back to the mighty and the sometimes forbidding River Trent with its promenade of steps stretching away on either side. The place where people used to gather in their hundreds on a sunny Sunday afternoon to feed the swans, and play on its miles of recreation grounds stretching down to the river. Back to the mining village in Warwickshire, where the colliers used to walk home down the hill from the pit as black as the coal they had risked their lives in cutting. To the school which I loved, to the master who brought me on from a complete dumbo to pass my eleven plus in twelve months. I must have been miles away because I didn't hear my mother come in until she spoke.

'Penny for them, John,' she said with a smile.

Snapping from my reverie I gave her a grin and confessed that I was miles away. She was beautiful then, my Mum. Full of vibrancy and the joy of life, not like the shrivelled husk when I last saw her, taken over completely by Alzheimer's, not knowing or understanding anything. But that was far into the future; today I worshipped the ground on which she stood.

We had a cup of tea and a biscuit together and I broke the

news that I wanted to go to school the next day, and despite her protests, I made it abundantly clear that I couldn't afford to miss any time. She understood this and I knew it would stand me in good stead at a later date. In any case, I might not be that hot on religion but I certainly didn't want to miss the weekend's gossip on the school bus.

That evening I pleaded with her to go to church, but to no avail. She had made up her mind not to leave me alone in that big old house after dark and disappeared into the kitchen to do some ironing, leaving me to listen to the wireless. Sunday nights were crap programmes anyway until the Sunday night play, which happened to be Sir Walter Scott's The Bride of Lammermoor. It was the final episode and as a family we were into it big time. I can still hear the cry, 'Where's your bonnie bridegroom now?' As if it was only yesterday.

Bidding them both a fond goodnight I left them and went up to bed for I had my usual early start the next morning. I read for a while, but gradually sleep overcame me and I was slipping into the land of nod. My last conscious thought was that no one had mentioned Saturday night's antics.

Sure enough I was up bright and early next morning and after a hurried breakfast I was ready for the off. Seeing the worried look on my mother's face, I quickly reassured her that I was perfectly alright and had no ill effects from my supposed cold. In fairness, my old man backed me up and I did wonder if he'd been shamming as well. If anything, it was even colder that morning but at last the bus came rattling around the bend. As I climbed aboard, my friend the driver exclaimed, 'By Christ, old chap, it's bloody cold this morning; in fact it's too cold to snow and it won't get any warmer till it does.'

This piece of nonsense amused me greatly and I wondered to myself did he know what he was saying. However, his next prediction caused me to stop and think.

'Bloody hell, old chap, if it does snow you won't see me for at least a week out here in the bloody wilderness!'

I wondered if he was having a joke or would I get a week of enforced holiday thrust upon me? The day passed quickly enough for a Monday but it was so cold nobody much went outside but we all huddled in the corridors and classrooms during the breaks. At last the final bell heralded the end of the day's lessons and we all trooped like a herd of cattle down to the waiting bus and wound our weary way home. Later on that night, I was tucked up in my nice warm bed, buried in my book, when I heard my parents coming upstairs to bed. Hearing my door open, I looked up from my reading. My mother's face was a picture of wonderment.

'Your father's just let the dog out and it's starting to snow, but he doesn't think it will come to much,' she said.

I sat bolt upright, the driver's voice ringing in my brain. Well who knows what tomorrow will bring? I thought, as she bade me goodnight and see you in the morning.

Six forty-five and my alarm went off with a terrible clang. God, but I hated that bloody clock. Banging it down, I clambered out of bed and made my way across to the bathroom, candle flickering in my freezing hand. I opened the bathroom door and the warm glow of the oil lamp greeted me. Thank God they were up and had lit the lamps. Roll on, I thought, when the village gets electricity this spring. Quickly dip in the lukewarm water, remembering to wash behind the ears, scrub the teeth up and down, so they will last you all your life. What a load of rubbish we get told by grown-ups. Race back across the landing, trying hard not to spill candle fat on the carpet, climb quickly into my school clothes, knot the tie and push the comb through my hair. That's it, we are ready for breakfast.

As an afterthought I pulled the curtain aside and tried to peer through the window but, foiled again, it was frozen solid and I couldn't see a thing. Dad and Mum were working together in the kitchen, reminding me of a couple of marionettes, each carrying out their allotted tasks. One made the tea, one buttered the toast and so on. The Rayburn was going full bore and the kitchen was marvellously warm. Sitting down at the table, I pulled the curtain back and nearly fell off my chair . . . everything was covered in a deep carpet of snow.

Snow the like of which I had never seen. The branches of the firs were touching the ground with the weight of snow on their needles and the shrubbery was non-existent as it was completely covered. Although prone to exaggeration, I guessed there must be at least nine inches of flat snow and it was still snowing heavily.

I turned to look at my parents. 'Have either of you looked outside this morning?' I asked.

They shook their heads.

'Well, you had better come and have a look at this lot, because there'll be no school for me this week.'

My old man, always the optimist, looking out of the window replied, 'Now come on, son, you've got to try. You can't let that bus driver come all this way and you not bother to turn up.'

I looked across at him pityingly. My mother was giving it goodness gracious and saying she'd never seen snow like it.

Gulping down my second cup of tea I shrugged into my duffle coat, wound my scarf around my neck and headed for the back porch where we all kept our wellingtons. Holding them upside down, I knocked them against the wall to get rid of any unwanted guests, such as mice and spiders and clambered into them. Opening the back door, I realised when I saw the two steps covered over, just how deep it was and how futile was the trip I was about to take.

At least they kept the curtains open so I had some light as I stumbled around the corner, both waving goodbye. I didn't bother to reciprocate but bent my head into the wind and reached the drive gate. I felt like Scott of the Antarctic as I looked across the snowy waste that was the road. It was no use trying the church path as the snow had drifted halfway up the gate. Taking care not to lose my shoes, which were shoved into the side pockets of my coat, I lurched down the lane. My biggest problem was that every time I came to a break in the hedge the snow had drifted across the lane, and the depth could vary up to about four feet in places. I finally reached the church corner where some of the lights from the houses cast their reflection over the snow and I could see one set of half covered footprints meandering down towards the bottom of the village. Bearing in mind that this was the mid-fifties, there were only about four cars in the immediate village with a few on the outlying farms. Trudging onwards I made the bottom and stood, trying to see up the hill. I knew it was useless and to be truthful, felt a right prat as those words kept echoing back to me: 'Bloody hell, old chap, if it does snow you won't see me here for a week.' For all this I felt a sense of achievement, for at least I had tried, but then again I hadn't become a seasoned campaigner as yet.

It was snowing harder as I made the return trip and halfway up the hill, I met my friend, the farmer, crossing the yard.

'You've never been down to catch the bus in this lot?' he asked incredulously.

'The old man thought it would probably get through,' I replied.

'Listen, I've lived here all my life. We get bad snows here that sometimes last for weeks. As you know, there are two very steep hills on both roads into the village and nothing can get in – not even the bloody postman – and if it freezes tonight, there'll be no buses for a week. So go on home and get warm and tell your old man not to be so fucking stupid.' With that, he was gone, disappearing into the swirling snow of the yard.

As I approached the house, I thought how best to pass on this information and decided to omit the last sentence, much as I would have liked to repeat it word for word. I kicked my wellies off outside the back door and having knocked the snow off them, put them in the porch, for I would need them later. I entered the house and made straight for the Rayburn, a habit I was to regret later, but stood there warming my hands as the folks came in with questioning looks on their faces.

'The bus didn't come then, Sunny Jim?'

Looking at my father, my face a mask, I replied that it did not and neither would it be here for a week and that if he didn't believe me, he should take a walk down the village and ask someone else. He pooh-poohed this and my mum, catching my eye, shook her head so I ignored the whole thing and put the kettle on the stove to boil.

It was just breaking light outside and we could see the extent of the snow. It was easing now and the sky looked a leaden grey. I wondered about my mountain and how it would look in its covering of deep snow.

'Give me a chance to get changed and drink my tea and I

will go out and clear a path,' I said to my father. I noticed the look of relief on his face, and it was at this point, as young as I was, I realised that for all his bluster, how vulnerable he was, but how he hated someone younger and fitter to take over in certain circumstances. Indeed, as the years progressed, this became more apparent and I learned to handle each situation with kid gloves.

'Sunny Jim, that would be marvellous,' he replied.

Gulping down my tea, I rushed upstairs and changed and was all set to brave the elements again. Finding the shovel and a broom, I set to clearing a path from the back door to the gate, then from the front door to the gate with the old man following behind with the broom. It was good to be together, father and son, and we were like old mates. It's wonderful to find yourself growing up; I knew I was getting stronger and my body was changing. My arms were very strong for my age, with all the stone throwing and bow pulling I was doing and I felt good in myself. I could see my old man watching me as I bent my back to the snow, revelling in every moment.

We finished in what seemed no time at all and retired to the warmth of the kitchen for a cup of tea and a biscuit. The old man was talking about going down the village to speak to his flock, but I was insistent that he leave it until later, when the snow had been flattened by other walkers before he tried it. For once in his life he listened and I was glad he had, for he wouldn't have got ten yards in those conditions. Looking back, I think he was somehow grateful that I had talked him out of it. Anyway, he retired to his study after lunch and stayed there until teatime.

Meanwhile I had changed into some dry trousers and socks and walked down to the village but I could have saved myself the bother; there was no one about. In fact there had hardly been anyone up or down as there were few footprints but rounding the corner, I stopped in my tracks and held my breath for there he stood . . . my mountain, magnificent as he gazed down. Frozen in time, he reared up in icy splendour beneath a clear blue sky. A pair of ravens circled his peaks, small black dots as they tumbled through the clean cold air, the ultimate in aerobatics. Lost in time, I stood drinking in the scene, wondering where the sheep had hidden from the snow in his valleys and clefts, until the sound of a far off tractor broke into my trance. Slowly, I tore my eyes away from him and turned to head back home. Kicking at the top of the nearest drift, it broke away in one piece so I bent to scoop up some snow to make a snowball and found the top had an icy crust on it. Again I heard those words, 'And if it freezes tonight there'll be no buses for a week.'

I headed for home, content in the knowledge that everything I'd been told by these countrymen had been correct Later that night, as we sat down to our cocoa and biscuits I said, 'Well there's no need to call me in the morning, its freezing hard out there.' And guess what? Nobody argued.

BOOK TWO

Losing My Religion
(REM)

CHAPTER TWENTY-SIX
Teenage Heaven
(Eddie Cochran)

On Christmas morning I was up with the lark, and not ashamed to say so. I still had a stocking which I explored with great gusto and anticipatory pleasure. My mother came in with a cup of tea plus a huge smile and we shared a hug and wished each other the compliments of the season.

The old man had gone over to the church to get everything ready and knowing how much pleasure it would give them both, I decided I would accompany my mother to the early morning service. Rushing across to the bathroom, I completed my ablutions which had recently included pinching the old man's razor to remove what he termed bum fluff. Climbing into my best suit, I raced down stairs to see my mother's eyes light up as I told her that I was coming too. We went together, mother and son, down the drive and churchyard path into the freezing depths of an ice cold church. I think that this was probably the last morning we would do this together for many years; the next time would be a much more sombre journey. However, this was Christmas morning and everyone was smiling and nodding to each other. The church looked beautiful that morning with my mother's candles all lit and the warm glow from the many oil lamps reflecting down across the age worn pews. I knew my mates would all be home in bed, so I could relax and enjoy the ambience of the building and the atmosphere of the season as I had no witty comments to make and no one to prove myself to. The old man was well pleased when he saw me sitting in my usual pew at the back and for one heart stopping moment, I thought he was going to come down and invite me up to the front, but thank God prudence ruled supreme that morning.

The service was very well attended and went smoothly with the old man trying to out sing everyone from his usual spot in the Chancel. There is something magical about a Christmas morning with everybody in a kind of trance like state, letting the joy of Christmas wash over them and allowing nothing to mar their day. At this stage of my life I was a becoming a great observer of human behaviour and also beginning to question my own religious beliefs as it seemed to me that this world I was growing up in could be a very cruel one, and not the wondrous place I had believed in from my childhood days. On top of this, there seemed to be a lot of confliction in my elders' views and as an avid listener to other people's conversations, I was slowly becoming totally disillusioned with Christianity in general. Watching my mother as she returned from taking her communion that morning, I saw the reverence in her face as she walked back down the aisle. It was as if she had received new life from her experience. What happened ten minutes later, however, had a profound effect on me, and was probably the one of the main factors in my subsequent fall from grace.

We sang the last carol, put our offering in the collection plate and with a final blessing, were out of the door. I knew my mother would be some minutes talking to various people, so I drifted around the corner of the church. There, having a pee, were a few male members of the congregation, lighting up fags and having a conversation.

'Fucking hell, I was pissed last night,' said one. The rest were all agreeing on their varying states of drunkenness. Saying nothing, I dived back round the corner, my heart racing. How could this be? On the one hand was my mother, still quiet and thoughtful from her experience while on the other hand were people who had taken the same sacrament and had not been affected in any way. In all probability I was too young to understand the ways of the world and having grown up in a somewhat sheltered environment, was unable to cope with situations I was not used to. My mother had finished talking and we rushed back home to put the kettle on so the old man could have a quick cup of tea before he set off for his other parish Who'd be a parson on Christmas Day? Still, I thought, he would have the rest of the year to get over it.

I took Kim down the field and returned to the house where mother was stuffing the chicken and as I had requested a harmonica for Christmas, retired to my bedroom to practise. I remember it was a Horner Chromatic, quite the thing in harmonica circles and I soon got the hang of it.

It was a tradition in our house that as the old man was so busy in the morning we would open all the rest of our presents around the tree after tea. Being brought up with this idea, I am a fan to this day as it prolongs the spirit of the day. With my many uncles and aunties from South Wales I did very well and after the presents were all handed out we settled down to listen to the wireless and after a good variety of programmes I retired to bed with my selection of new books I'd had for presents.

My parents always gave me a wonderful Christmas and I always said a big thank you to them at the end of what was a very nice day. I'm sure that the youth of today would think it was a boring time, but there was not much money around in those post war years and we had to make our own enjoyment. There was no television but the families were knit closer together.

The next morning dawned cold and clear and after a nice breakfast I went down to the school with the old man to help him get it ready for that night's dance. Some others were coming later but I knew he was tired and wanted to get home, for there was a long night ahead. The top man in the area was coming from the local town to provide the music and all the village had been looking forward to it for months. There were only two classrooms, so our first job was to slide the moveable partitions back to the sides to make one big room. Then the turtle stove had to be set ready for lighting and big scuttles of coke were brought in, lamps were filled and all the desks stacked in the girls' and boys' cloakrooms. Chairs had to be placed all around the room and finally, a local lady swept the floor and put soap flakes all over it. This intrigued me and when I asked why, I was told that it would make the floorboards slippery for dancing. With all these tasks completed, I was let off the hook and joined my mates about a mile up the road who were trying to catch a glimpse of the local hunt who were in the vicinity that day. I also had a well-earned smoke as I caught up with the latest gossip. Promising to see everyone that night, I headed home to a lunch of cold chicken which I always enjoyed. Meagre fare by today's standards; however we couldn't afford goose and no one I knew had ever eaten turkey. We only had chicken once a year and considered ourselves very lucky. Myxomatosis was about to hit us in the spring and up until then, many a family depended on rabbit for their Sunday lunch, and what is nicer on a winter's day than a plate of rabbit stew hot from the pot? I really cannot remember what exactly I expected to happen that night, but I mooned about all afternoon wondering what I should wear . . . not that I had a lot of choice, but who knew? Some ravishing bird with big boobs was probably waiting around the corner just waiting to take me off to some barn and roll me in the sweet smelling hay. Some chance, hey? Oh, the fantasies of youth!

I waited for the old man to finish in the bathroom so I could nick his razor, and spent a long time on my appearance. Slipping into my new powder blue, crew-necked sweater, a Christmas present, and my silver grey trousers, I looked at myself in the mirror and thought, you handsome swine, go get 'em. Just who or what still remains a mystery to this day.

The three of us walked down the village together, past the pub, which was full to overflowing, a great source of concern to my parents but, speaking personally, I longed for the day when I could get in there and join them. Around the corner and we could see the lights of the school which meant that someone was already there.

The main doors were open but opening the second door, we were met by a warm blast of air and it was obvious that the turtle stove was doing its job. The school was looking very festive in the light from the Tilley lamps placed all around and with all the decorations hanging from its ceiling and walls. All the lady helpers were there and greeted us warmly as we entered, but gave me a glance now and then. I read their thoughts: I wonder what that little devil's got planned for tonight? The music man had already arrived and I looked with interest at the big ornate record player with its huge horn speakers. He was trying it out and I was amazed as a couple of the ladies took to the floor for a foxtrot while another said, 'Come on, John, and have a dance with me!' Talk about embarrassed, I nearly shit myself, and muttering some inaudible excuse, I hurried outside to see if any of my mates were on their way. Around the back of the school I lit up a cigarette and gradually came back down to earth, but for the rest of the evening I kept well away from the dancers and spent a lot of the time outside, eavesdropping on the young men's conversations on who they were going to take home and what they were going to do to them At that age, one has so much to learn and is so impatient to practice what they have, or think they have, learned.

One man had a bottle of beer in his pocket and spotting me, said, 'Hey, kid, want a drink of beer?'

Is the Pope a Catholic? I took the bottle as I had seen the men do and took a great big swig. It was bloody horrible. I was so disappointed and went to hand it back.

'It's alright,' he said, belching, 'have some more.'

I made the pretence of having a deep swallow, handed the bottle back with a grateful thank you and walked away, wondering why I'd bothered to come at all. What with no girlfriend and to make matters worse, the debacle with the beer, I had drawn blanks all round.

Later that night, tucked up in bed, I thought, I'm never going to be able to drink that stuff. How little did I know, with the New Year a few days away, that I was heading into another stage of growing up.

It proved to be a most eventful and informative year for yours truly, but sleep took over my thoughts and turned them into dreams of scantily clad ladies, drinking pints of beer in the pub and loving it, mixed up with warnings from my mother as to the error of my ways.

CHAPTER TWENTY-SEVEN
HIGH SCHOOL CONFIDENTIAL
(Jerry Lee Lewis)

Back in my village the rest of that Christmas holiday passed by quite quickly. The weather, although bitterly cold, remained dry and we spent the time making a general nuisance of ourselves in the evenings, and searching the surrounding countryside during the daytime looking for something to shoot with our catapults. The churchyard wall was the favourite meeting place for us at night and we used to spend hours freezing to death, smoking cigarettes and making crude remarks about what we'd like to do to the local girls. I think that at that stage of my life, if one of them had propositioned me I would have run a mile, and I'm pretty sure the rest of my mates would have done the same. Not that there was the slightest chance of this ever happening so our adolescent dreams were never to become a reality.

By now I had managed to get out of going to church, except for Sunday evenings, which I didn't mind, for my mates and I who were all sitting in the back of the church could fool around and ogle the choir girls. In those days, on Sunday nights it was a meeting place for the villagers, with everyone congregating down the path having a good gossip, and the girls who were courting met their boyfriends after the service and headed off to their secret places. So we who were left walked down to the bottom of the village, engaging in mindless chatter and smoking the occasional cigarette. The village pub was closed on Sundays so most people walked over the hill to the neighbouring tavern, which did a hell of a trade.

January 1955 and I was making my way down to catch the school bus early that morning on the first day of term. The bus arrived bang on time and I could see instantly that there was a new driver at the wheel. Asking where the other one was, he invited me to sit in the front and told me the old chap had finished. I was genuinely sorry about this but the old guy had obviously told him all about me, for he said, 'Smoke if you like, boy, as long as there's no one else on the bus.' Taking up his offer, I held out the packet but he declined, saying he only ate sweets.

Telling me that his name was Cecil, he quizzed me about my old man's job and remarked that it was a long way out in the sticks and should it even look like snow, I wouldn't see him until it had all gone. I told him I didn't give a shit whether the bus came or not, which finally seemed to break the ice and from then on we got on like a house on fire. As soon as the next pupil got on the bus I moved down to my usual seat at the back of the bus and as it filled up, I found myself in deep conversations about what had happened over the holidays. Born with a vivid imagination, I managed to invent a few items which once again helped enhance my already dubious reputation.

Down in the bottom cloakroom, I was having a pee when one of the prefects came in and said the headmaster wanted to see me before assembly. Knowing something must be wrong, I walked towards his door, wondering if Cecil had dropped me in the shit with the smoking. Walking in through the door into his study, I saw that my form teacher was there as well. I thought, Christ, what the hell's gone wrong now? but he gave me a watery smile and asked if I'd had a pleasant holiday and I replied that I had.

He then said, 'Your form teacher and I have been discussing your progress since you joined us and we both feel that, through no fault of your own, you are falling behind in class and therefore we are putting you back down to form two, to give you a chance to catch up with some of the curriculum. Now, how do you feel about that?'

My instant answer could have been, 'Bollocks! Blame my old man, because he's been dragging me all over the country like a fucking gypsy,' but I swallowed instead and although my brain was reeling, I answered that whatever they thought was right was okay with me This seemed to satisfy them and I was told that my parents would get a letter confirming this and was dismissed as if I was the drain cleaner.

Walking towards the gym for assembly, I thought to myself, well old mate, that has just about finished the job for you. Hang on in there until you can get out of this place. A few verses of 'Lord behold us with thy blessing,' and I was out in the fresh air. Hearing someone shout, 'John!' I turned to see a new member of staff hurrying towards me. She introduced herself and asked if I had spoken to the head. When I replied that I had, she asked me how I felt about it and I said that I wasn't happy.

She looked straight at me and said she hoped we'd get along, for she was my new form teacher and that was that. Her name was Miss Daniels and we got on all right but when I entered the classroom she asked for silence and introduced me to the class. All the lunatic fringe cheered me and I thought my reputation had spread before me. Getting on the bus that night I was dreading the comments but to be fair, no one ever mentioned it and for that I was extremely grateful.

There's an old saying, 'Loaded for Bear', and I was certainly just that as I walked through the door of our house that January evening. There was nobody in the house although I could see Kim's lead had gone from its usual place, so I went upstairs to get changed and could see from the landing window that they were both down the paddock with mum throwing a stick and Kim barking.

Changing out of my uniform, I got into an old pair of slacks and a warm sweater and went back down the stairs just as I heard Mum coming in through the back door. Coming into the warm kitchen, she took one look at my face and asked me what was wrong. Although I told her there was nothing, I knew she didn't believe me and I changed the subject by enquiring where my father was. Hearing that he was out in the parish and would be home for tea, I made the excuse that I was going to do some non-existent homework. I went back upstairs and after I'd had a bit of a think I settled down to read until I heard my father's deep voice calling me for tea. The old man was in a benevolent mood and telling my mother about someone he'd been visiting that afternoon when I came in and sat down. I picked up my knife and fork and idly picked at my food waiting for the storm to break.

Sure enough, as I caught my mum's eye, he asked, 'Well, Sunny Jim, how did your first day back go?'

Taking a deep breath, I said that it had not gone at all and that I had been put down to a lower form because it was considered that I wasn't up to the standard of the rest of the class.

I thought he would throw a fit and from the corner my eye I saw Mum's head go down. I let him rant for a minute until he'd exhausted himself and then let go.

'What the hell do you expect?' I asked in deadly quiet tones.

That shut him up and got his full attention.

'I've done my best,' I continued, 'having been to four different Grammar schools in two years, all of them doing different work. I have spent half my life copying up only to be moved on again. Well no more; I am sick to death of you expecting me to be a brilliant scholar when I don't stay long enough in one place to catch up with what I've missed!'

There was a deathly hush and my mother's hands covered her face. The old man looked thunderstruck and muttered that it was their fault and that he would go and talk to the headmaster. That was the last thing I needed.

'That will do no good at all,' I said. 'Don't you see they are right? It's an impossible situation as it is. Today I was asked to learn the school song . . . that will be my fourth, and the work I would have to do in the evenings would take me twelve months and anyway, I'm not prepared to do it.'

That finished the conversation and I walked out through the back door and down the paddock in the dark – anywhere to get away from the frustration of having to explain myself any more.

When I went back in, the old man was in his study. Mother, meanwhile, was making herself very busy in the kitchen and humming to herself, always a sign that she was agitated. Having calmed down I asked her was she all right and turning towards me, she replied that my father was very upset and blamed himself.

Selfishly, perhaps, I thought, so he should, but instead I said, 'Look, Mum, there is no way out of this and the only thing I can do is bite the bullet and get on with it until I get fed up. After that, I'm not promising anything.'

This seemed to appease her for she said, 'Don't worry, I'll speak to your father later and explain things.'

I gave her a kiss and went upstairs, thinking it best to keep out of the way for the time being. There was no doubt I was in crisis, and I really had no one to talk to who would understand. Growing up is a strange stage of one's life and at that moment, I'd had a gut full of the process. I had been fighting a constant battle with the old man's job and the only way around that was to use shock tactics on everyone I met. At least this got me noticed, but for all the wrong reasons. In the second place, my faith had gone for a box of dirt, and if I really came clean, I didn't believe any more. Thirdly, my education had gone downhill at a frightfully fast rate; once again I knew deep down it was just a matter of going through the motions. It was only going to take one more thing to tip me over the edge and this was, unknown to me, coming along at a gallop.

The next day I must have been pretty quiet at school, because if anything was going down I was expected to take a lead, but for the next few days I kept my head down, and let them get on with it .Getting off the bus and walking home was something I didn't look forward to for I wondered what sort of reception I would get from the old man after my outburst the previous night. Well, I didn't have long to wait. As I opened the drive gate he was bending down looking at something in the flower beds.

Looking up at me, he said, 'Hello, Sunny Jim, and how was your day?' just as if nothing had happened.

'So-so,' I muttered.

'Well, I expect you'll give it your best shot,' he replied and that was that; end of story, as if it had never happened, but I could see my mum's hand in it and wished we could all have our say and talk it out round the table. Still, it wasn't to be and I went in to get changed.

As I went into the bedroom to get out of my school clothes I saw a new razor, shaving brush and a stick of Ever Ready shaving soap on my dressing table with a note: 'To save you ruining mine, Dad.' Another step forward on my path to manhood and I smiled as I realised that the peace was made.

The next morning as I walked down to catch the bus it was bitterly cold and I could feel the wind finding a way through my several layers of clothing. Standing there at the bottom of the village, I noticed how quiet it was and except for the occasional bleat of a sheep, there was dead silence. Suddenly, I heard the roar of the bus as it rounded the corner and started to climb up the far side of the hill. I thought to myself, God he must still be about a mile and a half away, and it's so still I can hear him at that distance.

At last he came into view and Cecil shouted, 'Morning, Johnny Boy! By Christ, lad, it's cold this morning.'

Agreeing with him, I clambered aboard and we had the crack until the next stop hove into view.

The first two lessons went by quickly enough and we were doing our thing in the break time when suddenly the bell rang and the head appeared. Calling for silence, he told us to get our things and go quickly and in an orderly fashion to the bus as it had started to snow out in the country.

I couldn't go either quietly or orderly enough and for once I thought someone had been looking out for me, as it appeared I was going to get an extra few days holiday. As the senior girl got out at her stop I bade her goodbye, saying that I would see her next week.

CHAPTER TWENTY-EIGHT
ROCK AROUND THE CLOCK
(Bill Hayley and The Comets)

The journey home that day was bad enough, but after dropping the last two pupils off it became horrendous as we struggled through blinding snow and hurricane winds. Cecil, in fairness to him, was fighting a battle to keep the bus on the road, and every time we stopped it skidded all over the road in an effort to get a grip.

Lighting up a fag, I grinned at him. 'Only three miles to go,' I joked.

'Johnny boy, I'll never get this bus up these bloody hills!' he exclaimed. 'You'd better come back with me and I'll get the staff to find you digs in town.'

'You've no chance,' I replied, 'just get me to the bottom of the Crabtree and I can walk from there.'

Reluctantly, he agreed and we lurched on until we finally reached the place where I was leaving him. Watching him back as he reversed into a wide track up into the woods, I waved and shouted,' See you in the spring!' and with a roar he was off, swaying down the road and soon lost to sight in the snowstorm.

Taking stock I thought to myself, what a stupid prat you are! You've got low shoes on, a mile and a half to walk and the snow is already four inches deep. Then I thought, you could be lodging with the headmaster, pal, so just count your blessings, and away I trudged, soaked, cold and tired, but happy in the knowledge I was heading in the right direction.

If you have never walked a long way through deep snow in

low shoes and with a blizzard blowing in your face, don't try it unless you have to. I was young, fit and very powerful for my age and my leg muscles had developed well from hours of walking up and down the various hills around us, but with icy snowflakes constantly hitting me in the face coupled with the struggle to keep my shoes on, it was a very tired lad who pushed his way through the drive gate and stumbled to the back door. My mother was looking through the kitchen window and saw me coming and I could hear her calling the old man. As I hung my coat on a nail in the cool room and kicked off my shoes and socks, they looked on in horror at the state of me. Into the kitchen and huddle up to the Rayburn me, as quickly as I could, and both my hands and feet started to tingle as warm blood returned to my veins. Gulping down a hot mug of Ribena, I blew out steam.

'I walked from the Crabtree,' I said, 'over a mile and a half and snow up to your ankles, never mind the drifts.'

With that statement I got a barrage of questions as to the Why's and the Wherefores of this amazing piece of information.

'They wanted me to stay in town but I refused,' I said. 'I wanted to come home but the bus couldn't get any further so I walked.' This really pleased them and I felt like a returning hero, so I finished off with, 'Well, when this lot stops somebody's got to help dig out the paths.'

They were now grinning like a pair of Cheshire cats and the old man was saying 'I expect he's hungry, Duck, you'd better make him some food.'

I smiled at them both and said it was great to be home and went upstairs to change out of my uniform. Wondering idly about Cecil, I hoped that he had got home safely for it was still snowing hard and my footprints of half an hour ago had almost disappeared. Never mind, I thought to myself, I won't be seeing the inside of that school for at least a week, and I went down stairs to have my food.

After a lovely hot meal, I asked Mum if Kim had been outside. Getting a negative answer, I pulled on my wellies and my old top coat and let him out though the back door, for he loved the snow. I felt in the pocket of my school coat only to remember that

I'd left my fags and matches on the front seat of the bus. Shit, I thought, now I'll have to walk down to the shop and get some more.

Kim soon got tired of playing in the snow and left big yellow stains everywhere on the stark white background of the paddock.

Back in the kitchen, I asked my parents if there was anything they wanted from the shop before the snow got too deep and it got dark. More Brownie points as the old man was nearly out of tobacco and Mum wanted several items, so off I went again. There had not been any vehicles through the village and it was deserted as I walked down to the shop. Getting everything that was wanted, I quickly added twenty Woodbines to the list.

When she reached for them, the lady behind the counter remarked, 'The vicar smokes heavily, John . . . both a pipe and cigarettes?'

I answered, 'Yes, my mother's trying to get him to cut down.'

She just gave me a knowing smile and I was out of the door and lighting up before you could say 'Jack Robinson'. I kept a watchful eye out for unseen snowballers lying in wait, but all was quiet and dousing my fag, I was through the gate and back into the warmth of the kitchen.

That January day, it snowed all day and was still snowing when I went to bed that night. With no exaggeration there must have been at least nine inches of standing snow on the ground and huge drifts where the wind had blown it.

'Don't bother to call me in the morning,' I said to my folks as I climbed the stairs. 'Looks like I can have a nice lay in for a change and if it freezes later I won't be back for a fortnight.'

They both looked concerned but smiled and bade me goodnight I must have read for at least an hour and a half before I put my book down, and switching off the bedside light, lay there in the dark for a while, wondering vaguely what the light from outside was. Finally, I crossed to the window, thinking the old man must have left the outside light on. Peering through the curtains, I caught my breath in wonder, for as far as I could see, the whole of the grounds were bathed in bright moonlight. Not your normal, run-of-the-mill moonlight; this was like daylight. It was a fantastic sight, the trunks of the trees standing out against their blanket of snow, their branches almost touching the ground, giving shelter for any small creature that passed them searching for food, as they themselves became victims in catching the eye of an owl, perched on high in the snow laden branches. Through the trees, I could make out the rows of ancient gravestones, some capped with snow, and standing like sentinels, guarding the entrance to the churchyard. The sky was inky black and cloudless with the Milky Way glittering like a jewelled carpet stretching as far as the eye could see. How long I stood there I don't know, but feeling the chill of the room envelope me I hurried back to bed, realising that it must be freezing hatchets outside. Glad to be back in the warm, but loath to leave that fairy-like scene outside, my last thoughts before falling asleep were that there would be no school for some time to come.

Next morning, I was awake as bright as a button and crossed to the window to make sure the scene would still be there, but it was just breaking dawn and my window was frozen over. After a few minutes spent blowing on the glass I managed to get a peephole big enough to squint through and one look outside was enough to tell me that we'd had one hell of a frost. Hurrying across to the bathroom, I met my old man coming up the stairs, still in his dressing gown and carrying a cup of tea, which I thought must be for Mum, but instead it was for me. Thanking him, I gulped it down gratefully and sped into the bathroom. This room, being directly over the kitchen, was always warm from the heat of the Rayburn, and peering through its latticed window I could see for miles across the open countryside to the hills in the distance. It really was a wonderful sight, just like a Christmas card, the only difference being that you couldn't feel the deep penetrating cold on a Christmas card, or have to shovel away mountains of snow with fingers and toes numb from the cold, in order to be able to walk about.

Downstairs, Mum was getting my breakfast which consisted of my favourite, three rounds of Bovril on toast which, by the way, I still enjoy to this day, washed down with two mugs of scalding sweet tea. Kim, as ever, was anxious to get outside and do his business so, opening the back door, I braved the icy blast which met me and shuffled through the snow to the paddock gate where he plunged ahead and, completely covered at times, disappeared to find his own secret places. Then, with much barking and shaking the snow from his body, he came back to me, tail wagging nineteen to the dozen.

The old man was having his breakfast when I went back in and looking at me hopefully, asked how bad it was outside.

'It's as bad as I have ever seen it,' I replied and saw the disappointment in his eyes. He hated being housebound but was not strong enough now to battle through conditions like this. It was getting obvious, although he would never have admitted it, but he was becoming more and more reliant on me to carry out the heavier tasks that cropped up. For my part, I loved being able to show off and prove just how fit and strong someone could be at that age.

'Don't worry,' I told him,' just stay in the warm and finish your breakfast. I'll start to clear the snow and make a path for us to get out.' I caught my mum's eye and winked. 'There won't be any room for two until I've gone a few yards,' I said and turned to the back door, picked up the shovel and started to work.

It was monotonous work and also still freezing underneath but I finally got to the drive gate and started back on another path to the front door. The old man came out after a while and started to brush behind me, but in fairness it was too cold for him and he went back in the warm. Finishing the snow clearing, I threw some more logs in the shed and noticed the woodpile was getting low, but that would have to wait until tomorrow, for when Reg had gone back this time he had left me the twelve bore and some cartridges, so I was a mite anxious to go across the fields and murder something. Kicking off my wellies, I hung my coat and gloves in the cold room and went back in the house to check the time.

Christ, it was half past twelve already! Where had the morning gone? I may as well have dinner before I go out again, I thought, and found Mum polishing in the sitting room. The old man was nowhere to be seen so I guessed he was locked away in his study.

'What time's dinner, Mum?' I asked.

Looking at the mantelpiece clock she replied, 'Good gracious, is it that time already? I'll just put the potatoes on to boil they won't take long.' As an afterthought, she said, 'Your father's ever so pleased with you doing the paths, son.'

So he should be, I thought, there's a hell of a lot of work shifting that lot, but I just smiled sweetly and went upstairs to get my latest book.

After dinner I put on my thick coat, picked up a handful of cartridges and with the twelve bore resting in the crook of my arm, went out of the back door and around the corner of the house. Feeling like a modern day Davy Crockett (who, by the way was in the hit parade), I skirted the house and there, sitting on a Rowan tree branch was a nice fat wood pigeon. I felt the kick of the gun against my shoulder and Mr Pigeon was no more but, on hearing a shout of anger tinged with fear, I hurried to the fence to see what was the matter. The ground on the other side of the fence dropped away very sharply about fifty feet to a footpath running by the side of the brook.

Looking down, I could see a little man with a stick, trying to fish his cap out of the brook. By his side lay a dead pigeon in the snow. It was obvious what had happened; the pigeon had plummeted down, hitting him on the head and knocking his hat into the brook. It must have been a hard blow, for it fell a long way.

'Are you alright?' I shouted down as he retrieved his hat.

He glared up at me, muttered something about a fucking hooligan and stormed off along the snow covered path. Making a mental note to keep out of his way for a while, I thought that perhaps I had done enough shooting for one day and returned home to clean the gun.

We had a week and a half away from school that January, followed by a further week in March and believe it or not, were sent home again on 17th May, the day of Knighton and Hay May fairs, when there was six inches of standing snow in the village. However, I am getting ahead of myself.

Going back to school after the first break, my new found friend said to me, 'What do you think of my new hair style?'

Looking at his hair, I couldn't see a lot of difference.

'At the back,' he said, 'at the back!'

Then I could see what he was getting at, for it was quite long by the standards of those days and he had a parting down the back which he proudly told me was all the rage and was called a DA. I asked where he'd had it done and he told me at a barber in the next town, which was nearer to me than him, so I resolved to get mine done the same.

The next day he brought in a magazine showing this hairstyle and also several articles on a cult who not only had this hairstyle but also wore the drape suits, bootlace or Slim Jim ties, luminous socks and the famous brothel creepers. This cult called themselves Teddy Boys after the Edwardian style of dress they wore, and it appeared they carried a lot of bad publicity. Their trademark was a flick knife and there was an aura of danger about them that fascinated me. On top of all this we had started to hear the American music which was thrilling to say the least, and come what may, I was determined to find out all I could about the Teds and their music and to become one of them as quickly as I could. This objective was not as easy as it sounds for a young man growing up in an isolated village in the Welsh Mountains.

My new found friend, whose name was Brian, was a fount of knowledge and soon had me finding Radio Luxembourg broadcasting on 208 metres medium wave and our vicarage was soon echoing to the sounds of Fats Domino, Bill Haley and Little Richard, much to the horror of the old man who called them a bunch of heathens and me a nutcase for listening to them.

I remember the first time I heard Fats singing I'm in Love Again, when the hair stood up on the back of my neck. Another regular of the time was Lonnie Donegan singing Lead Belly's Rock Island Line. I was now completely hooked and when I heard Elvis singing Heartbreak Hotel it put the finishing touches to my dream.

You cannot imagine, if you weren't there at the time, the excitement of that music after hearing nothing but the post-war ballads of the day. I was soon memorising the words and singing the music, which to my ear sounded like a carbon copy, whereas to others it must have seemed a dreadful racket but my mates all liked it and the girls on the school bus gave me nods of encouragement. I also visited the said barber and kept peeping through the window until the shop was nearly empty, but this was all to no avail because while I waited for him to finish with the last customer, another lot came in so I was back to square one. At last my turn came and I shuffled self-consciously to the waiting chair. Putting the cape around my shoulders he asked me in a quiet tone what I wanted. Red as a turkey cock, I asked him could he change my style and put a DA in for me.

'We'll certainly do our best, son,' he replied and busied himself with razor and scissors. I noticed that he had pulled the front forward in the beginnings of a quiff, but I couldn't see what was going on at the back until after spraying and combing he got out the mirror and showed me the back. I was that chuffed I nearly pissed my pants, for instead of the short back and sides of yore I had a styled back, cut in deep with a parting running down from the crown to the bottom.

'How's that, son?' he asked.

Blushing with pleasure, I thanked him.

'Now son, that's for free,' he said, 'on condition that when your friends ask where you had it done you send them here?'

As I nodded my agreement, he finished, 'You let it grow for three weeks and come back and you'll have a brilliant hairstyle!'

As I left his shop I felt ten feet tall and looked in all the shop windows on the way to catch the bus, but couldn't really see anything. Arriving home, I ran upstairs and pinching a small mirror from my mum's dressing table, I ran into my room and checked out my hair. Horror of horrors! My parting had disappeared. Returning to the bathroom I wet my hair and recombed it, using the two mirrors. Perfect. Hurrying downstairs I met Mum.

'What do you think of my new hair style?' I proudly asked.

She didn't look impressed and said she preferred the old one, stating that he hadn't cut enough off. Feeling somewhat deflated, I walked away. My battle to become a hooligan had just begun.

CHAPTER TWENTY-NINE
Whole Lotta Shakin' Goin' On
(Jerry Lee Lewis)

Back down the village I went, to seek out my mates' reaction to my new haircut and although it was quiet, those that hung around the corner were suitably impressed, or said they were. When Reg got home late that Saturday it had already got around the village and when he saw me he laughed and pointed.

'Hey up,' he said, 'there's a Teddy Boy in the village!'

I was extremely pleased about this and silently vowed to myself, just wait a few weeks and you will see what a real hairstyle is all about.

That Sunday we were sitting up on the mountain, looking down on the village with its comings and goings. The short mountain grass was still quite damp but we found some large stones to plonk our arses on, ignoring all the advice about piles and chills. There was only Reg, Adrian and myself sitting there like the three wise monkeys and taking the piss out of anyone who chanced to come into our view. From up there they all looked like ants, scurrying around getting their morning papers.

Adrian, who was the wise man, didn't smoke and I wished later in life that I'd been the same. However, a strange looking packet of fags suddenly flew over. This was no surprise as Reg, working away, always had a new kind of smoke to try. We'd already tried Fifth Avenue, Texan, Camel and Lucky Strike which were my favourites with their toasted tobacco flavour, but these were in a light purple packet with a Cavalier on the front. Looking at the name, I saw they were called Passing Cloud and looking inside noticed that they were oval in shape. Taking one, I chucked the packet back to Reg and lit up. Not bad, I thought, when Reg spoke.

'Have you ever tried inhaling?' he asked.

'Never heard of it,' I replied. 'What the hell is it?'

Reg explained that you took a mouthful of smoke and breathed it into your lungs.

I instantly took a huge drag and took the lot down. Well! You should have seen it . . . my chest was red hot, my eyes were streaming and I was gasping for breath.

Reg had collapsed with laughter as I cursed and blinded him and everything in sight.

'You have to take it steady,' he said as I returned to normal.

I tried again and this time it was a lot better. Carrying on, I got down to the last inch or so and suddenly felt as sick as a dog and as giddy as a churn. Reg assured me that this would pass, which it did, but I didn't want another smoke that morning. As we climbed down the mountain in readiness for our Sunday dinners, little did I realise that I had covered another milestone along the road to ruin, be it health or money, but I was finally caught on the hook of cigarette smoking.

Mind you, looking back, wherever you looked, tobacco advertising was telling you just how good for you smoking cigarettes was. The one I liked best was, 'You're never alone with a Strand' and I always tried to copy the man lighting up, but a trilby hat didn't suit me. After lunch, when my parents had gone out to their different duties, I lit up a Woodbine and inhaled the lot with no bad effects, and that was the end of that.

That night after the evening service we all met up under the churchyard wall and after clumsily, and I might add completely unsuccessfully, trying to chat up the choir girls, we decided to walk over the hill and into England to try our luck at getting a pint. Our local hostelry was closed on a Sunday and I wouldn't have tried it anyway, in case some kind soul saw fit to bubble me to the old chap, so we decided to head for the next village, where I thought no one would know me and I could possibly pass for eighteen. Being a very virile chap, as every boy is at that age, I was getting quite desperate for some feminine company, and couldn't understand for the life of me where I was going wrong, but I put my thoughts to one side as we sauntered along the dark lane, with only the glow of our fags to show us the way.

On we trudged, for what seemed like forever, each one of us confiding in the others our different hopes and fears for the future, who we fancied, what we hoped to do with our lives and how we were going to achieve it. Looking back, if a modern day careers officer had been eavesdropping he would have been appalled at the lack of commitment and concern we had for the rest of our lives. Our main concerns seemed to be how quickly we could get to eighteen and be able to drink in peace, and the various members of the opposite sex we could seduce, while reaching this seemingly far away age. My personal dream was to become a dyed in the wool Ted with plenty of money, girls and nothing to do but hang around the dances listening to rock music. This fantasy, I hasten to add, was not shared by my parents, who were observing my apparent downward spiral with increasing alarm and not being sure how to stop it. Regardless of all these mere nuisances, I walked on with my mates until we saw the lights of the next village ahead of us. There were five of us that Sunday night as we approached the pub and from the noise coming from within the lighted windows, it seemed to be packed out.

Reg was the oldest, with the rest of us well under age, but, faint heart never won fair lady so, taking a deep breath, I pushed through the door and followed Reg inside, closely followed by the other three. The room which I entered, I found out later, was the public bar and it was packed to the rafters. Peering furtively through the cigarette smoke, I realised that half the customers were from our village and if they didn't know me, they certainly knew the old man.

Reg bought me a bottle of light ale which, as learners, was our usual tipple and as I sipped it I could hear the various comments of the older customers.

'Fuckin' 'ell, 'e's a nice bugger,' and 'At least he'll have a drink, different to his old chap!' echoed in my ears. They were all looking at me and grinning, with various words of greeting, and I suddenly relaxed and started to feel quite at home in this smoke-filled and very noisy environment.

I grinned as the door opened and our other three friends walked in. I saw the landlord looking at the one lad closely. He was a good lad and almost as old as Reg, but he had a small school mac on and to be fair, looked about thirteen.'

'What can I get you, son?' asked the landlord.

'A pint of cider, please,' he replied in a trembling voice.

'How old are you, son?'

'Seventeen, sir,' was the answer.

I thought to myself, bollocks, he's had it now.

'Right, son,' said the landlord, 'you can have one pint tonight as you're under age, but when you come in next week and I ask you again, I expect you'll have had your birthday, okay?'

To this day, I don't think our mate got the gist of it, and I half expected him to say he didn't have a birthday next week, but thank God he kept his mouth shut, and all credit to the landlord, he played a blinder that night. I never understood why, but he never asked me my age once. Come to that, I was never asked once in my younger years. Perhaps I had an invisible sign on my forehead, Natural born piss head, readable only by landlords. Walking up our drive later that night, sucking hard on a pear drop, to get rid of the fumes, I thought, well old mate, life's not so bad after all.

Bidding goodnight to my parents, I went up to bed and fell into a dreamless sleep. Indeed, that year would prove to be a very good year for me in some ways and a very bad one in other ways, as I would soon find out.

Waking up the next morning, I thought things were definitely on the up. For a start it was getting slightly warmer and both the mornings and evenings were lighter as spring began the struggle with old man winter, and seemed to be breaking his icy grip at last. My whole life seemed to be centred around rock and roll now, at the expense of everything else and I couldn't get enough of the music, the dress and all the literature that accompanied it. By today's standards it would seem to be pretty mundane, but after the darkness of the post-war years it was heaven on earth to me. Apart from the excitement of the music and the artists, everything was more colourful and both cars and motorbikes became more powerful with a vibrancy that we had never seen before.

Getting ready for school that Monday morning, I took longer to get ready with my new hair style, plastered down with Brylcreem and combed into the infamous DA at the back. I always carried a mirror in my pocket now and thanked the Lord that I had started shaving so early, for I had grown a wonderful set of sideboards, much to the disgust of others. I had also noticed the way some of the teachers looked at me sometimes and guessed it would just be a matter of time before a showdown ensued.

Grabbing a piece of toast on the run, I managed to gulp down my cup of tea and get out before my mother's questions and looks of distaste at my hair and sideboards. Grunting that I would see them later, I was out of the back door as quickly as I could go, giving Kim a hug on the way. I lit a fag as I hurried on my way down to catch the bus, wondering what the day was about to bring forth. It was just getting light as the bus hove into view and with a great crashing of gears, came to a grinding halt.

'Morning, you old fucker, what have you been up to this weekend?' shouted the driver, grinning.

I answered, 'Not a lot. Had a few pints last night, but apart from that, quiet.'

'Lying bastard, bet you were getting your end away all weekend,' he laughed.

If only, I thought to myself. At the moment it was a definite no-no in that department. We were now good mates, Cecil and myself, and continued our banter until the next pick up. I was lucky in that I was accepted by all the senior pupils, including the senior girl, who was to become head girl the following year and we had some good fun on the journeys both to and from school, with endless banter and mickey taking between us all and I enjoyed these times more than any other part of my school life.

That morning, as I walked around the perimeter path to assembly, I spotted the headmaster standing watching as we walked up the steps into prayers and I had a premonition that I was probably in some more shit of some kind, and wracked my brain to think what the hell I'd said or done. As we drew level, I looked out of the corner of my eye and caught a glimpse of him staring at me from behind his bottle bottom glasses. However, I passed by with no comments being made and breathed a sigh of relief. Assembly over, we trooped out once more like a load of animals heading for the Ark, all heading for our designated classrooms where I was met by my form teacher with a request that I was wanted in the head's study before lessons commenced. I knew now that something was definitely up and walking down the long corridor towards the hall of the mountain king, I again wondered what could be wrong.

Knocking the door, I was commanded to 'Come in!' and taking a deep breath, I stepped inside and closed the door behind me.

He sat there ignoring me and studying some scrap of paper on his desk while I stood waiting for the shit to hit the fan. Finally, he looked up with his best Heinrich Himmler expression.

'I'll have Paul Brown's pocket knife, please,' he requested and held out his hand expectantly.'

'I gave it him back this morning straight after I got off the bus,' I replied. That stopped him in his tracks.

'Right then, I'll have that bicycle chain I'm told you carry around' was the next shot.

'Bike chain? The only bike chain I've got is on my bike at home,' I replied, patting all my pockets for good measure.

I could see from the look in his eyes he knew he had dropped a bollock and he immediately went on the defensive. Gathering himself, he fairly spat out the next words.

'Both myself and my staff have been watching you very carefully and are not very happy with your conduct of late. Furthermore, I have reports constantly on your sympathies with the bane of our society which are called Teddy Boys. This is made more apparent by the hairstyle you have developed and by your general attitude. I will tell you this once and once only, I will not have the Teddy Boy culture in my school so I want to see a marked improvement in your behaviour and your appearance, and you can start by getting rid of those sideburns. Now get out!'

Giving him the dead eye, I didn't give him the satisfaction of a reply, but backed out, closing the door behind me. Returning to my class I thought, I'll have that bastard Brown, if it's the last thing I do. I'll wrap the bike chain around his fucking neck; good job I gave him his knife back this morning. I should have stuck it up his arse, the conniving little shit. You had better keep your head down for a bit, son, or you'll be out of the door. This bastard's only looking for an excuse.

Fuming inwardly, but outwardly calm I knocked and entered my classroom, and giving my teacher a beatific smile, I took my seat and planned my revenge.

CHAPTER THIRTY
Slippin' and Slidin'
(Little Richard)

As days go by, and also considering my earlier conversation with the head, it just about passed by, but I had plenty to think about with regard to my future. I did notice an occasional glance from some of the teachers, but then again I could have imagined it but at the same time I was wondering which of them were in league with the head. I thought all this was getting me paranoid, but what the fuck? I was not going to bend the knee to anyone. My main problem was how to get even with the little bastard who had dropped me in it in the first place. He now knew he was in the shit when I put the dead eye on him, but I knew that any attempt on my part to coffin him would bring the walls tumbling down.

I must have been in pensive mood on the way home, as when the girl sitting behind me got out, my friend, the senior girl tapped me on the shoulder and beckoned me to come and talk to her.

She asked quietly, 'What have you been up to today then, John? I saw you coming out of the head's study this morning?'

I explained what had been going on and what my intentions were.

She told me in no uncertain tones to draw my head in and keep well away from Mr Brown. Promising to keep quiet, she also trusted me with the information that the seniors on the bus had been asked to report any misconduct from yours truly, should it happen.

At this, I was dumbfounded. 'Sylvia,' I said, 'you know me, I've never caused any problems on the bus, and I certainly never carried a bike chain.'

She insisted that I must keep my head down and that none of

them would drop me in it. With that I cheered up a bit and it was soon time for her to get off. Two more drops and I walked down and sat by Cecil, the driver, but I was just about to light up when I thought, perhaps he's in on it, too and reporting back. He looked at me as I stuffed the fag back into the packet.

'I made up my mind to pack them up for a bit,' I said.

He made no comment and we jabbered on about nothing in particular until it was my stop and I headed up the road for home, lighting up as soon as I heard the noise of the bus as it headed back home.

At tea, I had the usual questions as to what sort of a day I'd had and lying through my teeth, said it had been great. Slipping the lead on Kim, I decided that I needed some time on my own that evening, so together we set off across the fields where, lost in my own little world as they say in Ireland, took my time and had a look at the day. Later that night, as I lay there in the dark trying to get some sleep, my mind was awash with the day's happenings and I went through them a dozen times. What could I do to be right? I certainly wasn't cut out to be the simpering, whimpering parson's son, but whatever I did, I just didn't fit in. All right, if they wanted a scapegoat I would be their man and my first priority was to get a bike chain. As I drifted into an uneasy sleep, my mind took me back to Nottingham and the trials and tribulations I had encountered there. It was becoming crystal clear to me that with my background, I was expected to fit in to everyone's idea of what I should be like. The moment I stepped outside the mould, I became the focus for gossip and character assassination, so I would give them plenty to talk about, no matter what the cost.

Waking up the next morning, I thought, I feel great: bring it on. Whatever, I'm ready for it. Checking my hair and sideboards in the mirror, I marched downstairs for my breakfast, humming the latest Bill Haley number.

My mother looked up as I came into the kitchen. 'My word, son, you are in a good mood this morning!' she exclaimed.

'Never better,' I replied as I shouldered my satchel, thinking there will be another row today as I haven't done any homework. Giving my mum a kiss, I stepped out of the door to meet the day.

Boarding the bus, I lit up and the driver remarked, 'Bloody hell, that didn't last long!'

'No, sod it,' I replied, 'life's too short to worry.'

Shaking his head, no doubt at the fallibility of idiot schoolboys, he engaged the gears and we headed for the bright lights. My friend, the senior girl, boarded the bus and she took one look at me and said she could see I had come to a momentous decision about the rest of my life. In fairness, she was a very good friend to me but I didn't need the hassle at the moment and was gradually withdrawing into my own little world. Everyone left me to my own devices that morning and I was glad that they had.

Walking into assembly, I felt the eyes of the head fall upon me once more and fully expected him to call me out of the line, but he left me alone which was fine for both our sakes. Looking back though, it was his school and he did have the right to lay down the rules. By this stage I was very proud of my hair, for I had a superb DA, and my sideboards were nice and thick. All of the people in my class that mattered gave me respect for my outlook even if they didn't agree with me, whilst all of the junior school gave me a very wide berth. This did not faze me in the slightest and I did not force my opinions on anyone, but was constantly being approached by others who desired information on the new type of music, code of dress or newspaper headlines that flooded the school.

It was blatantly obvious by now that times were indeed a-changing as the great Bob Dylan was to immortalise some years later. As for me, I was firmly in place on the band wagon and nobody was going to pull me off. On the bus going home that night, my thoughts drifted back to Nottingham, which was the only big city I had ever lived in and I thought to myself, I bet there's hundreds of Teds there and I bet I could get a suit of clothes there with no trouble at all.

I walked down to the village after tea and had a chinwag with the various villagers who were gathered about the churchyard wall, but my mind was full of the happenings of the day, such as they were. Realising that I must not let them get to me was one thing; carrying it out was a totally different matter and I did realise that not one of the staff would back me. Who to trust in the class was another matter, but I suppose once again the answer was no one. So it appeared I was completely on my own, stuck in a school I now hated. Why the hell was I there? Answer: my folks. What were they hoping for . . . some genius who would suddenly arise and take over everything? Answer: not a bloody chance!

CHAPTER THIRTY-ONE
I'm Not a Juvenile Delinquent
(Frankie Lymon and The Teenagers)

The month of March can be deceptive and from sitting on a mountain top smoking fags on one Sunday morning, the following week found us huddled up in the tin shed in the school playground as it was freezing the dog's bollocks off, with icy winds that went right through you. Coupled with sheets of icy rain it wasn't fit for a dog to be out, but there we were, the stalwarts, planning our campaign of misdeeds and winding Reg's Lucky Strikes into our lungs as if there was no tomorrow. I'm certain that any unsuspecting person who was unlucky enough to be out that morning would have thought the shed was on fire.

That coming year, although unknown to any of us at the time, was to prove to be a very critical one for me, both in terms of my education and also my whole outlook on life but for the moment today was the day and it was bitter, so we decided that we wouldn't walk to the other pub that night, but stay local. With this momentous decision made we left the warmth of the shed and headed for home and Sunday lunch. That afternoon it snowed again and as we stood on the corner of the churchyard wall that night I knew we would all be meeting up the next day as there would be no school.

The following morning, after clearing the snow around the house and sawing some fresh wood for the fire, I ventured down the village to find everyone engaged in making a slide on the road, much to the horror and disgust of the senior members of the community, for by the time we had finished it was about thirty yards long and you couldn't stand up on it. As soon as we had finished skating on it, we got our bikes and tried riding up and down it without falling down. Finally, having got bored with the whole thing we retired to our wall, standing around the corner where we couldn't be seen, lit up a fag and watched for the first person to walk down the road and fall arse over tip. After waiting for a considerable time I got bored and retired for lunch, returning a couple of hours later to find all hell breaking loose as some old chap had nearly broken his neck and they had put salt over the lot, so that was the end of the day's fun.

Some new people had moved into the village that March, who were to have a considerable effect on me later. The council had added two new houses to the existing ones and the first people to move in were the new headmaster and his wife who were going to teach at the village school, followed closely by our mate from the house by the church, whose mother had also been allocated one. Both the schoolmaster and his wife were cracking people who were to become close friends with my folks, and who also had a television set which was almost unheard of in the village.

The second lot of people were two retired ladies who came to live in a little house at the top of the village and must have been horrified at their peace being disturbed by everyone playing football and swearing outside the house, but they were nice ladies and never complained. The one thing they kept saying was that they were waiting for the furniture to arrive, so I don't know how they managed and I don't think anyone believed them.

Back at school after the snow and that was another week gone and Easter just around the corner. I seemed to be attracting less attention and a few more hairstyles were to be seen around the school. By now I was the proud possessor of a bike chain which was polished to perfection, and at the same time I was reading a book called No Mean City which was all about the razor gangs of Glasgow's Gorbals. This was perhaps not the best reading at my age, but I was in awe of the main character and resolved to get myself a cut throat razor as soon as I could.

By now we were getting the American rock and roll programmes and the airwaves rang to Little Richard, Fats Domino, Charlie

Gracie and of course the man himself, the great Elvis Aaron Presley and like so many more people of my age, I just couldn't get enough of the music. The older generation were appalled at the way our generation was, in their words, being seduced by the devil's music, while every Godbotherer from Land's End to John o' Groats was pummelling the pulpit and demanding for it to be banned. The Teds were also getting into the newspapers with tales of terrorising dance halls and insulting old ladies, but our generation didn't give a shit. From my own point of view, I had never been disrespectful to old people, and to this day have shunned anyone who was. However, the papers of the day were having a field day. On the brighter side we could fantasise about the ladies of the day, Diana Dors, Jayne Mansfield and Sabrina, to name just a few. The old folks were forever moaning about me and trying to get me to cut my hair, but all to no avail for I was a child of the time.

Just before Easter, I was home for a day and walked down the village on my own. Leaning on the bridge, I lit up a fag and hearing the kids playing football in the junior school, walked up to have a look. While I was watching, the new headmistress came out through the door so I held the cigarette behind my back. Of course she must have seen the smoke going up for she shouted, 'Put that cigarette out at once!' Giving her the dead eye, I very slowly dropped the burning dog end and ground it out with my foot. Turning on my heel, I walked away back down to the bridge, wondering if she would tell the old man. After giving it some thought I decided that she would keep it to herself and promptly forgot it. The days passed and nothing was said and it gradually slipped from my mind.

Before I knew it, we were on the bus heading for home with the Easter holidays in front of us and with the weather having taken a turn for the better, everyone was in a good mood on the homeward journey. Although happy to be away from the school itself, I was sad to be leaving my travelling companions for a fortnight and was well aware I would miss all the ribaldry and one-upmanship of the journeys to and from school.

Back in the village, I soon forgot my melancholies as I heard

Reg was coming home for the holidays the next day. Everybody was tearing around getting the church ready for Easter and except for meals, I was left to my own devices. The only thing to mar the week was Good Friday, with our house like a morgue and everything closed. I had a big stack up with the old man that evening when I put Jack Jackson on Luxembourg and he kicked off with Little Richard singing 'Jenny Jenny'. I seriously thought the old man was going to throw a fit as he ranted on about the seriousness of the day and how I should be ashamed. So let that be a lesson to all who live in a vicarage; do not play loud music, especially rock and roll music on Good Friday.

The Saturday was not much better but I spent my time with my mates up on the mountain and kept well out of the way. Funny how things and people change and on Sunday morning, everyone took on a different personality. Everyone put on their new hats and outfits with the old man leading the way, smiling and laughing and calling everyone Brother . . . probably hoping the collection plate would be full as it went to the vicar at Easter. The house was also filled with sunlight and my mother was full of bonhomie as she prepared lunch. My take on this, for anyone who was interested, was if that was Christianity I was glad I had ditched it and become a heathen.

The following Tuesday afternoon, we were all standing on the corner smoking and telling filthy jokes, when a large furniture van pulled up outside the two old ladies' house. A man got out of the driving seat and knocked the door, whereupon the two old ladies threw their arms around him and he was followed by his wife who got the same treatment. Lastly, a vision of loveliness climbed down from the cab and they all went into the house. I thought I must be dreaming as no one else seemed to have noticed, but after a few minutes they all trouped out of the house and going to the back of the van, started carrying bits of furniture into the house.

Judging my moment, I walked across as the vision was carrying out an armchair. I asked if I could help and she put the chair down on the road and I could feel her eyes appraising me. She must have liked what she saw because she gave me a brilliant smile, and said Alright, thank you,' in a strong Midlands accent. She disappeared into the house, but not to be discouraged I waited for her to reappear, which she did, accompanied by her old man, who said something to her and she blushed and laughed, looking straight at me. At this stage nothing could put me off, so after he had gone back into the house with something else I asked if she was staying over.

'Only for tonight, we're going back after lunch tomorrow, but I'll be coming up for a week in May,' she replied. 'I can't stop tonight as I've got to help with this but I'll be free after breakfast tomorrow.'

Well, faint heart never won fair lady so, quick as a flash, I offered to show her around the place the next morning and she agreed and gave me another of those brilliant smiles. That night she was on my pillow and was to remain there for some considerable time. Strolling back up to my mates, I was greeted with hoots of derision and cries of, 'You bastard, how did you get in there?' as well as many other obscenities which are best left out. I just grinned and remarked there was nothing doing there, which seemed to pacify them and we sloped off down to the bottom of the village for another round of fags and ribaldry, also managing to scrounge a couple of bottles of beer from one of our older mates. We drank them and hurled the empties into a convenient ditch and headed for home. In truth we were a motley crew and I would imagine every mother's worst nightmare.

The following morning found me scrupulously completing my toilet and splashing on some aftershave and dusting myself down with talc, slipping on a powder blue sweater and a clean shirt which in those days seemed to be always white, and a pair of black jeans with sixteen inch bottoms, I took another fifteen minutes doing my hair, using my two mirrors to make sure the parting was just right down the back. I took a final look in the mirror and happy with what I saw, went down to meet the day. As I entered the kitchen, my mother nearly fell over with shock and to be honest, the smellies must have taken her breath away. Lying through my teeth I told her I was going into town with Reg and we had got a lift with his uncle and I would be back for dinner. Whilst wolfing down my breakfast I found out the old man had gone to a meeting at his other church and wouldn't be back till late afternoon. I thought that everything was working out okay, baby, and I could just about get away with this and not lose any credence with my mates. Looking up at the clock, I realised I must get going and making a fuss of Kim, headed out of the gate for my date with destiny.

It was a beautiful morning and the birds were giving it some as I strolled down the churchyard path to the spot where I had arranged to meet her. As I rounded the church porch I saw her walking towards me. Not having seen me yet, she was idling along reading the tombstones, which gave me time to study her. Dressed in a light blue blouse and jeans with her long hair combed into a ponytail, she looked the business with a lovely figure and fresh face with a pert little nose. I was instantly smitten. Looking up, she spotted me and walked towards me, smiling. My mouth suddenly dried up and my heart was hammering in my chest. She asked where I was taking her and I, tongue-tied for once in my life, stammered that I would show her around the village. Putting her hand in mine, she said, 'Your name's John, my aunties told me all about you.' This relaxed me and made me laugh and I suddenly felt as if I had known her for years and that holding hands was the most natural thing in the world. As we walked down towards the church gates she told me her name was Vivienne and that she lived near Coventry. This totally broke the ice as I had lived in the same county and realised where I had heard the accent before. I asked her what, if any, trouble she had got into meeting me and she replied that her old man had said that I looked a right tearaway, but her auntie had told both her folks that I was a really nice boy. I didn't know whether to be pleased or not with this and hoped that this was not how the rest of the village saw me, but I needn't have worried, I was pretty safe on that score.

That morning I took her everywhere and introduced her to my mates, who stood there with their mouths hanging open, obviously in shock, but she handled it like a professional whilst I was praying that they wouldn't come out with any swear words. It's always the same when you're enjoying yourself, for it was soon time for her to go. I was feeling quite pissed about this but she snuggled up and gave me the most amazing snog as she left and pressed a piece of paper into my hand. As she went through the door she shouted, 'See you in a month; write to me!' and was gone.

Walking up the path for home, I opened the piece of paper and it showed her address with the words, 'Will you be my boyfriend?' written in a small neat hand, with a load of kisses underneath. Stuffing it safely away in my innermost pocket, I felt a warm glow and thought to myself, Roll on May, Johnny boy, the sooner the better. To this day I cannot get over the way a smile from a pretty face can temporarily change one's character.

Back at the churchyard wall that afternoon, I was strangely quiet and didn't join in with the usual banter and for once, my mates left me alone. The lorry had gone from the ladies' house and I imagined her on the long journey home, being quizzed by her parents about me and I vowed to be extra polite to her auntie from then on. The rest of the week passed by. I spent a lot of the time high up in the rookeries, winning bets on various nests until Reg said, 'You won't be happy until he has killed himself so try yourselves for a change.' This was met with shuffling feet and more bad language.

On the Sunday night as we walked over to the pub after church, I knew it was back to school tomorrow and was not looking forward to it. Reg was off back tomorrow as well and wouldn't be home for a fortnight so it looked like being a quiet old time. That night when I got to bed, I wrote a long letter to Vivienne, full of romance, and prayed that her folks wouldn't open it. My last conscious thoughts were, thank God my mates couldn't see it!

CHAPTER THIRTY-TWO
Bad Boy
(Marty Wilde)

Living in a small village has its perks, which are enormous, but occasionally it also has a downside. In this case the downside was that everybody knew everybody's business and sure enough, as I sauntered down to catch the bus on Monday morning, I met a lad who worked on a local farm. He was a lot older than me and I didn't see him very often, so it came as a bit of a shock when he asked me how long I had been 'doin' a bit of courtin'.'

My immediate thought was, bloody hell, I've only been out with her for two bloody hours, but I grinned and told him he must have got it wrong. Lighting up a ciggy, I climbed aboard the bus and for the next ten minutes sat talking to the driver about the past week, leaving out the bit concerning my liaison.

As the bus started to fill up I went to my customary seat at the back before the senior gang got in. Imagine my horror when my friend, the senior girl, got in, sat down and said, 'I heard you've been enjoying yourself last week. Anyone we know?'

I was now seriously pissed off as I had begun to fancy her and didn't want anything to wreck my chances. 'Who the bloody hell told you?' I asked.

'Now, now, don't get upset so early in the morning! So it must be true?' she quipped, doing nothing for my temper.

Slumping down into my seat I stared out of the window at the passing countryside, desperately trying to think who the hell had spread this lot around. I racked my brains throughout the journey but got nowhere and as we were approaching the school, I felt hot, sweet breath on my cheek and a voice whispered sweetly in my ear, 'What's her name then, John?'

I knew I had to play this cool or I would never live it down. Turning back in my seat I saw my friend smiling at me and looking her straight in the eye, replied, 'Can't tell you that, darling, but don't worry yourself, she couldn't hold a candle to you,' and gave her a broad wink at which she turned bright red and looked quickly out of the window.

Those nearby that heard, cheered and I thought, round one to you, son, and then it was time to leave the bus.

I went straight down to the toilet block and had a quick drag on a dog end I had in my pocket and started to feel better. Several of the juniors looked at me in awe, but my friends and I were used to this and tended to ignore them. We felt we had reached that lofty status where we could get away with anything and had long finished hiding behind the bike shed for a drag. Crushing out the end, I flushed it down the toilet and headed for assembly, hoping to Christ I was to have some peace for the rest of the day. One of my mates slid me a copy of the New Musical Express on the way out and I hid it inside my blazer pocket. We had maths first thing and I knew I wouldn't get away with it but following on, we had science and the teacher was a dozy cow who couldn't keep control, so I could read it in peace while the fall guys played her up. True to form, I read my magazine but being senior to the rest, wondered how long it could go on. The racket was tremendous. Sure enough, we had geography that afternoon and as well as being our form master, the teacher was the most respected man in the school. I never heard him raise his voice but I had great respect for him.

He said, in his quiet way, 'Before I start the lesson, I had the upper sixth in the classroom next door this morning and I couldn't hear myself speak for the racket you were making. In the end I had to pack the lesson up . . . the first time ever and if it happens again I will bring the wrath of God down on you.'

There was a stunned silence and I wondered how long it would take for the grasses to drop their poison but I knew one thing for sure, the teacher's card was marked as well as ours that morning. Getting on the bus that afternoon, I was in a better mood and sat looking out of the window at the way the countryside was changing as it got warmer. The fields and hedges had taken on their summer mantle of lush greens and where the meadows had been put for hay, the grass was like a sea as it rippled in the breeze, full of buttercups and other wild flowers, a sight you no longer see today in a world of pesticides and fungicides and God knows whatever else.

Suddenly I felt a tap on my shoulder and turning, saw our most senior lad grinning at me.

'Hey, John. Were you in that science class this morning?' I nodded and he continued, 'Bloody hell, Gogger was pissed off; he had to abandon the lesson.'

Replying, I said, 'Yeah, I know, he had a right go this afternoon. It's her fault, she's got no control and neither have some of these wankers I've been saddled with, but he was in a shit mood and it's bound to end in tears.'

He nodded and we had a long discussion about the problem and I knew it would go back but I didn't give a monkey's fuck, I had enough problems of my own.

Our senior girl had been studiously ignoring me all the way home but as the kid next to me got out, she slid into his seat. I just looked at her and grinned, but I could see she wasn't too happy.

She said 'Look John, I didn't mean any harm this morning and was only having a joke. There is no way I want us to fall out, I know you're having a rough time, but let's be friends?'

I looked at her and gave her a grin. 'For Christ's sake, Sylv, I'm not mad at you, it's just everything and everybody at the moment. I hate this bloody school and I'm trying to find my own identity, so take no notice of me.' I was looking at her straight in the eyes at that moment and I saw her face soften and I realised just how pretty she was and I fancied her like hell, but swallowing, I knew she was already courting a bloke in the sixth form and she was not for me. All the same, we were very close at that time. Seeing her get off at her stop and waving, I felt very strange as I made my way down the bus to be greeted with, 'Well, Johnny boy, how's your day been?'

Blowing a stream of smoke at the windscreen I replied that it had been as usual, and he then said, 'You need to calm down, my friend. There are a lot of people worried about you and also a lot of questions being asked.'

With eyes narrowed through the tobacco smoke, I weighed him up and again realised that I had misjudged him. Getting off the bus I gave him a grin and said I'd see him in the morning. Walking up the road, I resolved to write a long and explicit letter to Coventry.

The weeks passed by and I got into minor skirmishes at school, but nothing terrible and I began to think they were giving me a break. However, back at home I got into more shit than I could imagine and although most of it was down to me, some things were not. The weather was really warm that May and I was looking forward to Vivienne coming back in the last week, but in the meantime a couple of things happened that kicked me off.

One night I was sitting in the front room twiddling my fingers, when my father said, completely out of the blue, 'For the Lord's sake, Sunny Jim, stop fidgeting. If you want a cigarette, have one. Your mother and I have known for months that you smoke and while we don't condone it, we understand that you young men are just the same as we were at your age.'

I very much doubted that but nearly fell out of the chair at this statement, but needing no more encouragement, got out my Woodbines and lit up. It felt very strange for the first few minutes and I had heard all the stories of stunting your growth many times before. So what; I would grow up to be a pygmy? However, my mother then let slide a little bit of information that stopped me in my tracks when she confided that they had known for months as the school teacher had told them. I quickly confirmed it was the right school teacher and bang went another reputation down the drain. It was far, far better to know who you could trust and who you couldn't.

Although most of my waking hours were taken up with combing my hair in front of the mirror or two, and learning every rock song I heard off by heart, I was also quite good at tickling trout, having been shown how the previous summer by a local farmer's son. As my auntie and uncle were coming to stay the next day, I thought I would try my luck as the weather was very warm. Lying on the bank above one of my favourite pools, I carefully felt around the tree roots under the bank and sure enough, there were two nice fish coming into the warmth of my hand. No grabbing here, but stealth as I let him ease through my hands and then return. Slowly, I slid my hands up his plump body until reaching his gills as he opened them, and it was goodnight Mr Trout as he lay on the bank with his neck broken. His buddy swiftly followed the same fate and threading them on a stick, I moved on to the next pool for I needed two more. In no time at all I'd got my fish and had just vaulted the gate out onto the road when the schoolmaster pulled up with his wife.

'Good gracious, John, have you just caught those fish?' he asked.

Replying that I had and that they were for my relations' tea, he stated that they loved fresh trout if I ever had any spare. It was in my mind to ask if they liked them smoked, but I thought better of it and returned home.

One evening about a week later, I was up the brook at the bottom of our garden and caught five beauties. Threading them on a stick, I walked up to the schoolmaster's house but there was no one at home. Spotting a fanlight window open, I leaned down and opened the main window which was over the kitchen sink. Filling a bowl with water, I dropped the trout in, which I had already gutted and closed the window.

The next afternoon, I was walking up the village from school when all hell broke loose. The schoolmaster's car screamed to a halt, as much as a broken down wreck could screech and he shouted at me, 'I want a word with you! Did you break into our house last night and frighten my wife to death? I was putting the car away and she happened to walk into the kitchen and put the light on. I heard her scream from outside.'

I was instantly on the attack and told him it was he who had asked me to get them some fish, and putting them in water was the only way to keep them fresh. All to no avail and I seriously considered telling him to fuck off, but I knew his relationship with my folks, so I just gave him the dead eye and left him sitting there. I thought, yet another beautiful friendship gone down the tubes. Still seething, I walked into our house and Mother asked what was wrong. When I told her she laughed and said not to worry it would soon blow over. Ever the peacemaker, my mother, but I think she was fighting a lost cause as far as I was concerned.

I had now managed to scrounge a coil of rope and had it hidden in my bedroom, behind some cases. This was wonderful because I would come in about ten on a Saturday night, feign tiredness and go to bed, tie the rope to the bed leg and out of the window and back out down to the pub, where I could now have a drink with no one dropping me in it. I would tiptoe back across the lawn later when my parents were sleeping the sleep of the just and let myself in with a spare key I had stolen. One morning, however, my mum brought me a cup of tea after the eight o'clock service, and spotted the rope curled up under the bed. Eyes wide she asked what it was doing there. Quick as a flash I explained that we had found a badger's sett on the hill opposite and went up there to watch them. Bless her, she thought it was wonderful, but I made a mental note to be more careful in future

As per usual, we went over to the pub later and had a good evening as all the locals knew about my latest escapade and were all offering me a pint. As I climbed into bed sometime later I thought, one more week and Vivienne will be coming.

Fortunately for me, most of that last week in school was taken up with trials outside in preparation for sports day, and I made a name for myself throwing the cricket ball and breaking the record, but I kept right away from the track events. Everyone seemed to be in a good mood and we were all relaxed on the bus going to and from school. I had a letter from Vivienne saying she would be back at her auntie's on the Saturday afternoon and secretly, I couldn't wait to see her.

At last it was time to board the bus for the last time for a week and although I was glad in one way I was sorry in another. I would miss my friends, especially Sylvia, and was getting closer to her as the weeks went by. Reg would be home on Saturday morning, so all round it promised to be a good week. Saturday morning I was going into town for my three-weekly visit to the hairdresser, so I hoped I would be at my best for the holiday.

CHAPTER THIRTY-THREE
Sealed with a Kiss
(Bryan Hyland)

Saturday morning and I was headed for town and my mate, the barber. By luck, Reg's uncle was going in, so I had a lift both ways and having had an early wash and shave, I headed down into the village to meet my lift. I felt good that Saturday morning as I lit up the first of the day, and took the nicotine deep into my lungs. My hair was now the envy of my mates and I had acquired some fifteen inch bottom jeans which I was pretty pleased with and along with my powder blue sweater I felt I could take on the world, but more likely the world was going to take on me. Wandering down the village, exhaling smoke and singing to myself the Platters latest, I was thinking that Vivienne would be here tonight or Sunday at the latest and I couldn't wait to see her. I felt a warm flush stealing over me at the thought of her pressing against me as she had on that last morning when we parted. Pretty naïve me, in the ways of women, but thought I knew it all and knew nothing.

I bent over the bridge and was looking for trout when I heard the car pull up and a voice shouted, 'You getting in, or what?'

I turned around to see Reg grinning at me from the back seat of the car. Quickly throwing the butt into the stream I jumped in beside him, asking when he had got back.

'Last night,' he told me. 'I came down on my new bike.'

I nearly fell out of the car. 'Jesus Christ! That must be all of sixty miles,' I said to him.

'Yes, I must admit my arse is a bit sore this morning,' he replied.

It took us about a half an hour to get into town and pulling into the car park, we arranged to meet in an hour and a half, which gave me plenty of time to do what I had to do.

Walking into the barbers, I was pleased there weren't many in that morning and took my place. My turn soon came around and as I sat in the chair he asked me if I wanted the usual and started cutting my hair into shape, all the while carrying on a conversation, asking me different questions. Suddenly he asked if I was doing a bit of courting, to which I replied that I was, and felt very grown up when he bent down and said if I ever needed any rubbers to just say: '. . . and the usual, please...'

Knowing that my girlfriend was coming down, I replied that I would like the 'usual, please' and he went to his cupboard and slipped a small packet into my hand with a wink. He then sprayed my hair with some stuff out of a bottle and showed me the results in the mirror. I was chuffed to bits with my hair and thanking him, paid up and sauntered out of the shop, clutching my ill-gotten goods in my trouser pocket and smelling like a brothel keeper's clerk.

Halfway up the main street was a café where all the Teds hung out and lighting up a fag, I walked up to the counter, got myself a coffee and joined some others who were sitting around listening to the jukebox. Some of these lads were a lot older than I was but they accepted me as one of their own and I was well pleased to be with them, especially as a couple of them had fair reputations. We had the crack and I put a two shilling piece in the jukebox, putting on one each of Elvis, Little Richard and a new one which I had only heard once on Lux called 'Last Train to San Fernando' by a bloke called Johnny Duncan. It also turned out to be the first record I ever bought. Having listened to the records and drunk my coffee I said my goodbyes and headed for the street, noticing some of the older customers looking me up and down and quickly turning away, which gave me a tremendous buzz.

I had half an hour to kill and spent it eyeing up the local talent and seeing which one I fancied the most. As I stood there lost in my own little world, Reg came up and tapped me on the shoulder.

'Bloody hell, mate, I thought you were going to have a haircut?' he said.

I protested that I had and he remarked that I'd only had an oil change! We stood there watching the people moving around us and it was soon time for us to go back to the car. As we returned along the road and up into the hill country, I put my hand into my pocket and felt the small package that I'd bought, wondering if I would get the chance to try them out in the coming week.

Pulling in at the top of the village I thanked the driver and telling Reg I would see him later, bounded up the path and into the grounds. Entering the back door I saw the look of disappointment on my mother's face.

'John! I thought you were going into town to get a haircut?' Replying that I had, I headed upstairs to get out my mirror and check out my DA. I was well pleased and it had certainly grown, standing way over my collar and I thought holy shit, there will be hell to play come school time, and then again . . . what the fuck!

During lunch I could see the old man looking at my hair but nothing was said and I finished my meal and went upstairs to change and then made my way down the village. Standing under the wall, I lit up and Adrian must have spotted me from his window as within a few minutes he had joined me. '

Christ, John, your hair looks well,' he said.

It's alright, I suppose,' I said nonchalantly, but inwardly gloating. 'Let's go down the bottom,' I said, 'because if Viv arrives, her old man will think all I do is stand here smoking against this fucking wall.'

So off we walked to the bottom of the village and were soon joined by Reg, the conversation going from girls to motor bikes to rock and roll and who would be the first to get a record player.

About this time there was a kind of a toff who, although he lived outside of the village, had a farm within the village limits. He used to drink a lot of gin and was pissed most of the time, but he seemed to have it in for me, as I had heard him shout as I went past on several occasions. However, this afternoon as he came down the hill he pulled up and looked at me.

'You're a bloody teddy boy,' he shouted, 'and we don't want any teddy boys in our village.' Whereupon he crashed the gears and roared off in his Landrover. This was starting to unnerve me as he was a man of about forty years of age and he had got the Indian sign on me as I hoped I would not bump into him on my own. However, if I had any illusions of this problem going away I was much mistaken as time was to tell.

Later on, we went for a walk along the brook but couldn't see a thing as the water had been stirred up by something upstream, probably cattle drinking, so we decided it must be coming up to tea time and headed for home. As I passed the house where Vivienne was staying, I had a good look but there was no car around so I surmised that she had not arrived yet and continued on my way home for tea. I suppose that anyone bothering to read this is thinking, 'My God, what a boring existence' but it was the middle fifties and miles out in the sticks so we had to make our own fun, which we certainly did and I would not have changed a minute of it. Anyway, if I'd lived in a town at this stage of my life I would probably been locked up at the very least.

Tea on a Saturday was always a solemn affair with the old man deep into his sermons for the following day and I was glad to finish eating and take myself off upstairs for a read. About seven, my mother knocked the door and came in with a cup of tea, asking what my plans were for that night. Never one to give too much away, I said I was going down in an hour to meet my mates. She left the room saying that it would be nice for me and hoped I would have a nice evening.

Mulling it over in my head, I wondered if Vivienne would arrive tonight or in the morning, so I had a wash and put some smellies on and headed downstairs, checking my hair in the big hall mirror as I went. Mum was in the sitting room listening to the radio and the old man was locked up in his study, so I muttered a goodbye and headed for the village. The nights had really drawn out now and it would be light until at least half nine. Lighting up a fag, I checked if the car was outside Vivienne's house, but there was nothing there and the top of the village was empty, so I walked down past the pub and heard a shout. One of the older men was coming out of the door and asked if I fancied a pint.

'He won't serve me,' I said. 'He knows I'm not old enough.'

'Step into the porch,' he replied, 'and I'll get you one.'

So I walked in and sure enough, he was back in a couple of minutes with a pint.

'Get that down you,' he laughed and I took him at his word and swallowed it as fast as I could, this not being a good practise but I was learning the trade. I offered him one back but, refusing, he said he'd see me on Sunday night at our local, so I left, warily glancing up the road in case the old man was coming down for a stroll. I walked down to the bridge and stood there deep in thought. When I looked up to see the dreaded Landrover coming down the road towards me, I must confess I felt very worried as it slowed down to approach the bend, pulled up almost to a halt and I heard the dreaded voice through the open window of the vehicle shout, 'We don't want any fucking teddy boys in our village!' and pulled away again.

I remember turning away, lighting up a fag and looking down into the brook, saying to myself, 'You've got to do something about this bastard, old mate.' But what? I was only a boy and he was a full grown man, and pissed or not, he would be too much for me. Leaning over the bridge and lost in thought, I didn't hear anything until a cool pair of hands went around my eyes and as I jumped nearly out of my skin, a voice said, 'Where's my welcome kiss, then?'

I turned around and there she stood, lovelier than I could remember or imagine and I'll leave the next five minutes to memories.

CHAPTER THIRTY-FOUR
Guess Things Happen That Way
(Johnny Cash)

Back at the ranch, Mum was humming to herself as she prepared the vegetables for lunch and after a swallowing a copious amount of water, Kim got into his basket for a nap. The kettle was boiling on the gas ring and I sat down with Mum and had a cup of tea. I have to admit that all my life I've never understood why women are so nosy, but true to type, within a few minutes the comfortable silence was broken.

'How long is Mrs Jenkins's niece here for, and are you seeing her today? You ought to bring her round to meet your dad and me, we'd love to meet her.'

With this last statement I swallowed the remainder of my tea down the wrong way and after nearly choking, gave her a withering glance. Bless her, she just gave me a knowing smile and returned to the vegetables, while I ran upstairs to check my appearance and then headed out through the back door.

I was early and wandered up the side of the brook, ensuring that I didn't disturb anything. It was indeed a glorious morning and the alders that lined the stream were full of glorious birdsong. Making my way back to the footbridge, I looked at my watch. She was late again and I wondered if the directions I had given the night before had been clear enough. I also realised that she would have to pass the bottom of our ground and I wouldn't put it past my mother to just happen to be around somewhere. Then, looking through the gaps in the trees, I could see her swinging along in that easy fashion that she had. Wearing a pink blouse and drainpipe jeans, she looked good enough to eat, and as I was lying in the long grass she was almost on top of me as I said Hi. Stopping dead in her tracks, she had her hand to her mouth and I could see her change colour before she realised it was me and then lying down beside me, punched me on the arm as we were lost in each other. Drawing apart, she laughed and breathlessly asked if I was alright this morning.

Auntie asked if you were a bit off colour as she thought you were very quiet last night,' she said.

Pulling the heads off some grass, I replied, 'Well I expect your folks think I am some lunatic with the hair and the attitude.

Grinning, she replied that they had all thought what a lovely boy I was, so if we had a good week, they were going to ask me down to Coventry for a week.

Trying hard to look totally unconcerned, although secretly I was chuffed, I rolled over and we lay like that, quite comfortable, and the world carried on and we didn't give a shit. Realising I was becoming very aroused, I turned over on my stomach and tried in vain to think of her old man and what he would do to me next Saturday if I didn't behave myself. She grinned at me and suggested we walk on down the brook and I showed her a pool where the trout lay.

Lying on our stomachs, I let her edge forward until her head was over the bank and as her eyes got accustomed to the water she gasped, and looking around at me, I could see the excitement in her eyes as she asked what they were.

'Fresh brown mountain trout,' I replied. 'The best eating you could ever have.' If she hadn't been there I would have slipped my trousers off, but gentleman that I was, I stepped out of my shoes and socks and she gasped with amazement as I slowly entered the water and it came up to my knees. The cold water soon calmed me down and I waded slowly over to the far side where the deepest part of the pool was and where the roots of the alders gave shelter beneath the water. Slowly, oh so slowly, I let my hands feel around and under the roots where I could feel the fish as they circled around my open hands, not trying to grab them but letting them come to the warmth of my hands. Then I would slide my hand along the belly and up to the gills, into the open gills and it was Goodnight, Mr Trout. Holding him under the water, I quickly broke his neck and held him up for her to see.

Talk about delighted, she was ecstatic as I threw him onto the bank and returned to the pool for another. I managed to get three out of the pool that were a good size, swiftly gutted them, threaded them through the gills onto a piece of elder branch and off to the next pool, telling her to keep them wet and away from the sunlight. I finally caught five and was the hero of the hour.

Threading them through the gills on an elder twig, I gave them to her and told her they were for her and her auntie's supper that night. My trousers soon dried and after a good snogging session it was time to go as lunch would be ready. Seeing her safe with the fish and arranging to meet up that afternoon, I headed back home for Sunday lunch and various questions as to what I'd been doing all morning.

I wondered if I could get away with taking her over to the other pub that night, but I needn't have worried as when we met later, she told me she had to go out with her auntie in the car that night to see some relations, which was all for the best and let me off the hook with my mates. However, I was flavour of the month with the fish and was invited round the next morning.

The whole of that week was wonderful, both weather wise and company wise but like anything enjoyable, it flew by and I took her up to the house to meet Mum when the old man was out on his rounds and we all got on a treat.

On Friday afternoon, we were down on the bridge when I heard a car sound its horn and sure enough it was her folks, and she ran to meet them. That night I called for her and went in to meet Bob and his wife who were all smiles and said they had heard about my fishing exploits, but added that if I lived by them I'd be locked up and the key thrown away. Anyway, I was told that I could come to stay if I wished. When I took her back that night the house was in darkness and she was right down in the dumps so after a tearful goodbye, promises to write and a last kiss, I was away home.

Early next morning, I ran down to the house but the car had

gone so, lighting up a woodbine, I walked disconsolately around the road towards home. Passing a familiar part of the wall, I looked and found the stick I had pushed in there last week and retrieved my packet with a wry grin. Well, there's always next time, I thought to myself and carried on home for breakfast.

I was totally miserable all weekend. Three of us caught the bus into the local town on Saturday night and went to the pictures. I think we saw Carve Her Name with Pride, but I cannot be sure. We had to bike for three miles to get the bus and afterwards had some fish and chips before getting the bus home, which left half an hour after the picture finished, so there was no chance of a pint or anything else, for that matter. Shouting goodnight to each other as we got to the village, we headed our separate ways. Big adventure, hey? I had a good lie in the following morning and didn't even bother to go out that night but instead went to bed early, mulling over the events of the previous week and I finally dropped off thinking of having to go to that bloody school the next morning.

Sure enough, I was up at the crack of dawn and washed and dressed by the time my mother surfaced.

'I've put the kettle on and made the Rayburn up,' I said as she came into the kitchen.

'Your father's not very well; he thinks he's coming down with a heavy cold,' was her quick reply.

Looking at her, I could see she was worried about him as he was not that strong to fight off these illnesses. She said she was fine and I gulped my tea down, kissed her goodbye and headed off down the road to catch the bus.

On the dot it arrived with the driver laughing as I mounted the steps.

'Johnny boy, how have you been you old bugger?'

Grinning, I jumped into the front seat by the side of him and lit up a ciggy. I was genuinely pleased to see him and replied that I was just fine except for coming back to this poxy place.

'Now listen, Johnny bach,' he said, 'you didn't hear this from me, but I had to go to a meeting at the school when I got back last Friday week and they wanted to know if you were behaving all right on the bus and if I had any worries.'

I looked at him straight in the eye as he said, 'Of course you were okay and I had never had a problem with you, so that was it and they didn't keep me there, but there was something going on, so keep your head down and say nothing.'

Well fuck me, I thought, what have I managed to do now? I would hold my hand up to anything if it was my fault but this was persecution and I'd had a gutful but being the peacekeeper, I knew I was almost fifteen and could bail out at any time. However, I needed to cut the old man some slack and leave on my terms, not theirs. Pretending to be looking out of the window, I watched Sylvia as she boarded the bus and she looked absolutely stunning. Thumping me on the arm, she asked if I had a good week. I must confess that all thoughts of Vivienne went clean out of my mind at that moment as I looked into the brown pools of her eyes, sensing that she was pleased to see me.

'Pretty quiet, really,' I answered, 'but it's lovely to see you again.'

Going bright red, she laughed and looked quickly away and I thought, old mate, either you've got an amazing imagination or this bird really fancies you. Changing the subject, she told me that there had been a meeting at the end of term and that they had been asked if there were any worries about any people on the bus, but nothing else had been mentioned. I confided what I'd heard and she could see I was worried, but there was nothing we could say and the bus started to fill up. The head was missing from assembly and I hoped he had fallen down a well, but sadly we were informed he was laid up with influenza. At least I was off the hook for a few days.

The week passed with no further problems but I came out of the bottom cloaks on Thursday afternoon and bumped straight into the head. You could sense the atmosphere between us and I thought, here we go, as he looked me up and down. But you could have knocked me down with a feather when he smiled and said, 'Ah, Elias. How are you and your mother and father?'

None the better for you asking, I thought, but answered, 'Fine, thank you.'

He nodded. 'We had a meeting at the end of term and I am

writing to your parents with a suggestion that you may possibly be better travelling to another school, than having to come all this way. How would you feel about that?'

Stone faced, I replied that a decision like that was up to my parents.

'Quite right,' he replied. 'Well, I expect I'll be hearing from them in due course.' With that, he turned on his heel and strode off.

I shot back into the cloakroom and going into one of the stalls, lit up a dog end. You cheeky bastard, I thought. The school he had suggested was about twenty miles further each way and I couldn't wait to get home and tell the old man. There was no way on God's earth I was going to move now and that was the end of it.

I bumped into Sylvia in the sports field and told her what had gone down. She was amazed and wondered how much more devious he could get. As we were in sight of his study window, I suggested that she shouldn't be seen talking to yours truly and we went our separate ways.

Sitting down to tea that evening, I told the folks that they would be getting a letter and its content and couldn't believe the old man when he said he wondered if it would be advantageous to me to change. I was just about to blow up completely when I caught my mother's eye. Sitting there in stony silence, I let her have her say, commenting that it was ridiculous to have to travel any further than I was already. I could see the old man wasn't convinced, so I laid it on the line, for once quite calmly. In the first place, nothing would change my mind; I hated the place and was only there on sufferance. I would under no circumstances go to any other school whether I had to travel or not and the sooner I could get out of the one I was already in, the better. I knew they were waiting for a change of heart but it was not going to happen and as far as I was concerned, I'd been sold up the river long before.

The old man went on about how I was throwing away my life, etcetera, but it was far too late and at that time I would sooner have shovelled shit than be a cleric, but I couldn't say as much. So there we had it. The old man promised he would write a letter to the head once he received his letter, telling him in no uncertain tones that I would not be changing schools under any circumstances. My mum, bless her heart, totally agreed and as for little old me . . . well I couldn't wait to see the expression on numb nut's face when he found his plan had gone down the tubes.

CHAPTER THIRTY-FIVE
Sympathy for the Devil
(The Rolling Stones)

The music was really starting to come into the country now and we were getting to hear a lot of American groups. We were listening to Frankie Lymon and the Teenagers, the Great Fats Domino, Elvis's 'Heartbreak Hotel' and he had released a fantastic ballad called 'I Want You, I Need You, I Love You' and I think it still is one of the best ever, but what do I know? We spent hours learning the words and I think we all imagined we would be rock stars one day. Not if our seniors had anything to do with it, however. All we heard was a load of total rubbish about the devil's music and how it should be banned, but the biggest laugh of all was that nobody took a bit of notice.

Reg had gone back to work and we had a quiet weekend for a change, but I had conceived a plan which nearly became my undoing. Adrian's mother was apparently the maker of some lethal home-made rhubarb wine and its fame was legendary. I found out that his mum and sisters were going on a visit to Mid-Wales the following Friday and as he had the house to himself, I persuaded him to let me sample it. This was all planned for the following week, so I had to contain myself until then.

So this was it, then, the final weeks of term with mock O-levels being the order of the day and me, not giving a shit, revising zilch, with a capital Z. I thought to myself that really I should have been sitting the real thing if I had not been put back a year. Things were all quiet at school and it was a stalemate because we still had not received the letter from the head so a strange kind of peace reigned. As we were now well into June, most of the seniors on our bus were getting ready for their final exams and hopefully a place in University, so the bus was half empty most of the time. I received a letter from Viv on the Saturday morning telling me how much she had enjoyed her week and she was going to the sea with her folks in the summer holidays, but hoped to be down in the Autumn half term and how much she thought of me. I'm afraid, though, it was a case of out of sight, out of mind and my devious little mind was centred on someone closer to hand. With this thought, I resolved to write to my auntie and ask if I could go down there for a few weeks. Newport would seem to be the in place and I might be able to get myself some gear.

Sure enough, Friday night found me heading down to my mate's house to try the rhubarb wine. He also found a quart of GL cider in the pantry and I got a pint of that down my neck and two large glasses of wine as I sat on the sofa. I am not kidding, you could smell the strength coming off it and within about five minutes, I started to feel very strange and couldn't even get up off the sofa. I was vaguely aware of the door opening and his mum and sisters all looking at me. With that, I shot the cat all over the floor and thank God it was flagstones or I would have been in some serious shit with his mum. Well, they got me out of the door and he and his oldest sister walked me up and down the road until I gradually became coherent again. He told me his mum said to get me out of sight in case the old man saw me, and fair dos I was back to normal within an hour and worrying about the mess I'd made in her house. The next morning I knocked on the door and apologised and she gave me a very old fashioned look and said there was no harm done.

Needless to say, I didn't go far that weekend and was glad to get out of the way on Monday morning. After a cheery greeting from the driver, I related my weekend adventure and I thought he was going to piss himself he laughed so much.

'Fucking hell, Johnny boy, do you think we'll ever rear you?'

I grinned and muttered some expletive and went down to my usual seat. Most of the exams had finished now and there was a lot of preparation for sports day, while all the seniors on our bus were getting ready to leave and I wondered where I would be sitting next term, that was if there was going to be a next term for me.

The following Friday we were down on the corner, raising Cain and I think I must have had a death wish in those days, because I said to Adrian, 'What are you doing tomorrow afternoon?'

He replied nothing as usual and I told him my plan. The main church bells were never rung on a Sunday morning, only a small, single one, but on Sunday night the peal was rung twice; once at six o'clock and again at twenty five minutes past six. This meant that we could go up into the belfry on Saturday afternoon and muffle all the clangers, which would hopefully cause consternation in the village.

Sure enough, come Saturday we were up in the belfry with a load of old woollies, but we found it easier to loop the ropes around the clangers so that they couldn't ring. Not being very clever, we both walked down the village on Sunday night and there was silence at six, which we pointed out to people in a questioning way: 'No bells tonight? There can't be any church then?'

Just before six-thirty, the peal rang out and I knew we'd been rumbled. Adrian remarked that he was off home out of the way as there would be, in his words, a hell of a fucking row, and I was left on my own to face the music.

Skirting the churchyard I could hear the sound of them singing and knew I was safe for about three quarters of an hour, so I jumped the stile and came up through the paddock, working out my plan of campaign. It didn't seem long before I heard the sound of voices and saw the first of the congregation coming out through the church door. It was like watching a kettle boil, waiting for them to disperse, but finally there were only two groups left, with my mother talking to the one lot and my father talking to the other group which also included the verger. I thought if the shit was going to hit the fan, I had better face it now and walked down the path to meet my fate.

I was amazed at the response, as Mum smiled and asked if everything was all right and carried on talking. So far so good, but I noticed the verger had his navy suit covered in cobwebs – not a good sign – so, keeping him furthest away from me I spoke to the old man, who seemed oblivious to any problems. However, out of the corner of my eye, I could see the verger edging round to me. Saying cheerio, I beat a hasty retreat and just got out of his reach when he said in a low voice, 'Yes, you little bugger, I'll catch up with you one of these days, don't you worry.' And I was gone, whistling down the path without a care in the world. I thought it prudent to keep out of sight that night though, so after being called a hero by my mates I decided against the pub and retired home for an early night, amazed that I had got away with it so easily.

The following morning I boarded the bus and had the driver in fits over the escapade of the previous night. Strangely enough, I will mention here that I met a lad recently who remembered the incident all those years ago.

When I got home that night there was a letter from Wales saying I was welcome so I wrote back, giving the day when I would arrive at my old village, Croesyceiliog.

That week was a strange old time, with a lot of pupils leaving to go to college and everyone looking forward to the long summer holidays. The good news was that Sylvia had been made up to head girl and everyone was delighted, as well as being a little bit in awe of her, but she really deserved it and was studying hard for her final exams next year and university.

Cecil the driver and yours truly shared our usual conversations on the home run and he was full of queries about my time being spent in South Wales. Finally, the last stage of the journey and it was just Sylvia and I left on the bus. She was explaining what she would be doing in the holiday and, looking earnestly at me, asked me to try and keep out of trouble for the next six weeks. Laughingly, I suggested that I could bike over to see her, but she evaded an answer as we pulled up by her house and giving me a peck on the cheek, was gone.

Climbing into the front seat next to Cecil, his eyes were full of questions but I simply told him bollocks and to leave it alone. We had four miles left to go and chewed the fat as he drove until we descended the last hill and the bottom of the village came into view. Shouting at me to take care, he was gone and I was left alone with my thoughts and for once, feeling a little vulnerable, although I wouldn't have admitted it to anyone. I walked up the road through the village, which was deserted and my thoughts were very much on Sylvia, but it was strange, for although there were only four miles of hilly roads between us, there was no means of communication as there were no phones in our houses.

I am ashamed to say that by the time I had finished my cigarette and drunk my tea, my eyes were closing. This always happened to me for the first couple of days in South Wales. I guessed it must be the air down there, with all the works polluting the atmosphere. Anyway, I woke with a start, hearing Auntie's voice calling me for lunch. Sitting down at the table I could see them both smiling at me and they remarked how sleep always overcame me when I first arrived.

After a nice lunch, I retired upstairs to my bedroom to unpack my suitcase. Looking through the window, I noticed my uncle down in the garden. I joined him for a cigarette and we chewed the fat for a few minutes. He was working four to twelve, or continental shifts as he called them, but was finishing that night and going up to stay with my folks for a week while I was down with my auntie. I knew he would love going around with my folks and that they would love having him. I sat down with the South Wales Argus for half an hour and also noted that Rock Around the Clock was showing all next week at the Odeon. This being a must, I set off down the road to see if my old mate, Rob, would come and also called on my other auntie and uncle who lived close by on the Turnpike road. Having checked my hair at the back with my second mirror and being pleased with the DA, I thought of how much time we spent with these new hairstyles, but we were at the very least of smart appearance. However, I digress . . .

As I walked up to Rob's front door it was opened by his mother, who must have seen me coming up the path. Standing back, she looked me up and down and remarked how I had grown up since she last saw me. She told me that Rob was up in Abersychan with his father at the moment, but to come down after tea and he would be back. Leaving her, I walked around the corner to see my auntie Olive down the garden pulling a few weeds. My auntie was looking very frail these days and having lost her only daughter some years ago, had never got over the shock. Seeing me, she hurried up to give me a hug and I joined her for a cup of tea. Noticing that the bedroom curtains were drawn over I asked if my uncle was working night shift. Being familiar with these work patterns, I kept my voice down and, appraising me from head to toe, she told me I had grown into a man since last she saw me.

Explaining that I would come and have a chat on the Sunday morning, I said goodbye and turned down Woodland Road or the Black Road, as it used to be called from the far off days when it was first constructed with cinders and spoil from the old collieries. Well, like it or lump it, a lot of the older folks still called it the Black Road.

Walking to the bottom of the road, I followed my old haunts. Being faced with a half built roundabout and behind it stretched the muddy horror of what was to be called The New Town Cwmbran. Again, wherever I looked there was a gaping hole or a pile of soil and shuttering by the mile. Knowing this was the last time I would see the bottom of the village, I thought of how the trees used to meet in the centre of the road to Pontnewydd. Turning right, I passed St Mary's Church onto what is now North Road and was again met with houses in various stages of construction. Seemingly going on for miles, I reached the Garw, walked past the Cambrian pub, on to a small row of houses telling me that their name was Florence Place. To this day I do not know who Florence was, that they were named after, but I did know this was where my grandparents lived and brought up four children. After my granddad died, my mother who was the youngest, moved in the Highway with my auntie and uncle, my auntie being the oldest and my granddad died in their house. This was also where I was brought to from the nursing home as a baby.

Standing there, I contemplated these far off times and the tales my mother told me as a youngster . . . the family Christmases, the snow, the roar from the forge of the blacksmith's shop as he pumped the bellows for heat and the old cottage down the road where some of the Chartists stopped to dry out their powder in the baking oven before their fateful march to the Westgate in Newport. I remember that Victoria had just come to the throne. Walking on around the corner I was out on the highway, past the Upper Cock Inn and back down to my auntie's house. A full circle and man, was I tired. Going up the front path and through the gulley, it was as if I had come back home. However, it was over twelve years since my mother and I set off on what seemed a never ending journey to live in Hampshire.

Looking down at my watch, I saw the time was five-fifteen and realised my uncle had left for work over an hour ago. As I lowered myself into the easy chair my auntie asked me what I would like for tea. Good old Auntie Gertie looked after me like a prince but I was still full up from my lunch, so I settled for a cup of tea and a few of those nice chocolate fingers she kept in the biscuit barrel. Settling down with a cigarette and listening to the local news on the wireless, I was aware of my tendency to drop off so I asked her to give me a call about half past six as I had promised to see Rob later on.

Rob was a good lad and we had known each other for a long time. He was a little younger than me and passed for Abersychan grammar school, where he was doing well and good luck to him. Being respectful, I was always on my best behaviour around his folks, certainly not letting them know that I smoked and drank as they may have worried he was running around with a lunatic.

I must have dozed off again and jumped when I heard the mantel clock chime the half hour and saw my auntie looking to see if I was awake over the top of her People's Friend magazine. Going upstairs, I had a quick wash, put on a clean shirt, checked my hair and was ready for the off.

Rob must have seen me coming down the road and was out of the door in a flash. He had grown tall like his father and looked really good.

'C'mon,' he said and we set off around the fields and out onto the Black Road, exclaiming how we were growing up and what had happened to the old Cross. He grinned when I lit up and said he could see I hadn't changed my bad habits. There was no doubt about it that the old Croesyceiliog had gone forever and in its place was growing a monster of offices, factories, shops and all the furnishings of a large town. The only difference between us was that in two weeks I would be jumping on a train and back to rurality, whereas he was stuck with it. He had found himself a part-time job but we made arrangements to see some films, kicking off with Rock Around the Clock on Monday night. After a long conversation I left him to go indoors and headed up the Highway and home. Walking up the hill I wondered what, if anything, was going on in my village, and swearing to myself, bloody hell, you only left it this morning.

As I walked into the house I was asked what I would like for supper and thought, at this rate I will be a stone heavier. We talked for a short while and making my excuses, I climbed up the wooden hill to Bedfordshire and goodnight.

CHAPTER THIRTY-SIX
You Can Go Your Own Way
(Fleetwood Mac)

Walking up the village that afternoon, my mind was full of the day's events. Was Sylvia telling me the complete story or was her new found position of head girl playing on her conscience and she was afraid to break confidences? Well that was alright, I didn't blame her, she was a topping girl with a great future in front of her and good luck. I also wondered how much longer I could hold out at school and was under no illusions that I was under constant surveillance by the staff who, it would appear, were just waiting for me to put a foot wrong. Well, what the hell, I thought, there was nothing I could do to change it and I had expected it, anyway.

I was so deep in my own thoughts that I had reached our gate before I realised and opened the back door to be welcomed by Kim, who was losing a lot of weight recently, but I thought at least somebody is pleased to see me. Mum was in the kitchen getting the tea ready and the old man was out somewhere, so I went up to change and take Kim out for a short walk as he was not so well.

Opening the bedroom door, I could see all my clean clothes on the bed in readiness for my long stay down in Croesyceiliog the following morning and I looked around my room with mixed thoughts. I had been looking forward to my holiday for some time but I felt that in some ways, now the time had come, perhaps I would rather be at home and keep my eye on things. I checked my money that Mother had been saving for me and was pleased how it had mounted up. Adrian and I had a good little scam going where we wandered the farm hedges, watching out for hens laying away and kept collecting the eggs. His mum used to sell them to a visiting egg man by the dozen so that it soon mounted up, plus the odd jobs around the place kept me in profit as well as paying for my fags and a few beers. Going back downstairs, I put Kim's lead on and with warnings from my mum to go careful with him, I set off across the paddock and out into the fields.

Tea was a sombre affair that evening with my folks avoiding any mention of school or the dreaded report. The main topic seemed to be my journey the next morning, and what I would find to fill my time. I thought of the town of Newport with its many cinemas in those days; the shops and the friends I had down there and knew exactly how I would spend my time. I was catching the twelve o'clock train from Hereford the next day and Reg's uncle had offered me a lift so the old man, who wasn't the safest of drivers, was thankfully let off the hook. After tea I wandered down the village but there was no one about and I thought I would have an early night anyway, so I headed back home and went to check the pools for trout and my return. Saying goodnight to my folks, I was up to bed and reading until my eyelids started to close. Putting the light out, I lay there listening to the sounds of the house, my mind full of thoughts about the various things happening in my little life until sleep took over and I didn't hear my parents coming to bed.

The next morning dawned bright and clear and I was up with the lark, sideboards trimmed to perfection and hair combed to my satisfaction. Reg's uncle was picking me up at nine-thirty so I had my case down in the hall in readiness and went into the kitchen for breakfast. Everyone was cheerful and the old man greeted me with, 'Well, Sunny Jim, this time tomorrow you will be sitting down with your Auntie Gertie. The Lord only knows what she will think of your new look.'

I quipped back that if she didn't like it I would be back on the return train, but guessed she already knew all about it from my mother's letters. Having consumed my Bovril on toast and two mugs of tea I went back upstairs to check I hadn't left anything behind. Looking around the bedroom I felt a strange feeling of contentment and realised how much I loved this house, its grounds and the village below. It had been a struggle but I had managed to make friends with people and was at last accepted for what I was and not the 'Parson's Son' as was the case when I first arrived. Back downstairs I said goodbye to the old man and gave my mum a hug and carried my case out to the gate, to save the car coming up the drive and having to turn. Looking around, I saw the old man coming down the drive towards me and I thought to myself, look out for a final lecture, but I couldn't have been further from the truth.

Holding out his hand, he said, 'Here you are, Sunny Jim,' and passed me three pound notes adding, 'There is no need to hide away; have a nice time in South Wales.'

With this he was gone, back up the drive, and I looked down at the money. That was a lot to give and I felt the back of my eyes burning then, suddenly and with a toot, the car pulled in and I was away. Hey ho; boys trying to be men before their time. After an uneventful journey along the country lanes we finally arrived at the outskirts of Hereford and headed for the railway station approach. Looking back now, it is frightening to think how the lovely old city has grown. So much for progress. Anyway, I was dropped off outside the station in plenty of time, bought my ticket and crossed the footbridge to await the Cardiff train.

Lighting up, I sat on a bench scrutinising the various people coming through the entrance. Just my luck, I thought, as it seemed anything half tidy was catching the up train, whereas on my line it seemed to be middle-aged men or ancients. Suddenly the loud speaker announced, 'The train now arriving at platform two is the twelve o five for Cardiff Central, calling at Abergavenny, Pontypool Road, Cwmbran, and Newport,' and around the bend she came. I never tired of this journey and watched how the landscape changed, from fields and hedgerows and finally giving way to the eastern valleys industry with smoke from the works climbing across the sky. It won't be long for me now, I thought to myself; off at Pontypool Road up the hill and down to Croesy on the Jones bus, stopping ten yards down the road from my auntie's front door.

Climbing on board, I walked down the corridor and finding an almost empty carriage threw my case and bag into the rack and settled down in a seat by the window. All too soon my reverie was interrupted by the sonorous voice stating that we would be arriving in Ponty in the next few minutes. Looking up, I saw the cemetery and felt the train slowing and retrieved my case and bag, ready to disembark.

Jumping out onto the platform, I immediately smelled the difference in the air from the various works which were all around Ponty and stretched right up the valley into the collieries. This was a familiar smell to me, far from the pure air of rural Radnorshire, and while some might have found it offensive it was like coming home to me in those days. I walked under the tunnel and up the hill to the T-junction at the main road and waited for the Jones bus to Newport. I hadn't long to wait and climbing aboard, paid my fare and sat down, listening to the familiar sing-song of the voices all around me. Down through Upper New Inn we went, then Lower New Inn and then along the straight mile, approaching Croesy as we called it and down the hill past the Upper Cock pub.

Shouting above the hiss of brakes, the conductor called out, 'Anyone for the highway?'

I was out of the door and walking up the path.

I could see my uncle in the window and the front door opened and we were shaking hands, then I walked across and gave my auntie a hug before carrying my cases upstairs to the old familiar room. I was back.

Downstairs they were waiting to hear all the news from home and as I drank a welcome cup of tea I was told that dinner would be about an hour. My uncle, who had been a heavy smoker all his life, grinned as he offered me one of his Gold Flake cigarettes, saying he had heard from my parents that I had started. So here I was like a seasoned campaigner, sitting in my auntie's front room, smoking, drinking tea and relating all the gossip. Looking out of my auntie's window, I could see the mountain in the distance. Twm Barlwm's topmost peak looked quite grim with the rain clouds swirling around his head.

CHAPTER THIRTY-SEVEN
What in the World Has Come Over You
(Jack Scott)

Oh, the eastern valleys! Oh, my beloved South Wales! I woke up early that morning and realised I was homesick for my little village. Also, in truth, I couldn't wait to get back home and show off my new gear. Walking down the garden that morning after breakfast I thought to myself, Jesus H Christ, the old man will have a bloody fit when he sees you, but you're only young once so bollocks to 'em all. Walking back up the garden path I thought, you'd better make the most of your time down here, son . . . there's nobody watching you, and you can have a bit of fun without somebody grassing you up to the school. I knew I had changed and that I wasn't an angel, but I wasn't a bloody monster either, well not yet anyway, but I had noticed the way older people looked at me and then quickly looked away again. Rob's mother, for example; in her case, I would bet a pound to a piece of shit that if I was living permanently down here she would stop me seeing him. However, I wouldn't blame her as he was doing well at school and wanted to go places and good luck to him.

That week passed quickly by and we went into Newport to see a film on the Friday night, which wasn't much cop and not worth the mention, but we had a good night and I was also thinking of going back down on the Monday to get my knife. I awoke early on the Saturday morning and looking out of the bedroom window, saw that it was pissing down. After washing, dressing, combing my hair with the help of two mirrors and pleased with the DA, I went down the stairs to be greeted by my auntie with a cup of tea and the Argus, which was the paper with the mostest. Looking out of the front room window, I could just see upper Cwmbran, and the mountain. Old Twm Barlwm had his head buried in cloud and years of experience told me that it was going to be a wet one.

Auntie had got the fire going like a blast furnace and I knew that breakfast would not be too long. Uncle was on six till two and would be back home by two-thirty. By then, the whole house would be cleaned and sparkling, maybe twice over. After breakfast I was at a loss what to do and so I wandered back up to my bedroom. Lighting up a fag, I opened the window one latch and blew a stream of smoke through the gap, watching it swirl and disappear. Lost in time, I remembered my schooling up the road, and the teacher who taught me to read. Now it had been turned into a day centre. The old Willow tree was still down the garden where I used to climb up and sit for hours, fantasising about my years to come. Long gone were the ducks and the chickens which the neighbour used to keep down his garden. Poor old sod; he was dead now and his wife had gone loopy.

The old Croesyceiliog which I knew as a child, was rapidly disappearing, lost in the endless roar of the shale lorries en route to the new Llanwern steel works, which was going to be the biggest in Europe, or so they said. On the other side of the village they were knocking Avondale Tin Works down as fast as possible to make way for hundreds of houses ready for the new light industry which was coming in. Drawing heavily on my cigarette, I reflected on my village back in Radnorshire, wondering whatever they would think of this?

Smiling to myself I doused my fag and flicked it away down the garden. Pulling on my coat, I was away out into the rain, closing the door behind me. The air seemed fresher and cooler with no smell of the works. Walking down the Black Road I passed Arthur Peak's the undertakers and supposed he had put most of my ancestors under the ground. As I walked along I found myself humming Fat's 'I'm in Love Again,' but don't ask me why. Good job there was nobody about or they would probably have thought I should be locked up. I swiftly changed it to Lonnie Donnegan's

'Wont You Bring a Little Water, Sylvia'. I wondered what she was doing and what the weather was like with her. Probably cleaning and then later getting ready for the dance in Presteigne, no doubt being met by the opposition, I thought bitterly. Little did I think at this moment that this time next year we would be gone our separate ways. Also that my life would be completely different and the lane that I was now walking on would become a dual carriageway leading to the new town centre and not only would there be no trees meeting over the road, I would be very hard pressed to recognise it.

Going on towards Pontnewydd village centre, I took the road up the hill to the White Rose cinema. It was just over twelve months since I last visited here. The billboard was announcing A Star is Born, starring Judy Garland and James Mason. Well, never heard of either of them, I thought, but hey ho I had nothing doing tonight so that was it. It was still chucking it down with rain so I caught the Western Welsh down to Crossy and walked up the road from the turnpike.

Lunch was early as Uncle was due back later that afternoon and I knew Auntie would cook him something special for his tea, so I took myself up to my bedroom and read a few chapters of my latest war book called Boldness Be My Friend by Richard Pape, and before long I had fallen fast asleep.

I was awakened by a knock on the door some time later and Auntie came in with a cup of tea and a biscuit. Looking at my watch, I told her I thought I would catch a bus up to Pontypool station and carry his case. Auntie thought that this was a great idea, so half an hour later I was waiting outside for a Jones bus to Pontypool Road. In roared the bus bang on time, and I was headed for the station. As we went through New Inn I saw that the sun was breaking through the clouds and thought with any luck it would clear up.

As the bus stopped at the top of the road, I walked down the hill and under the line. Looking at my watch I saw I had a quarter of an hour to wait. Sitting on a bench seat I lit up a ciggy and wondered how things were back at home. Lost in my thoughts I was thinking it was time I was homeward bound and hearing a rattle on the line, looked up to see the train approaching. As it slowed I could see my uncle grinning as they came to a halt some yards further up the platform. As I took his case he asked if everything was alright at home and I told him that it was. He said he had thoroughly enjoyed his break and everything was fine back in Radnorshire. As we walked up the hill he told me about some of the characters he'd met during his stay. Just as we reached the bus stop, along came the bus and within ten minutes we were pulling up outside the house. Carrying his case to the front door I did not go in but went round the back so that they could have a good chat.

That evening, after a lovely tea, I excused myself and spent an hour in the bathroom and changed into my black jeans and a powder blue sweater. After looking in the mirror for the umpteenth time, I left the house and boarded the Western Welsh for Pontnewydd. After climbing the hill I saw that the foyer doors were open and walked through to get my ticket. Sitting close to the back I took a good look around the dimly lit auditorium and was surprised to see it was nearly empty. Although this was odd for a Saturday night, I presumed they would all come in after the Pathe News. Something caught my eye as I looked around and I noticed a nice looking bird sitting about four seats from me. She quickly looked away as I caught her stare and lighting up a smoke, I ignored her, suspecting she was waiting for her boyfriend to arrive. The usual crap came on; first the trailers, then the news and then of all things, the Three Stooges or Amigos, or whatever they were. Having nothing better to do, I looked across at the girl and every time I looked across, she was looking at me.

After a bit of this, I thought sod it and proffered my ciggy packet to her. Well, quick as a flash she came straight over and sat down and I lit her ciggy for her. We missed most of the film, for we talked through most of it. She asked if I lived in Ponty, I answered I was staying in Crossy and it turned out she lived there too. Bloody small world, I thought, especially when she lived about five hundred yards from my other auntie. Her name was Joyce and it turned out that my family knew her family and they weren't exactly big mates. Anyway, James Stewart walked into the sea and was never seen again and Judy Garland gave a tearful speech and I found myself walking this bird back towards the Cross. I could see under the streetlights that she was a lot older than me and she was also firing questions so, full of bullshit, I told her I drove a tractor for the war agriculture, which one of the men did back home.

She told me she worked in a grocery store I knew and we arranged to meet in the cinema again next week. No snog, no nothing and she disappeared up the garden path of her folks Mulling all this over that night, I must confess that I fell asleep with her on my pillow. My God! Whatever would Sylvia think? Looking back now, I would say she would have nothing to say, but would smile with an expression of total relief.

The next thing I knew, I was wide awake and it was morning. My uncle was sitting in his chair in the front room reading the Argus and as I sat down he passed me an envelope.

'Your dad asked me to give you this, but I forgot to give it to you yesterday.'

Thanking him, I sat down and ate my breakfast. After a smoke and a chat with my uncle, who was off to church, I went up to my room and opened the envelope. Inside was a fiver and a brief note: 'Enjoy yourself, Dad.' I sat speechless for a bit and then went down the garden. I thought, Sundays . . . the worst day of the week; nothing to do and all day to do it in.

Monday morning found me climbing aboard a Jones bus and heading for Newport and the shop where I had seen all the knives in the window. This world in which we live is a very strange place; back then, the shop windows were full of switch blades, throwing knives and virtually any type of knife you could think of. Now, you can go to prison for just owning one. I went in the shop and looked at loads of them, finally settling on an Italian Rostfri with a five inch blade and a bone handle. It had a built in safety catch in the handle and a very powerful spring. As I went to pay for it the man asked was I over sixteen. Grinning at him, I said of course I was, and that was it. I slipped it into my pocket and walked to the bus stop, feeling somehow dangerous.

Back at the house I had a cup of tea with my uncle and auntie and a chat about the world in general, but what did I know?

Heading upstairs to my room, I wrapped the knife in some socks and looked at my watch. It was only eleven o'clock, which gave me ample time to amble down to the grocery shop where this bird worked and see if I could find her. Checking my DA on the way out, I called that I would be back for lunch and headed down the Black Road to Pontnewydd. The nearer to the shop I got the more nervous I became. I was thinking, what if she was horrible in broad daylight, and planned how I had to go back home to see a dying relative. I soon reached the shop, a lot quicker than I thought, I can tell you, and looking through the window felt daft as there was nothing to interest me in a grocer's window. I could see this old guy staring at me and gave him the dead eye. The next thing, the door opened and the lady herself came tripping out. She wasn't half bad, but a lot older than me. Stuttering that as I was passing, I thought she might like to go out. She replied that she'd love to but her sailor boyfriend was due home and she would be going out with him.

Covering my disgust, I said, 'See you around,' and beat a hasty retreat. Bloody horrible cow anyway, I thought, and sauntered home, my thoughts very much on Sylvia.

CHAPTER THIRTY-EIGHT
Like I've Never Been Gone
(Billy Fury)

Well, well, 'Let the good times roll' and my holiday was nearing the end. The last few days had been quiet and fair play, I'd seen almost every film, bought some super gear and was the proud possessor of an Italian switch blade, but more of that later. I was glad to be going home and my thoughts were very much on the school and my future, and if there was one thing I knew for sure, I was a marked man. I went down to see my mate on the Thursday night. We chatted and he told me his hopes for the future and I had a lot of respect for him. He was a real down to earth, genuine lad, who knew where he was going which was more than could be said for me.

That Friday morning, I said my goodbyes to Croesyceiliog and boarded the Jones bus for Pontypool Road, with my case somewhat heavier than when I came. Little did I realise that it would be some three years later before I visited again. The train journey was uneventful with no sign of a Diana Dors look alike boarding, so I spent my time looking out at the changing countryside as we hurtled along. Long gone now, the smoking chimneys of the valleys, replaced with fields and hedgerows, brooks and farmhouses, nestling into the surroundings as if they had been there since the world was born. Here and there the fields were filled with white-faced Hereford cattle, lying down amongst patches of thistle, contentedly chewing their sweet grass. It was a sure sign of rain, so the old country folk said. Here and there I saw little stone churches, standing all on their own, with no sign of any village, and my thoughts centred on my village, which was full of life, with the church, pub and chapel at its centre.

Lost in contemplation of all things rural we rattled through Pontrilas and up the main drag to Hereford, I heard the voice announcing that we were coming into Hereford station and thence to Ludlow, Craven Arms and Shrewsbury, names that I had heard, but never been to, another world about which I was blissfully unaware. Reaching my case down from the rack I went into the corridor, all ready to jump out onto home soil.

With much squeaking of brakes, the train came to a halt. Doors were banging as passengers left the train and I joined in, letting the window strap down, reaching outside and opening the door, to be met by the smell of smoke and engines and once on the platform, people busily hurrying to and fro. I passed my ticket to the collector and walked through the entrance and out into the approach. Lighting up a fag, I looked around to see if the old man had arrived, but there was no sign of him so I stood there and finished my smoke, wondering what had gone wrong. It was coming up to lunchtime and I had been far too fond of Auntie Gert's cooked lunches and was feeling quite peckish. I thought if the worst happened I could go across to the bus station and get a bus to Kington, but just as I was thinking I would do this, a car came scorching around the corner and it was Reg and his uncle. Screeching to a stop, they explained they'd bumped into the old man earlier in the week and he said that he had to go to a meeting. They told him they had to come to town anyway and would pick me up and here they were. Chucking my case in the boot, I jumped in the back and we were away. It was good to hear the old slow drawl again and they gave me some stick on the way back. Nobody had died, given birth or murdered anyone since I had left and so it seemed I was back to normal. I told them about the films I had seen and the nights I had enjoyed, but we made good time and I agreed to see them later that night. I was walking up the drive to the house when the door opened and my mother was standing there with her arms stretched wide and I gave her a big hug and lugged my case into the hall.

We sat down in the kitchen and I devoured a plate of sandwiches and two mugs of tea, and she said the old man had sent his apologies but he had to go to a Deanery meeting and would see me later. I took my case upstairs and started to unpack. At the bottom of the case were my pride and joy; my new drape jacket and a pair of fourteen inch bottom drain pipes. Also, my black and pink luminous slim Jim tie and some pink and lime green luminous socks. There was also a pair of black suede brothel creepers. I knew Mum was busy and thought I would try them on in my own room. This I accomplished and was admiring myself in my long mirror, when I thought I would call Mum and let her see how smart I looked. Going to the top of the stairs I called to her and she came to the bottom. Her reaction was not quite what I had hoped for; she put her hands to her face and let out a little scream.

'John!' she shouted. 'The jacket is miles too large for you and you can't seriously think of going out in your father's parish looking like that?'

I was totally horrified by this reaction and muttered that this was the gear to be seen in.

She made me promise to hide them in my wardrobe and not mention them until she had spoken to him, so that was that. I had only been home for half an hour and felt I shouldn't have bothered to come back at all, but I wouldn't let my mum down so I held my peace, for now at any rate. The one thing I was happy with was that I had booked an afternoon performance for Rock Around the Clock. As we walked across the bridge we could hear the noise and there must have been at least a hundred Teds there. Rob turned pale as he was conventional, but I was okay with my hair and drainpipe jeans. There was every colour you could dream of and the girls were hanging on their arms. The disturbing thing was they all carried switch blades and were constantly springing the blades out. One lad in a powder blue suit asked would we like to go to a café after the film, but I told him I would be back tomorrow and was coming to buy some gear. He told me where to go and we arranged to meet afterwards, but I nearly fainted when I saw where it was, right down in the docks. I told him I would see him later the next day. Needless to say, I did not go anywhere near the docks, hoping to keep my head on my shoulders.

Hiding my knife and a few other unmentionables in my drawer, I put on a pair of old trousers and shirt and descended the stairs to hear all the news and make a fuss of Kim.

One look at Kim and I could see he was looking far from well, and Mum came up behind me and said that they'd had the vet to him and he had kidney problems and there was nothing could be done for him. Poor little sod, I thought, only five shillings from the gypsies and all those years of love he had given to us. He looked up at me and slowly wagged his tail as if he agreed. I marched off down the paddock and felt the tears burning my eyes and savagely brushed them away. Come on, you dozy bastard, you are a big boy now; pull yourself together and get on with it. Calming down, I walked back up to the house and had a cup of tea with Mum and heard all the news of what had happened while I was away. As it turned out, sod all of it was any interest to me, whatsoever.

The peace was shattered by the roar of the old man's car. I looked out to see him revving it flat out and I thought if he lets the clutch out now he will demolish the church, never mind the garage. Having already had a go on several motor bikes locally, I had my sights set on the Royal Enfield he kept in the garage. Mum said not to breathe a word about the clothes and in he came, giving me a big smile.

'Welcome home, Sunny Jim. I hope you have had a nice time, and it's good to have you back home.'

I was waiting for something about school, but it wasn't mentioned and we spent about half an hour making small talk and having a smoke. Making my excuses, as I could feel my eyelids drooping, I went up to my room and lay on the bed, looking around at familiar things and I must have dropped off completely as the next thing I heard was my mum calling that tea was ready.

Tea finished, they made their way into the sitting room to listen to the news and I went out through the back door, down the paddock and followed the brook along over the little footbridge, looking keenly in all the deep pools for signs of fish. So this was what it was all about, far from the bustle of Newport, nothing but hills, fields and silence.

Sitting on a fallen tree I lit up a fag and, lost in contemplation, sank into a comfortable daze as I thought what the coming months would bring. Going back to school on Tuesday and looking forward to seeing my friends, but not in any doubt as to my position. Finishing my smoke I flicked it into the brook and wandered back to the house, I looked at my watch and it was almost seven o'clock, time for a wash and down the village. I was contented and had no wish to leave this little piece of heaven at this moment of my life.

Back in my bedroom, I took out my treasured flick knife and sprung it a few times before putting it in my pocket and with a hasty goodbye to the folks, strode off down through the churchyard to the village below.

CHAPTER THIRTY-NINE
No Particular Place to Go
(Chuck Berry)

I couldn't help but marvel when I saw him standing there in all his splendour as I walked down the churchyard path that Friday evening. He was always there, in your face, as he had been through the centuries and I made a vow to climb him again on Sunday, if the weather held. Lighting up a smoke, I stood for a moment looking up at him and my mind flitted back to the Cross and the constant noise of traffic and people and I wondered if this could ever happen here. I could hear mutterings coming from down by the churchyard gate and guessed the gang was there so I carried on quietly and shot down through the little kissing gate which took me out of their sight and I suddenly appeared virtually on top of them. Reg was the first to spot me and then all hell broke loose. Grinning, I pushed my way in between Reg and Adrian and tried to answer the barrage of questions that were fired at me.

Putting my hand in my pocket, I pulled out my prized knife, sprung it and handed it to Reg, who closed it and sprung it again a few times and putting the safety catch back on, handed it back to me.

'Jesus, John, you want to be careful with that, it's an evil bit of kit.'

The rest were looking wide-eyed and I put it safe and returned to telling them some highly embellished tales of my holiday. Gradually one and another drifted away and we three walked down past the pub to the bottom of the village, where they filled me in on the happenings of the weeks I had been away. By now the day's events were catching up with me and we very soon all went our separate ways and home to bed.

Saturday dawned bright and clear and after breakfast I tried Kim down the paddock. Bless his old heart, he did his best, but I could see how thin he had gone and I knew he wouldn't be around much longer. I also knew the old lady would be heartbroken when the time came and resolved to be the strong one. Taking him back inside he snuggled down in his box and picking up my fags and newly acquired lighter, I headed down the paddock, following the brook to some pools that I had been watching before I left. I was now on the land of the prat who kept shouting at me and threatening me and I was keeping a careful look out for him, but common sense told me he would not come down the fields in the old Landrover. Coming to the first pool, I lit up a smoke and sat watching the water and I could see a couple of nice fish laying deep in the current. I got up and they quickly swam for cover under the roots of an alder. I was just about to get down in the brook when a movement caught my eye, and there, walking backwards across the bottom of the pool was one of the biggest crayfish I had seen. We used to call them crabs and there were hundreds of them around but this was a big one and I thought to myself sod that, the bloody trout can stay where they are today.

I moved on up to the next pool and went through the same procedure and I could see a fair trout diving about all over the place but getting nowhere. Moving up the bank I could see why; it was on the end of a piece of line. I thought some bastard's laying night lines in my brook now; I'll leave it there and keep my eyes open as to who's laying them. Moving on again, the next pool was clear and I got three nice fish, broke their necks and threaded them on an alder stick, dipping them now and then to keep them fresh until I got home. Mum was pleased and said we would have them for tea that day so I gutted them and put them in a bowl of water. No fridges in those days, not in our house anyway.

After lunch I wandered down the village and four of us were standing against the wall when the Landrover came into view and the bloke shouted, 'I've told you before, we don't want Teddy boys in our village!' and roared off.

Reg looked at me and asked what the hell I had done to upset this bloke and I replied, nothing to my knowledge. I also added that I was going to have to do something about it if he kept it up. Little did I realise that I wouldn't have long to wait.

The three of us decided that we would have a stroll and see what the Weythel brook looked like. It was a bit out of our territory and was reputed to be full of crabs but we set off, heading up past the Lane house and followed the track towards the forestry fencing and toward Trewern's ground. We were now fenced in on both sides and I heard a roar and looked around to see my mate in the Landrover heading towards us at speed. My first reaction was fright and I took off, vaulting the forestry fence and leaving my mates behind, who must have been amazed. My heart was thudding in my chest as I ran, but he was catching me up. However, I knew he would not get over the fence. Slowing down, I thought, right, you bastard, I've had enough of you. With that, he pulled up by the side of me and started mouthing obscenities at me from within the vehicle. I jumped straight back over the fence and went up to his window.

'Come on then,' I said. 'You think I'm frightened of you? I don't give a shit for you, so come on, you've got something to say, get out and say it!' He was staring at me and his face was purple with drink, but I was past caring.

Suddenly he said, 'I think we've got off on the wrong foot, and I must have made a mistake. I'm sorry.'

I was really wound up now and replied, 'You've been making my life a misery and I have done nothing to you, but if you ever shout at me again I'll put you in hospital, so fuck off and leave me alone.'

With some difficulty he got the thing into gear and drove off slowly towards Trewern brook.

Reg and Adrian were standing some yards off and looked at me dumbfounded.

Finally, Reg said, 'Bloody hell, old mate, I know he asked for it but you certainly told him.'

Taking out my fags, I took one and threw the packet to Reg. My hands were shaking as I laughed and said, 'It had to come, but he knows the score now and I hope to Christ that's it.'

That night we caught the bus down to Kington from Stanner and went to the pictures. There was a hell of a difference after the plush cinemas I had been to in Newport, but I was back and happy to be so. We got back about eleven o'clock and as I let myself in through the back door I looked around on my way to bed and saw all the familiar objects and thought how lucky I was to live in a place like this.

Sunday morning dawned clear and I was wide awake as I heard the old man about, getting ready for the early morning service. A busy day for him, straight after morning service a bit of breakfast and a relax and then the eleven o'clock service, home for lunch and then off to his other church for an afternoon service, home for tea and then six o'clock evensong. Still, it was only one day a week. Mum brought me in a cup of tea on her way to church and asked if I'd enjoyed the picture last night and then was gone with a slam of the front door to join my father at the service. I drank my tea and got up to look through the window, made my way to the bathroom and then got dressed and was downstairs in the kitchen when they got home. After breakfast the old man disappeared into his study and I took poor old Kim out onto the lawn, got him back into his bed and set off down through the village. It was quiet with not a soul about as I walked around by the school, through the gate and up onto the hill. Getting up onto the first peak, I lit up a smoke and sat down to take in the surroundings. It was a glorious sight as far as the eye could see, with the heather clad hills stretching away into the distance and finishing my fag, I walked steadily upwards and out onto the tops. My mind was full of thoughts about the coming week and I wondered if Sylvia had enjoyed her summer. I thought I would soon find out and also I had a feeling that this could be a very eventful year . . . just how eventful I would find out in the fullness of time.

CHAPTER FORTY
Baby I Don't Care
(Buddy Holly)

Monday morning found me standing at the bottom of the village awaiting the bus, with my hair and sideboards still with me and my whole being awaiting a showdown with my friend, the headmaster. I could hear the noise of the bus as it came down the hill, pulling up with a flourish with Cecil crouched behind the wheel and a huge grin on his face. He shouted as I came up the steps.

'Jesus Christ, Johnny boy, the old man will have a fucking fit when he sees your hair this morning.'

I replied, grinning, that I couldn't give a monkey's arse and sat down by him, lighting up a fag. I watched with interest as we pulled in at the various stops, picking up the new kids all clad in their new uniforms, clasping their new satchels and looking frightened to death as they boarded the bus. I remembered only too well my own first journey, with all my hopes and fears as I set off for Atherstone on that far away journey. Pulling myself out of my reverie, we climbed the steep hill and there stood our new head girl and my heart did a little flip as she made her way along the bus into her accustomed seat. Laughing, she looked at me and exclaimed that I obviously hadn't changed my appearance since the end of the last term. After we had talked about the holidays and various other things, she asked me what my intentions were regarding my school career, or lack of it and I replied that in truth I had made up my mind I had decided to let it all wash over me and see what was in store, but advised that she should not be seen to be too friendly with me by the powers that be. For want of a better phrase, you never see a Robin flying with a Crow.

At this she laughed and said it was her decision. Having got that over with we were joined by more people, some who had moved back as others had left last term, and finally pulled up outside the grey stone edifice that had become my own personal nemesis. There were several members of staff waiting to welcome the new pupils to the school and as I pretended not to notice, I could see their eyes flitting over my hair and I thought this will be in the Hall of the Mountain King before assembly.

Trying to mingle with some of my so-called mates, I found myself somewhat alone as I headed for assembly. I was thinking that I would stand out like a sore thumb, walking on my own, but suddenly a lad I knew sidled up and told me he would walk with me. The lad died tragically at a very young age but he was a good scout and I will always remember him with fondness. As we rounded the curve in the path, I thought, here we go, giving a sidelong glance at the staff, but no head was to be seen. Wonder of wonders, I thought, I hope the bastard's had the sack or even died somewhere. As we all stood to attention, the deputy head made the announcement that the headmaster was very ill with a bout of influenza. I swear I could see a couple of the staff hiding behind a grin. I even managed a couple of verses of 'Lord, behold us with thy blessing, Once again assembled here,' but 'Pardon all, their faults confessing' was a bit much for me.

Going back to the classroom, I was elated. I had got some time to settle in before the old git got back and started on to me again. Although I was coming sixteen and could walk out if I wanted, I still did not want to upset my folks and really hoped that they would come round and see it from my side. The day passed quietly with much the same lessons and staff, but we appeared to have lost the lady science teacher, who was replaced by a young man who seemed to be alright, but I would love to meet him today, face to face, and gently remind him that punching those younger and not so strong as himself just wasn't really cricket, and I'm sure I could convince him quite quickly, hey ho.

It might have been just my imagination, but the whole

atmosphere seemed to have lightened considerably and climbing aboard the bus that night, everyone seemed to be in a joyous mood. Two lads had joined the school from further up, about three miles from my village and I could see by Cecil's expression that he was extremely worried about getting up there in the winter time.

When it came to Sylvia's stop, she said, 'I'm coming on up with you to see where these new lads are living. Naturally, I was chuffed to bits with this and we sat together having a talk and laugh there and back and enjoyed it.

Next morning as I boarded the bus, Cecil said to me, 'I think the little lady fancies you, Johnny boy, you want to play your cards right there.'

I just told him not to be so bloody daft and feeling my colour rise, lit up a smoke as we pulled up the hill out of the village. When Sylvia boarded the bus she was all smiles, asking whereabouts in the village I lived and how did the new lads exist in the remote farm where they lived. Gradually, everything settled down and we started to get back to normal with the loss of our people from the previous term. The week passed by quietly enough and before you could say bollocks it was Friday again and the weekend in front of us.

By now I had arranged with a mate to leave my new clothes at his house, thereby getting my mother off the hook and not causing any embarrassment to the old man. However, on the Saturday morning I got a lift into town wearing my new clothes and was walking down the street when, horror of horrors, there was the old man talking to the local undertaker.

It was too late to duck and in any case, I saw the undertakers eyes open wide when he saw me, so I crossed the road.

'Have you ever seen this chap before, Vicar?' asked the undertaker.

My old man looked me up and down replied, 'Never seen him before in my life, Bill.' Conversation over, I thought and crossing back over, I entered the coffee bar and fed the juke box a shilling. Three plays got me 'Great Balls of Fire,' 'Long Tall Sally' and 'Hound Dog'.

Perhaps it should have been 'Don't Be Cruel'. As I sat enjoying the music, I noticed a familiar face looking through the door and it was one of the older teachers at the school. I knew they must have seen me but as I looked up they were gone and I had a funny feeling that there was more to this than met the eye. My mind was in a whirl. Could it be . . .? But no, never would they stoop that low. However, it was on my mind and I thought if they really want to know, just ask me. This little episode certainly put the dampers on my good spirits, but I had to admit I was happy to be back in the village and back in the old routine.

I must admit that for one second I was tempted to catch him up and ask him what they found so interesting about me, but I thought better of it and reading this sentence, ask myself: who said it was a him anyway? Travelling back to the village, my mind was everywhere but running alongside the Hergest Ridge with the Gore bank on the right of us, I could relax a bit. As you passed Stanner Rocks, it was as if a green curtain came down behind you and you were entering another world.

Back in the house it was noticeable that Kim didn't get out of his box and he just wagged his tail, somewhat meekly. I noticed Mother looking at my hair as if she expected some miracle might happen and I would be parading around with a short back and sides. Not much bloody chance of that happening, I said to myself. I also knew in my heart of hearts that sooner or later there would be a war, and no way was I going to become the loser.

CHAPTER FORTY-ONE
OUT OF TIME
(Chris Farlowe)

I walked down to the bus that Monday morning in a far blacker mood than I had been when I left it for the Easter holidays. The old folks couldn't get much out of me, try all they might, and I could see a big black cloud out on the horizon that was getting darker every day.

Cecil arrived that morning in a mood almost as bad as mine. It appeared he had driven all the way up to pick up the new kids, but there was no one there. Apparently, they had found the long journey too exhausting and decided to move to a nearer school and I didn't blame them one bit as they would never have got out in the winter. However, their parents had notified the school but no one had thought to inform Cecil. I slid into the front seat and lit a smoke, taking it deep down and relaxed. He asked me what sort of weekend I'd had.

'Much the same, nothing jaw-dropping, half cut on Saturday, listening to music all the time and no swotting for the forthcoming exams whatsoever. In fact, fuck the exams, the school and all who sail in her!'

'Christ, Johnny boy, you have had a bad time,' he replied.

'Yes, and it's going to get a whole lot worse,' I told him, thinking to myself, I don't even know what I'm doing here any more.

Reaching Sylvia's place, there was no one waiting and a guy shouted that she was in bed with a bad cold. I immediately thought, thank Christ for that, at least there will be no lectures for a few days.

The journey went along quietly enough and I was studying the new entrants, as to where they lived and how they appeared to be settling in. Finally, we arrived at the seat of learning and being one of the last to leave the bus, I heard Cecil calling my name. I walked back to see what he wanted.

'Listen, Johnny boy, I shouldn't be telling you this, but for Christ's sake keep your head down this term as they are watching you, and don't let on I've told you, for Christ's sake.'

Thanking him, I walked off and thought, it's a good job he's read the Bible as the only expletive he knows is 'Christ.'

Watching me? I hadn't put a foot wrong in the bloody place since God knows how long and I was totally pissed off with everything and couldn't wait to get the day over and quiz Cecil on the homeward journey. I also wondered if this was anything to do with Sylvia's absence this week, but I thought to myself, keep this up and you'll find a bogey man around every corner, you're getting paranoid, my friend. The day passed with nothing out of the ordinary going on and the time came for me to go and sit down the front of the bus. In all honesty, I think Cecil wished he hadn't said anything that morning, but he said they had all been told to watch for anything out of the ordinary on the bus and my name had been brought up once more as a potential trouble maker. I jumped off the bus at my stop and thanked him for telling me and walking up the village, I thought that this couldn't go on for much longer.

The week passed boringly by and on Thursday, Sylvia was waiting at her usual place and as she got on the bus I could see that she had been genuinely ill. She was all smiles as she slid into the seat and asked me how things had been. I told her what was being said and she replied that there was something going on and the staff had been in a few special meetings with the headmaster towards the end of the last term. Replying that I had been keeping my head down for months but that it seemed to be the order of the day to blame me for everything, I said that this was pure victimisation and just because I chose to follow the fashion of the time and the bigot of a head didn't agree, I was being made a scapegoat and I'd had enough. This obviously worried her but there was not much she could do.

Friday came and I was very thankful to be getting off the

bus and back home to the peace and solitude of my village. That weekend I received a letter from Vivienne, again telling me that she would be down at half-term, but although I was pleased it didn't cheer me up much and I moped about across the fields, preferring my own company.

Saturday afternoon, Reg came home unexpectedly and came to the house and we walked the brook looking for fish, which although it was far too cold, gave us a fair idea where the fish would be when the weather warmed up. One thing I wasn't pleased to see were a lot of crayfish in the pools, but I supposed this meant that the water must be in top condition, a far cry from today when there is hardly anything left alive in the water. As usual, Reg had plenty of American ciggies and I just loved the flavour of Lucky Strike. We had a good chat that afternoon and I felt somewhat better when he left for his tea. I had been given a quart of Perry by a mate and I had a half bottle of scotch hidden in an old shed, so that evening found me hiding them down in the builders' yard at the bottom of the village. I really don't know just what was in my head at that moment, but there must have been something and that something was to get me in the shit over my head.

The next day being Sunday, I picked up the twelve bore and went round the hedgerows but apart from a few pigeons, or what we called quists around there, I saw nothing worth wasting a cartridge on. I contemplated my future, or what appeared to be fast becoming lack of it and sitting on an old tree stump, lit up a fag and thought to myself it was time I speeded things up a fraction. At that stage I did not mean a huge amount, but something, somewhere had to give.

I walked down to the village in the afternoon, but it was very quiet and as I was skint that day I didn't go to the local town that night, but preferred to go over the top on the Sunday and have a drink there, so we set sail as usual after church. I got talked into playing darts that night and won quite a few games at half a pint a game, so the end of that meant I drank more than I should and the following morning I felt like shit and could still taste the beer in my mouth.

However, my playing partner must have been chuffed to bits with all the free drink we won. Being extremely wary in case the old folks were up, I navigated my way along the bottom fence, checking that everything was in darkness and very quietly let myself in through the front door and climbed quickly up the stairs and into my room.

That night any sleep evaded me and lying there, my mind was a whirl of thoughts. So I had taken to the Edwardian era of dressing; to my knowledge, so had thousands of others. It was an exciting time with the music, the clothes and the carefree attitude on the street. Little did I know then of the trends that were to follow it . . . punk rockers, ton-up boys and various groups that were to make my era a laugh. So as I lay there I thought to myself, what has this dopey head got against me? What can I do to change things without giving in to anything? I was not stupid; I had not given him any reason for complaint with the exception of my hairstyle. Apart from my clothes, which I only wore to dances and town and that was nothing to do with the school or him.

Finally I could see it getting lighter through the bedroom window and resolved to put this to bed sooner rather than later. The next thing I heard was my alarm clock and very grumpily rose and headed for the bathroom. I always remember the words of the song, 'Good Morning, World, it's a brand new day.' Some chance!

CHAPTER FORTY-TWO
I'm Walkin'
(Fats Domino)

Walking down the village to catch the bus that morning, I felt terrible and said to myself, serve you right you stupid prat, that will teach you, getting too much down your throat with school the next day. But as I walked on, I thought I must have picked up a dose of Flu from somewhere, but thought again and came to the conclusion I would stick it out, thereby avoiding a ton of questions from the old folks. On nearing the bottom of the village, I suddenly remembered my stash of liquor in the shed and the next few minutes were to change the rest of my life forever.

I reached for the bottle of scotch and took several long pulls out of the neck, which took my breath away. I then had the brainwave of washing it down with some perry. This appeared to work and I had a few more sips of perry and replaced the bottles in my hideaway. Then I lit up a smoke and wandered outside to await Cecil and the bus.

Funny how one remembers things, but it's as clear as the day it happened and as the bus pulled in, I was filled with a gay abandon and mounting the steps shouted a greeting to Cecil, who looked both dumbfounded and horrified, trying in vain to get me to go and get my head down somewhere. I completely ignored him and collapsed in a seat halfway down the bus. I must have quickly fallen asleep and awoke some time later with vague memories of someone trying to wake me and looking around, I realised I was in an armchair in the male staffroom. Eventually I was taken to the toilets and told to wash my face and escorted to my class. I would admit to being in somewhat of a muddle as to what had happened to me, but was none the worse for it.

Apart from some very strange glances from members of staff, nothing happened that day; no questions or recriminations, nothing except for a very grim-faced Cecil who snarled that he hoped I felt better and would speak later.

This we did, for as soon as the last pupil got off the homeward journey he shouted, 'Come up here you dozy bugger and explain your stupid self.'

Sitting next to him I was very glad he was driving so he couldn't hit me but he was clearly very mad. Along the road of life, we meet the occasional good ones and he was certainly one of those.

'If you had listened to me and got your head down in the shed, you might have got away with it, but not you who had to pass out in front of a bus load of kids and I had to go and get the staff who carried you into school smelling like a fucking distillery! God knows what will happen when the head gets back, but I for one think it will be bye bye.'

Sylvia was back on Monday and didn't speak for a couple of days and I think we both knew it was the end of the line.

That weekend the local fair was on but it was pissing down with rain so I just put a pair of tight black jeans on. We went into our local and had a few pints until nine o'clock, when we headed for the fair. On the way we bumped into a local lad who said he would give us a lift from the top of the town at eleven-thirty. This was brilliant and meant we could stay until the end.

Standing on the Waltzers, watching the action I saw another gang across the way. I knew their headman, and although a bit of a rough crowd, they were as good as gold with us and we had shared many a night with them. I happened to look over the side of the Waltzer into the crowds and guess what I saw? Only the spy from the staff, standing watching me. I called to Reg, saying I was in two minds to go over and ask what they were doing, but Reg, always the wise one, said to leave it be. He suggested we go and have a last pint before getting our lift. Our mate with the lift was still in there and said he would be leaving in half an hour.

So in due course, we were heading back up into the hill country. Looking back, I am amazed there were no drinking and driving laws back in those days.

Saturday morning after a shave and wash and change of clothes, I went downstairs to have a look at Kim in the vain hope he might be a little better, but he just weakly wagged his tail and feeling very disconsolate, I lit up a smoke and walked down to the brook on my own. Drawing the smoke down deeply, I exhaled it into the fresh spring air.

Saturday evening found Reg and yours truly walking down the village to catch the Fair bus into Kington once more and after a couple of beers were on our way down to the fairground. The whole ground was packed and we headed for the Noah's Ark. I spotted a girl I always fancied on the ride with her friends and asked Reg to hang on while I watched where it would stop and she would get off. I asked her how she was and would she like to go to the pictures next Saturday night. She replied that she thought I would never ask. With that, I gave her a kiss and heard a roar of appreciation, looking round to see the local Teds from the night before, all cheering. She disappeared very quickly and I walked back to Reg who remarked that I would be all right there and I wondered how he knew, but suddenly remembered that Vivienne was coming down next weekend and that I certainly wouldn't be alright if she heard the story.

The local lads were sidling towards me and one of them remarked that he fancied the girl himself. After saying he was going to chat her up later, I wished him good luck and we wandered around for a bit and then headed for a boozer. All of the evening I was constantly looking around for the spy from the school but saw no one. We had a drink and a chat with the boys and headed for the bus home.

I decided not to go out on the Sunday night and was sitting at home listening to the radio when I heard my parents opening the front door and from the noise, it would appear they had brought someone with them. I hastily made up the fire and tidied the room when the door opened and in they came. They were a couple from another village, she being a retired headmistress and he being a justice of the peace and I wasn't fond of either of them, to put it mildly. The conversation, as always, got round to the importance of a good education.

Suddenly, the old man pointed at me. 'Look at him,' he said, 'he wants to leave school and throw everything away. He's mental, don't you agree?'

I suppose one look at me was enough and I swear the temperature of the room dropped considerably.

Mumbling a hasty reply they said their goodbyes and left as quickly as possible. By now, I had gone to a place of my own, mentally. I vaguely heard the old man apologising but I was way beyond any conversation or apology. It was getting dusk and I picked up my ciggies and lighter and headed out around the grounds.

I had been standing there smoking and looking out across the fields and hills for about half an hour when I heard a slight noise behind me and coming towards me was the old man, smoking his pipe. There was an ominous silence between us when suddenly, he spoke.

'Sunny Jim, your mother and I have been talking and firstly I wish to apologise for my remarks. Secondly, we have to admit defeat and so if you want to leave that dreaded school you can do so with our blessing, but please remember that we only want what is right for you. Also remember that it is a hard old world out there. Now if I were you, I would give it a lot of thought, both long and hard and whatever you decide, we will support your decision.'

CHAPTER FORTY-THREE
Bad Moon Rising
(Creedence Clearwater Revival)

Monday morning and I was walking down to catch the bus, my mind full of thoughts on what decision I should make. Really it was cut and dried on my part but on the old folks' side I was letting them down and felt a bit sad for them with all their hopes for my education. But then another little voice was ringing in my ears that in no way was it my fault and I hadn't been the one who wanted to travel the country like a bloody gypsy.

I lit up a smoke and waited patiently for Cecil to come clanking round the bend. Sure enough I heard the sound of the bus and flicking my ciggy into the brook, jumped aboard and slid into the front seat beside him. For once, Cecil was strangely quiet this morning and I was straight into him, asking what the hell was wrong with him this morning.

He replied that although nothing had been said to him, there had been a meeting after school on the last Friday and he was sure that yours truly was on the agenda, so he advised me to watch myself, but I should be alright as the head was away and therefore nothing should happen. Sylvia had two days off for exam revision and so I felt strangely subdued on the journey and was left alone with my thoughts.

Later that morning, during the break, I walked down to the changing room and one of the lads who was senior to me and was having a quick drag, warned me that he had just heard the head, whose study was adjacent to the changing room, ask one of the staff to fetch my report to his study immediately. This threw me completely as he hadn't taken assembly that morning and I thought he was still away. I instantly went on my guard and also thought, this is it old mate, but then you knew it had to happen anyway.

The journey home that night was weird as there was no Sylvia to talk to and I was lost in contemplation throughout the long journey and couldn't wait to get up the front and talk to Cecil. Finally the last pupil disembarked and I went up the bus to the front seat.

'Christ, Johnny boy, you're very quiet today. Is everything all right or are you missing Sylvia?' he asked.

Replying bollocks, I countered with the fact that the head was away, according to him.

'He has gone for a couple of weeks,' he replied, 'and he won't be back this week.'

I then told him of this morning's conversation, and he was totally gobsmacked.

'Leave it with me, Johnny boy,' he replied, 'and don't breathe a word to anyone, right?'

Reaching my stop I said cheerio and walked up through the village. Not a soul was about, not even the geese, and up through the churchyard I went, in through the gate and home at last.

The next days passed quietly with no sign of the head and I was left alone for a change. Getting home one Friday afternoon, I had the strangest feeling as I approached the house. Kicking my shoes off outside the back door, I stole quietly over to Kim but he was just lying there without opening his eyes. I thought to myself what a bloody great end to the week and walked into the kitchen to be greeted with a cheerful hello from my mother. Hoping to God I wasn't going to have any questions thrown at me, I sat down at the table to a nice hot mug of tea and some chocolate biscuits and felt the peace of home wash over me.

'We've had the vet out to see Kim today,' she said, 'and he says he is quietly slipping away, but he's not in any pain and won't last much longer.'

My mind flew back to the fat little bundle of fur that met me those long years ago in Hampshire and how he licked my face and the times we played together, and I shook with the deep feeling of sadness.

'Well, Mum, he has had a good life and at least he's with us,' I said.

Nodding, she turned away and I knew how upset she felt. Finishing my tea I left the room and ran upstairs to change, glad to be away from the atmosphere. Downstairs and out of the door me, through the paddock and down to the brook to look for the trout which were showing themselves in the clear water.

I spent about an hour by the brook alone with my thoughts and, finishing a cigarette, I started back up to the house and tea. The old man was seated at the table when I got in and asked if I had a good day. Replying that it was alright, the subject was closed and we ate our meal making small talk throughout and I was glad when it was over. I walked down into the village later and stood under the wall but there was no one about so I walked quietly back up through the churchyard, watching the first swifts as they screeched past, glad to be back. I thought, so am I, Mr Swift, so am I.

I walked into the house and the old man was in his study and my mother was nowhere to be seen, so I went into the sitting room and switched on the wireless. It was too early for Lux so I listened to the news and must have fallen asleep as I woke up to hear my mother crying and she came rushing in to tell me that Kim had died. Asking where the old man was, she told me he was in the room with Kim, so telling her to sit down I rushed in to find the old man ashen-faced, looking down at the dog. Bending down, I felt his side and he had obviously been gone for some time as he was getting stiff. I told the old man that I would carry him out into the wash house and bury him early the next morning.

I declined his offer of help. 'I can manage,' I said. 'Go in to Mum and leave it to me.'

This seemed to cheer him up and off he went to comfort Mum. I picked up the blanket with Kim inside and carried him out to the wash house and locking the door, went in to my folks.

My mother, although very upset, was a lot calmer now and realised the old boy had lived a good life and nothing can last forever. The old man was making a cup of tea for us and we sat there for some time without a word between us. At last, mother broke the silence, asking where we were going to bury him, and when. I quickly suggested that beneath the front lawn would be a good place and he would be aware of our comings and goings there and know that all was well. This being instantly approved by them both, I said I would do it first thing in the morning, and promised to give the old man a shout. So it was off to bed and I was painfully aware of an empty space in the corner of the kitchen for the first time since I was a mere scrap running around.

I was up with the dawn next morning and before it had got really light I had cut out a square of turf and was down into the soil, throwing it on an old tarp. I saw the old man coming round the corner of the house. Asked why I hadn't called him, I made the excuse that I couldn't sleep. He was amazed how much I had done and offered to dig a bit, but I had youth on my side and within no time at all I was down deep enough for nothing to disturb the old dog. We carried him round and laid him in his blanket and to be fair, there was nothing left of him after his long illness, I glanced up at Mother's bedroom window but all was quiet so I quickly started filling in the soil and having finished, re-laid the turf and tamped it down. The old man said he would brush over the lawn and that was that.

Returning to the house, I got cleaned up and had some breakfast before leaving to catch the bus. It's a funny old thing but with all that was going on at the school, I walked down that road and didn't give it a thought for I was away running with Kim through the heather at Pamber Heath and taking him across the fields at Ansley Common, or across the miles of recreation grounds by the Trent in Nottingham and it was a very sombre lad that greeted Cecil that morning. As we neared our destination, I thought, just let anybody start this morning. Please do, because I'm waiting for you.

Looking back, I am surprised that anyone spoke to me at all that morning and thankful for that, I retreated into my own little world for the rest of the morning. However, no one bothered me and I likewise. Lunch came and went with no sign of the head and

I began to think I was seeing a lot more into this and when the time came to board the bus for the homeward trek, I must confess to feeling somewhat easier. Everyone around me appeared to be having exam fever and were walking around with noses buried in books, but yours truly was having none of it.

Sylvia returned on Thursday and had a big exam on the Friday morning so I left her to the peace and quiet which she needed. Speaking with Cecil in the evenings when everyone else had left the bus, he was none the wiser whether the head was there or not and he certainly was not seen around the school, so I felt a little more at ease. Friday morning passed without incident and after lunch we had science for the first two periods. I was sitting quietly minding my own business when there was a knock on the door and our form master entered.

'Could I have John Elias, please?' and with a nod from the science master I found myself walking down the corridor towards the Hall of the Mountain King.

Looking down at me as we walked along the corridor, the form master said very quietly, 'Just tell the truth, my boy. They cannot hang you for it, but do not try to pull the wool over their eyes as it's a lost cause.' With that he knocked on the study door saying, 'John Elias for you, Headmaster.'

I entered the room and the door closed quietly behind me.

CHAPTER FORTY-FOUR
We Gotta Get Out of This Place
(The Animals)

I was facing the hanging jury or so it appeared, with no smile of welcome. Just a stony silence greeted me and I was shown to a chair facing the big guns. Now this happened all of fifty-five years ago so if I am guilty of a slight exaggeration, I beg forgiveness and after all, the head's study was not the local village hall but there seemed to me to be an awful number of people in it that day. I was facing a long table with my friend, the head, directly in front of me, whilst on either side of him were the school governors, both men and women. I was very formally introduced to the governors and taking a deep breath, thought to myself let battle commence, whilst in the back of my head a little voice was warning, don't let them sack you, but give them your option first, which of course was to leave this hallowed seat of learning as fast as I could possibly go.

'Now then, John, I would start this meeting by telling you that anything spoken of in this room today will not go outside these four walls and therefore you can speak quite freely in front of the governors and myself.'

I immediately noticed the shock in the eyes of a lady sitting opposite and thought, Hey ho, here cometh the lies.

'Now, John, certain things have come to light in the past twelve months concerning your behaviour and attitude, mode of dress and hair style both in school and out of school and such behaviour is not what we would expect from a pupil of this school. We, the trustees, feel that it gives a bad impression and is disrespectful, not only to the school and its staff and pupils, but also to the public and your parents, who have to behave with great dignity and compassion in the life that they have chosen.'

Hey ho, you sanctimonious sack of shit, I was about to say, but caught a warning glance from the lady governor, who appeared to be a human being, and a quite attractive one at that, so I gave him the dead eye and replied that what my parents did or how they behaved was absolutely nothing to do with him or me and I would have to leave the room should they be brought into any other conversation concerning myself. I could see his eyes hardening and again thought, go on then, but he controlled it and started on another tack.

'You have not hidden your leaning towards both being an admirer and dressing in the clothes of this Teddy boy culture that is sweeping our towns and cities, and have been seen on many occasions drinking, smoking and cavorting in very bad company. How do you feel about that?'

The Literary and Debating Society would have been proud of me as I replied that I was well aware of who had been following me, and in my opinion they needed help, but that I was in no way breaking any rules as I was not in school time or in school uniform and therefore as there was no dress code on the school notice boards for after school activities I could please myself.

This stopped them in their tracks and they mumbled to one another for a few minutes. Then, asking me how much alcohol I could drink, further hummed and ha'd, saying that was enough to knock a grown man over, to which I quickly replied I was a grown man and making grown men's decisions.

The next question threw me completely for they asked me if I knew of anyone taking drugs in the school. This was the middle fifties and the only drug I knew of was Aspirin, but this was obviously very important and they grilled me for a long time and looking at today's culture, I must admit that they were on the ball and for that I take my hat off to them. However, I was clean and green over this and then came flick knives, bike chains and other weapons, which I obviously denied any knowledge of.

After a lot more idiot questions, the head started his closing speech and I was wondering how I was getting home as the bus would have already left.

Summing up, he said that he was aware of my friendship with Sylvia and how she had tried reasoning with me but to no avail. Then one of the governors said that they would leave it at that, but looking at the head, he confirmed that he and his wife would be going over to see my parents that evening.

I completely lost it at this point and asked was this how they expected anybody to learn about trust and quoted the head's opening speech. I laid it on the line to them then and explained that with my folks' blessing I would be leaving the school as and when to be agreed and that I would not wish to be associated with them again. I was escorted to a taxi outside the school gates and climbing in, was amazed to find Sylvia sitting there. She was looking at me with those big brown eyes and asked how it had gone and I told her the whole thing. She said they had called her in that morning to question her about me, but was sworn to secrecy. I laughed at this for I knew she would not have said a bad word about me, and she said they had asked would she take the taxi with me as they felt I might need a friend after the meeting and I was very pleased she did just that.

All too soon it was her stop and I tried to make some small talk with the taxi driver but he must have been grilled not to engage so I thought bollocks. The small mindedness of some people . . . they just left me cold. We arrived at the bottom of the village and I asked him to drop me there, but he said he was told to take me to the house. I'd had enough by now and told him I would jump if he didn't stop, which he did. Pointing to the brook, I told him there was not enough water in it and not to worry. I bumped into him several times in later years and we had a laugh about it and got on fine, and you cannot blame a man for acting under orders.

So there we have it, all over and done with. As I walked up the village I thought of the hours spent copying up loads of different work, all to no avail, of the different uniforms I had to wear, of the master in Warwickshire who had seen me through. What would he be thinking now if he knew? I wondered would they let me see out the last weeks until the summer break up. Dependant on what had been said after I left the room, I supposed. I had not shown them much respect and certainly not given any apology. Possibly yes, out of respect for the old man, or maybe not; it was all down to the visit tonight and I would be long gone across the fields.

I arrived at my back door fully expecting a shed load of questions from the old folks. However, all was peaceful and after a few minutes I found my mother reading a book in the sitting room. Giving me a smile of welcome she got up, put the kettle on to boil and said the old man was out visiting around the village and would be back at tea time. I went upstairs to my bedroom and mulled over the day's events, also musing how the next few days would pan out. Suddenly, there was a gentle knock on my door and my mother came in, carrying a cup of tea and an anxious look on her face. Knowing she was dying to ask, I grinned and explained that it had gone alright and there was nothing for her to worry about. This seemed to please her and she went back downstairs to get the tea.

After changing out of my now hated uniform, I put on some casuals and descended the stairs. It's a funny thing with dogs and me, but for the last eight times with my dogs, when one dies I am straight away looking for another. I suddenly remembered Viv and thought, wake up sunshine, your gorgeous bird is arriving tonight and the whole world is yours to conquer so get out there and enjoy. Whistling a few bars of Rock I entered the kitchen to find the old man sitting there.

'My word, Sunny Jim,' he said, 'you're sounding a lot more cheerful than of late. By that I must conclude that things went alright today and you can have a little time to sort yourself out. Hopefully they will leave you alone now until the end of term.'

Replying that all was well, I ventured to say that I might try to get an apprenticeship to become a joiner and what did he think? He seemed genuinely pleased and offered me any help I might need to give it a try. Thanking him, I went for a walk around the grounds and thought this old world ain't so bad and when I sat down to tea later, there were no black dogs sitting on my shoulder.

Tea over, the old man retired to his study and I headed down through the fields and beyond. Alone with my many thoughts I wondered how my life would pan out and would I cope working with my hands for a living.

CHAPTER FORTY-FIVE
Standing at the Crossroads
(Elmore James)

As I neared the house my worry was that, no matter what, I did not want my folks upset knowing the head would shoot his mouth off to all and sundry. Secondly, I had dropped a bollock handing in my notice as I had told the old man I would give it serious thought and tell him my decision first, but I hoped that he would probably understand my reasons for this.

I walked in through the back door and there was no Kim, just an empty space where his box had been and I felt total shit at that moment. However, the door opened and my mother walked in, smiling at me and asked how my day had been. I confessed it had been worse than usual.

'Never mind, son,' she said and poured us a cup of tea and we sat down together, lost in our thoughts. I knew that she was missing Kim and was also worried about me but I had to sort out my own problems and was past the stage of running to my parents. Finishing my tea, I excused myself and went upstairs to change out of my dreaded uniform. Sitting on the bed in my room, I remembered my first night here and how I had been full of excitement with a new home and school and possible friends, and was lost in the dream of how it could have been and then the reality of how it really was and, sighing to myself, I went down the stairs for my tea.

Tea was a quiet affair with myself deep in thought about the oncoming storm and my folks trying to make small talk. In the end, we finished our meal and I headed for the fields and wide open spaces where I would be as far away as possible from the unwelcome visitors whom I knew were about to descend on my folks. I walked up through the Cwm wood and back around the side of Glanyrafon, avoiding the houses and then retraced my steps across the bottom of the wood and followed the brook for some way. Finally I sat down by a pool, wondering what was going on at the house. The mosquitoes were starting to bite so I lit up a ciggy and started slowly back towards home. It was now just past nine o'clock and I was sure the guests would be gone now, but I circled the gardens and checked for any sign of their car. It appeared to be all clear so taking a deep breath, I jumped the fence and skirting the back hedge, went in through the back door.

No one leapt out on me from the shadows; no shouting; no raised voices. All was quiet except for the muted tones of the wireless coming through from the sitting room. It was far too peaceful for me so I stole back out through the door and going around the side of the house, sat on the old bench under the hawthorn and lit up a ciggy. I sat looking out across the wood opposite, lost in my own little world when I heard a footstep and saw the old man walking towards me. Lighting up his pipe, he sat down by the side of me and told me that they had been visited by the head and his wife and that I was obviously the reason for their visit. They told my folks there had been a full and frank discussion with me and that I had no intention of changing my lifestyle and that we had reached an impasse. As I appeared to have grown out of the idea of learning, I had told them that I felt there was nowhere left to go other than leave the school. The head also felt that he should come and talk to them to see if perhaps they could change my mind in any way about moderating my appearance and behaviour and if not, were they happy to let me go ahead and leave at the end of the summer term, this giving me a chance to complete my exams. This latter offer was, I am sure, given out of respect for my parents' position and for which I was truly grateful. They had made no reference to my life outside of school, for which again I was grateful.

As to the exams, I felt he was having a laugh and I was trying to work out how I could avoid them, but I needed time to think and to organise a job for myself, so this would give me the time to look around. I apologised to the old man for not telling him first but after explaining the situation, he accepted it and said I had made my decision and it was up to me to stand by it.

We agreed that I would give in my notice of leaving the school on the following Monday morning, in a proper fashion to my form master and I resolved to keep my head down for the rest of my time there. The following Monday morning I met the bus as usual but with a feeling of elation, so much so that Cecil with his usual aplomb asked me what I was so bloody cheerful about. Telling him he would know tonight, he then quizzed me as to what had happened on the previous Friday as my form master had gone down to the bus to inform him that I would be late and that other transport had been arranged. He had also seen a couple of governors arriving that afternoon. These people he knew, and guessed there was something going down. But after a while he left it alone and was happy that I would reveal all later.

What a joy! No nasty stares as I walked into school and into my form room where I delivered my letter to the form master and told him the content. He looked at me straight and shaking his head, told me he would deliver it before prayers and that was the end of that, or so I thought. Now I am fully aware that at this time of my life I could be a little sod, but as far as I was concerned I was completely innocent and was being made a victim of sheer petty vindictiveness and I was soon to have this confirmed.

The first lesson came to an end and as I was leaving the classroom a mate gave me a shove and I struggled to get my balance. Instantly, the woman taking the lesson gave me the dead eye and telling the class to go, stood toe to toe and started telling me that I was a total layabout and should be ashamed of myself. I let her continue and then it was my turn as I quietly told her exactly what I thought of her and that my parents and I were none of her business. This left her standing gobsmacked and I believed I saw a few tears. Next lesson, and as I was letting my desktop down it slipped and made a bang. Instantly, I was told to get out and I walked out into the corridor when, surprise, surprise . . . who happened to come around the corner? Only the headmaster's wife, who looked at me and told me that it was obvious I was a waste of space and shouldn't have been given any leeway. I was fuming and standing there, guessed what was happening.

The rest of the morning passed quietly by and after lunch we were in an English lesson. The lad I was sitting next to had a plastic walking dog which he called Pongo. He was lifting the desk lid slightly and this thing would amble down the desk but he must have lifted it too high as it careered down the desk lid, crashed into an ink bottle and its nose fell off. This resulted in him bursting out laughing and me trying to stifle a giggle. The teacher who was taking the lesson and who I had a lot of time for, pointed at me and told me to get out. I walked out to the front and stood there, whereupon she told me again to get out. Repeating this three times, she asked me why I wouldn't leave the room. I replied that both she and I knew what would happen if I did and she told me to stand where I was until the end of the lesson. When the bell went, my mate with the dog told her it was in no way my fault and she just nodded to me and that was that.

Later that day I was in the woodwork class. I seemed to get on well with the teacher, I liked the practical side of things and was, apparently, very good at technical drawing as they called it in those days. I was cutting the shoulders on a mortise joint and as he came over to have a look, he remarked that I was doing a good job and keeping to the gauge lines. I asked him what chance he thought I had of becoming a carpenter and joiner, to which he replied that I should do very well at it and it was a very good trade to have. This set me thinking and I resolved to bounce it off the old man later.

The rest of the day passed quietly enough with most pupils and teachers leaving me alone and I was glad of the peace and more than ready to board the bus for the homeward journey. Sylvia gave me the usual banter as I got to my seat and I settled back and thought how everyone seemed to have gone quiet, as if waiting for me to say something. Looking up the bus to the driver's seat, I could see him looking into his rear mirror every now and then.

Talking to Sylvia, I told her about the day's happenings and added that I appeared to be public enemy number one for those who wished to ride on the head's bus. The only comment she made was my decision not to leave the classroom that morning would probably stand me in good stead, as it would certainly have got around the staff room and laughing, she said she must have had a shock when I refused to leave the room.

I knew Sylvia was off for a few days the following week and I had already decided to take the rest of the week off, so when we reached her stop I said I would see her a week on Monday and that was it. As we dropped the last pupil off, I walked down the bus to sit by Cecil, who tried to look unconcerned but I knew he was dying to know last Friday's events. Lighting up, I told him what had transpired and he listened and identified the governors I told him were at the hanging party. I told him how they had got me to open up and how they had broken their word and what I had called them, also how the head had been over to see the old folks. He said he knew something was going down as they quizzed him about my behaviour on the bus again. I then told him the goings on today and how they were jumping on the band wagon and he wasn't a bit surprised. I then told him I was not feeling too hot and not to bother coming over until a week next Monday, but to act surprised. Anyway, I was doing him a favour by saving him a long drive. Leaving him at the bottom of the village, I turned and shouted cheerio and saw him shaking his head as he started to reverse round.

I headed up the village and felt a great weight lifting off my shoulders and thought: I feel great, I'm kicking the dust off my feet with that bloody school and Vivienne is coming on Friday so get stuffed to all those jumping on the band wagon bar none.

CHAPTER FORTY-SIX
Something in the Air
(Thunderclap Newman)

I awoke at the same time as usual and rubbing my eyes, looked at the clock. It showed six-fifteen and I remembered it was Saturday and there was no bloody school. That was the trouble with getting up early, you got into the habit of waking and could not get back to sleep, but burying myself deep into the bed, I closed my eyes and was gone again. The next thing I heard was my bedroom door opening and my mum smiling at me, with a nice hot cup of tea.

Thanking her, I drank deeply from the cup and looked at the clock. It showed half past eight and I remembered Viv was supposed to be coming today, so after a wash, shave and struggling into my drainpipe jeans, I was back into the bathroom to get the hair right and then down the stairs for breakfast.

The old man was sitting at the table and after the salutary good mornings, informed me he had to go into town and would I like a lift. He dropped the hint that, as I was planning to go to see a potential future employer the following week, a call at the hairdressers would not go amiss. Thanking him for his oh so kind offer, I explained that I had already made arrangements, but that half the lads on the building firms were the same as me. With a look of disgust he bade me a disgruntled good morning and headed for his study.

Mum, bless her, just smiled and told me he had a lot on his plate that day. I finished my breakfast, lost in my own little world and without thinking went out to put the lead on the dog. Alas; no dog. I went out through the back door and shouting cheerio to

Mum, was on my bike and out of the gate before you could spit. Heading down through the village it was very quiet and I met nothing until I reached the top of the Wern pitch, where I waved to a passing tractor. I felt very much alive that morning as I sailed down the Crabtree pitch and into the drive, but once again there was no car and no sign of anyone about. I guessed the aunties were still asleep and that Viv might have been delayed in traffic, so I wheeled around and headed for home.

True to his word, the old man had gone to town and I hoped the local populous would be safe, when he approached in his car. Mum was up to her neck in cleaning and polishing and I was at a loss to do anything with the long awaited girl of my dreams, well some of them were unmentionable. Mother stopped what she was doing and came in to make a cup of tea and we sat there in silence until we both spoke at the same time, the subject being how quiet it was without Kim. I was all for getting another dog straight away, but she wanted to wait for a bit, so that was it. However, it was very strange as we'd had him for years and he was a great companion and always there in troubled times, giving you a lick. We had some chickens and a cockerel down in the paddock, and also some bantams, which were good layers. I wandered down to have a look at them and then walked down to the brook, which was in full spate and no chance of fishing. As I stood lost in thought beneath an alder, I felt a tap on my shoulder and turning around quickly was met by a big smile, a pair of arms went around me and I was lost.

Pushing her away, I laughed. 'Hell, girl, you frightened me to death then.'

Laughing, she told me my mum had told her where to find me and to try to cheer me up.

I eyed her up and down; she had grown up and was nearly as tall as me with a super figure. Asking me how I thought she looked, I replied that she looked perfect to me. Walking along the brook, we were lost in conversation of things past and present. Strangely enough, I felt a little awkward and hoped fervently that we could get back to how it was before. There was so much to talk about, so much to tell her about and I felt we needed to be on our own, away from the restrictions of my house and garden, which I suggested.

She had just arrived and her dad had dropped her off on his way back to Coventry, but she had to go back to her aunties to explain and spend the morning with them. We would spend the afternoon and evening together. So helping her onto the crossbar of my bike, I pedalled like a madman down to her house and told her I would be back down by two and away I went for home, with a little warning bell going off in the back of my head. No explanation of where she had got to last night; this morning a brief cuddle and chat and meet at two o'clock. Back home on Sunday? Something did not ring true or perhaps I was reading things wrongly, but I could smell trouble a mile away and resolved to be on my guard.

Tearing back home, I thought, if this keeps up I will be entering the local endurance contests, as I made it up past the football field and into my drive. I could smell the lunch cooking and washed my hands in the scullery, feeling ravenously hungry. There wasn't much conversation around the table and I was thankful for that as, finishing up, I made my excuses and headed upstairs to change my shirt. It had all the appearances of being a fine afternoon and I had an hour to kill before I left, so I took a tour around the garden and paddock and never being one to hang around, was back on my bike and away. What it is to be a teenager! Heading up the Wern pitch, my mind was in turmoil. Had she found someone else? Did she wish to be home rather than here with me? I swear I nearly went off the road a couple of times and then, heading down the Crabtree, I saw her coming to meet me. I could hardly believe it, I had the old Viv back again instead of the distant person I had seen this morning. We were all over one another and headed for the tree line of the wood.

Needless to say the afternoon was all and more than I had hoped for, and I also found out that her auntie had argued with the vicar over some triviality and felt it better if I did not come to the house this visit. Bloody grownups; I didn't give a monkey's you-know-what who fell out with whom as long as it did not get in my way. I begged her not to go back on the morrow but to no avail and finally, we parted with promises to meet that evening.

Arriving back home I had a walk around the churchyard to cool down, sitting on a log and lighting up a ciggy I blew a steady stream of smoke at the myriad flies hovering around. Today had been good, especially the latter part and I had the whole evening to look forward to. Stubbing out my ciggy, I walked to the house only to be confronted by mother with a command that tea was on the table. Tea over and I headed for the bathroom for a wash and change and a sweater, as it went cool pretty quickly at this time of the year. Deciding to walk over to Viv's I headed down the path into the village to find myself suddenly accompanied by Adrian and Reg. Asked where I was going, I told them and they said they were catching the bus to Hay Fair and why didn't I go with them? Not for me, was my instant reply, with them badgering me all the way down the village, and I could see the green back of the bus. The motor was running and they headed for the door as I walked around the back and jumped on just as the door was being closed.

Teenagers are all mental and pull some funny stunts, but that was the end of a budding romance and unfortunately, I have never seen Viv again to this day. Looking back, I thought this was a shame and that I must take the time to sit down and write to her in the next few days.

CHAPTER FORTY-SEVEN
The Great Pretender
(The Platters)

Going up the hill past the Colva turn I thought, what sort of bloody idiot am I and what am I doing on this sodding bus when I could be snuggling up to a luscious bird? Looking out of the window, I was thinking, it's too late now, you dozy git, you will never see her again, but there again, Hay Fair is beckoning you. Passing over the Wye, we could see clearly the different coloured lights of the various rides and sideshows.

Pulling in, the driver shouted, 'Be here for eleven o'clock or you will be left behind!'

Feeling in my pocket, I realised I only had a couple of pounds, but I knew Reg would lend me a fiver until I got home. Dismounting from the bus, we headed for the nearest pub, which appeared to be quite posh inside. Swanking up to the bar, I asked if they had any Flowers Keg bitter. The old guy who served me was obviously a seasoned campaigner and had seen hundreds of prats like me in his life.

'Sorry, son, we don't sell it in here but we have a brew which will suit your taste, young sir.'

With the 'young sir' I was his in an instant and asked what it was called.

'Worthington E, sir, and I don't think you'll be disappointed, but I can only let you have three pints each and then you will have to leave and visit the fair.'

'Three pints it is, then,' I confirmed and he filled three pint glasses with a beautiful head on them and passed them over to us. Taking a long sup, I thought I was in heaven. It was just like milk and I was sorely tempted to gulp the lot down, but had the common sense to enjoy it. In no time at all we had consumed our three pints each and I asked the barman could we have another. He replied that much as he would like to sell us another, rules were rules and not made by him, so that was that. I thought deeply about this statement over the following weeks and thought he must have been the shrewdest chap in Hay, for who in their right mind would want three hooligans, three parts pissed, staggering all over the bar and becoming uncontrollable, so I take my hat off to him. The truth of the matter was we got up to the fair, but were all the worse for wear, so we headed into the chip shop and had a meal.

This seemed to steady the ship but we were pleased to finally board the bus and head for home. As we came down into the village, I realised what a bad mistake I had made and vowed to write a letter of apology to Viv the next day.

Sunday dawned bright and clear and I got up for breakfast with queries from my mother was I going to see Viv today, to which I replied with a grunt that she had gone back home. No more was said and I finished my breakfast and walked down the paddock for a smoke and some peace and quiet. Alone with my thoughts, I blew a cloud of smoke out and cursing inwardly, vowed to write and apologise to Viv that morning.

Retiring to my room, I took pen to paper and wrote the biggest apology . . . correction: garbage, I could think of and scrounging a stamp out of the old man's study shot off down the village and posted it. That complete, I could only hope for the best and returned to the house and the smells of Sunday roast. Deep into Boldness Be My Friend, I must have dozed off, for the next thing I heard was the old man revving hell out of the car and I shot across to the bathroom and washed my face in readiness for lunch. Making small talk around the table, I then made my excuses and went back upstairs to my book. I had resolved not to go out that night and my mood was not good as I walked up the brook, across by New House, down past the ruined cottage called the Green, and over the fence into the paddock. Aware that it would soon be teatime, I sat on the bench in the garden and started to try and plan my week off from school which was starting tomorrow.

I wasn't left alone for long as my mother came round the lawn and looking surprised, told me tea was on the table. Just why she feigned surprise beats me as I had seen her watching me through the French windows in the sitting room. However, that's parents for you. I asked the old man what day he might go to town and he said that either Tuesday or Wednesday would suit him, preferably in the morning. This sorted, I resolved to ring the local builders first thing on Monday morning, hopefully for an appointment.

Monday morning I was down at the phone box and in my best manner, secured an appointment with the builders at eleven o'clock on Wednesday morning. Well, well, I would never have thought things could be so easy and it was plainly obvious to me that the old 'uns in my life didn't know how to handle things. I got back up to the house to be met by a deputation enquiring how I had got on and gave them the news. In truth I felt they were pleased in one way and very sad in another that I was going to get my hands dirty and there would be no doctor or solicitor gracing their fireside.

Taking the gun out of the cupboard and a pocket full of cartridges, I headed out of the back door and walked up the lane to Gobe Banks, where I knew there were a fair few rabbits up in the fern, free from the dreaded myxomatosis. On the way up the lane I met the farmer who owned the land. He stopped for a chat and asked where I was going and when I told him he said to forget it, there was a pair of polecats up there and they had cleared out all the rabbit population, so I left him and walked down along the rushy ground, around the fields and back home. I did manage to bring down a carrion crow, but that was the total of my hunting escapade for that morning.

Back home, I cleaned the gun and put it away before going into the kitchen to scrounge a cup of tea. Mother was humming to herself, a sure sign that she was not a happy chick and I asked her what was wrong. I gradually found out that it was the doctor/solicitor syndrome again and I explained that I knew exactly what

I wanted and was looking forward to it. At this she cheered up and we had a cup of tea and a chat at the table before I went up the stairs for an appointment with Richard Pape, the author of my book. I idly wondered when Viv would get my letter and supposed it might be by Wednesday. I then wondered what Sylvia might be doing. I thought she was going up to the smoke for an interview with a university and hoped she would get in and sock it to them. This got me thinking about school and also my stubbornness over the Teddy boy thing, also the total intransigence of the head and I opened the window and lit up a cigarette, wondering if it was the head or myself that I was most angry with.

Finishing my ciggy, I closed the window and went downstairs. I was bored to tears; all my mates were either at work or at school, so I got my bike and hurtled around a few lanes, had a look in some favourite pools, but it was too cold for fishing, got back into the village, dumped the bike in the yard at the bottom and quickly climbed to the top of the hill. I sat there looking down on the village and farms and counted my blessings. I heard the clang of the school bell and watched as a line of children streamed out of the door, some running to their waiting parents, some heading up the lanes and some climbing into cars and Landrovers, their day complete, with stories to tell and their day's happenings, should anyone listen.

I sat up here and watched the world pass by, but it was a very small world. There were more tractors than anything, with some cars going to the village shop, a few riders on horseback and the occasional person walking up or down the village lane. This was my heaven, if there was such a place. Wild and remote just the endless bleat of the sheep and the low of the cattle. It wouldn't do at all for the city dwellers, who would go mad. In my mind I went back to Newport and Nottingham with its endless streets and miles of shops, where everyone was a stranger and also in a hurry.

If only she could see me now, what would Josie think? The nearest picture house was seventeen miles away. No Saturday afternoon matinee for me, just a walk over the hills and I am at peace. With a feeling of contentment, I stubbed out my cigarette on a boulder and straightening up, began the descent to my bike.

Back home half an hour later, I walked in the kitchen to be greeted with a smile from my mother and a cheery 'Hello Sunny Jim' from the old man, and we sat around the kitchen table drinking tea with no stress and no arguments. Perhaps we could all be happy again.

Wednesday morning I was up, shaved and washed, wearing a clean shirt and a smart tie and clutching a mortise and tenon joint and a halving dovetail joint, wrapped in some paper. I was away with my father at just turned ten o'clock. I would be the first to admit I was somewhat wound up, but I knew I could give a good account of myself and I hoped for the best. At ten-fifty that morning, my father and I walked into the builder's office and were shown straight in to the hall of the mountain king. There were two men in the office; one with a large handlebar moustache and the other dressed in overalls with grey curly hair. Motioning my father and me to sit down, the man with the moustache asked me a few questions, but nothing heavy, I'm glad to say. Asked why I wanted to be a joiner, I told him of my interest in wood and handed him the joints I had made in school. He just looked briefly at them and passed them over to the overalls, who grinned and answered that of course this was very simple and there was a lot more to the job than just that. I bit my tongue and thought, you silly old git, I know ... that's the reason I need to be taught it, and the other man said they were a good start. My father butted in at this stage, addressing the boss man and asked him would he give me a chance and after a few minutes, the boss man said he would take me on as an indentured apprentice for five years and then one year's improver. This was all signed and sealed and settled with the clerk coming in and I was to start at seven-thirty on the first Monday in September.

Well that was the end of that and I shook hands with the boss man and the overalls and we left the premises. Not a bad morning's work, I thought and although Dad was pretty quiet, he shook my hand and said, 'Well done, my son; I hope your mother is pleased.' The journey home was quite uneventful and leaving my old man to break the news to my mother, I walked down the paddock and had a smoke and a think.

CHAPTER FORTY-EIGHT
I Go Ape
(Neil Sedaka)

The noisy clatter of the alarm awoke me from a deep sleep and I reached out and belted it before it woke up half the parish. The early sun was streaming in through the window as I grabbed clean pants and vest and headed for the bathroom. Looking out of the latticed bathroom window as I was washing, I could see the outline of Gobe Banks and cursed as I remembered Mr and Mrs Polecat had taken up residence and eaten all the rabbits. I shaved around the sides of my now prominent sideboards and toiletry over, headed back into the bedroom. I looked behind my bedroom door and sure enough, neatly pressed were my blazer, tie, white shirt and trousers. I did not know if this was a faint hope or total resignation and I struggled into them and combing my hair front and back in the two mirrors, descended the stairs and into the kitchen.

'Ah,' Mother exclaimed, 'I was just about to call you to breakfast.'

Grabbing a round of toast, I swallowed my tea and after giving her a peck, was away, round the back lawn and out of the gate. Reaching the bottom of the village I lit up a woodbine and inhaled deeply with satisfaction. Hearing the rattle of the bus I thought, he's late if he has to go up to the Lloyney turn. But obviously not, as he reversed into the Hergest road and I was met with a broad grin and a shout of, 'Johnny, you old swine! You are still alive then?'

Jumping onto the bus, I asked how it was so hot in there.

'I have had to close the windows all week because of the stink of dead rabbits,' he said. 'Jesus Christ, I don't know who invented this, but it's a bloody nightmare.'

'The local farmer by me has asked me to shoot the buzzards,' I replied, 'as he has lost forty pullets. The poor bastards have got nothing left to eat, except the occasional dead ewe up on the hill.' I asked him how it was he had not gone up to the Lloyney turn today and he said that the two lads had now gone to Llandrindod school. I then asked him what the crack was at school. He replied that they had asked him if he had any bother from me to tell them immediately, but he told them he had never had a moment's problem with me.

As we proceeded, we picked up pupils here and there in the little hamlets and outside the outlying farms. This caused me no end of amusement as when they got on they were laughing and noisy but when they saw me they went very quiet and ran to their friends and talked in whispers. It was obvious to me that word had got around, but I was somewhat perplexed as to what word. Pulling in at Sylvia's place, I grinned as she boarded the bus as she said she didn't expect to see me here today. Replying that I had to see it through to the end, we talked about the preceding week and made small talk until the rest of our mob got on and we headed up the road to perdition.

Arriving at the bottom drive, I walked up the path with my empty satchel hung over my arm, and was accompanied by two mates. It appeared the others had been warned off by their parents and good luck to them, I thought, at least you know where you stand and who you can trust. We walked into the classroom and there was a strange hush, but I hung my satchel over the chair and walked out to assembly. Walking around the side of the gym I could see the head, who pretended I wasn't there and I passed a couple of staff, who were watching him watching me. How bloody pathetic can you get and 'God bless us every one,' said Tiny Tim.

Prayers over and hymns sung, there were no speeches or events mentioned and I headed back to class with my two bodyguards, or that's what it felt like. English followed, my favourite lesson, and I just sat there listening. If I put my hand up in answer to a question it was missed. Maths was a hate, but I didn't need to worry as I took no part. Was I reading too much into this? Oh no . . . without a doubt I was public enemy number one.

Break time came and went and I strolled around the playground and out onto the sports field and only when I was out of sight of the head's study window did I get a quietly spoken, 'Hello, how you doing?' 'Kiss my arse' or anything. Back in class and the last lesson before lunch, I was dreading. Firstly, it was Latin and secondly, the teacher hated me. I knew that if anyone was going for a gold this would be it, and away we went.

'Mr Elias, are we going to sleep? Mr Elias, could you at least look interested?'

I thought to myself, bollocks, you are not going to draw me out. As the bell went and I was walking out the chance came. A couple of girls were pushing by me and one tripped.

'I might have expected it would be you!' she almost spat the words out.

I just stood there quietly with my bodyguards behind me.

'It wasn't him, Miss,' I heard one say.

'Not happy enough without causing someone harm!'

I am ashamed to say I turned and said, 'I know that you don't like me. I know that you have been reporting back on me on what I do outside of school and also know nothing would give you more pleasure than to see me kicked out. Well it's hard luck because I am leaving in a few weeks. Until then, I suggest we keep well away from each other before someone gets really in the mire . . .' I turned to my mates ' . . . and no one has heard this conversation, have you?'

This was met with a loud, 'No, we haven't heard a word!' and we three pushed past and left her standing there open-mouthed.

All afternoon and the next morning I fully expected a call to the Hall of the Mountain King, but all was quiet and I never went to or saw her close to again. At dinner time I wandered down to the playing field and the nets were up and some of the seniors were having a bat. What they didn't know was that I was very quick and had a very good command of the balls that I bowled. As if by magic, a ball came rolling by me and picking it up, I joined the waiting bowlers. Watching the batsman, I saw him punish anything on his leg, but weak on the off.

Taking a three step run up, I bowled short and the ball reared up into his chest. This frightened him somewhat and with the next ball that someone handed me, I yorked him, middle and leg stumps out of the ground. By now a few had gathered around and I had balls being handed me. I was in my element and taking a middle length run up, I began to speed up and dismissed our top bats in quick procession. What a change! I had people putting their arms round my shoulders and asking where I learned to bowl like that. I saw one of the lads talking to the sports master and pointing to me and for ten minutes I had become a human being again.

Walking back into school, I was half expecting a summons to the head's study over the morning's foray, but all was quiet and I met the lady in the corridor several times and she studiously ignored me, which was fine by me. The next day after lunch, I was back at the nets again and in the afternoon, the school captain of our house asked me if I would bowl for his side in the end of term House matches. Still feeling pretty raw, I said I would think about it and left it at that.

On the bus home that night, I overheard one of the seniors telling Sylvia that I was a demon with the cricket ball. She asked me about it and I told her it made a change from being a demon at everything else. The weeks were slipping away and I actually felt sad that it was all coming to a close. However, I did realise that all the people closest to me would be gone about their different ways, so I had no regrets. Tomorrow was the last day of term, the final day for me at my seat of learning. Everyone was in a good mood with the euphoria of the last time we would all travel together on this journey and I saw the bus was slowly emptying. The one thing I knew was all the seniors on the bus had stood by me and for that I was truly grateful.

CHAPTER FORTY-NINE
The Wanderer
(Status Quo)

Dinner that day seemed somehow quiet and I gathered from looking at my mother that she was none too happy with the morning's results. Also, it appeared that my father had an urgent lot of papers to read and therefore disappeared into the study as fast as his legs would take him, which in fairness wasn't very fast. This left me wide open so I thought I might just as well get it over with. So, I gently pushed open the scullery door, Mum put a plate down on the drainer and here we go.

'Your father and I did not want this for you, but it seems like we are going to have to tolerate it,' she began and then carried on with her father spending all his life as a furnace man in the steelworks and how it probably killed him. Trying to explain that I was going to become a qualified joiner in six years, earn good money and might even start up on my own, did nothing to pacify her. As I went to leave I had another barrage across the bows and turning, I let it all out. How I had slogged my guts out catching up with years of work as we roamed the country and wherever we ended up, getting nowhere because I never had the time. Met more people than you would normally meet in a lifetime and never had time to say goodbye, but it was always going to get better round the corner, which was obviously rubbish because it never was.

Although I loved my mum very much, I found great difficulty in keeping a cool head when discussing my future or past, come to that. I made a move for the door and out the back where I jumped on my bike and pedalled furiously down the road. I wondered what my old master at Ansley would have thought of all this. I covered a few miles of lanes and stopped in various gateways to look across the fields and gradually cooled down until I felt ready for the ride home. Coming in through the drive gate I was wondering what sort of reception I would get, and hearing a voice behind me, looked down onto the tennis lawn and there was my mum with a bunch of late primroses.

'Aren't they lovely?' she said and holding them under my nose, she laughed. 'I'm just going in to make a cup of tea and I'm sure you would like one.'

'I would love one,' I replied and with that we walked round to the back door together and sitting on the garden bench, I lit up a smoke and gazed out over the Glanyrafon hill to where a pair of buzzards were circling and mewling to each other. Poor buggers, I thought, they must be starving now with the rabbit population gradually disappearing.

The last two days slipped away and I woke up on Saturday with the weekend in front of me and wondered how things would pan out. After breakfast I wandered down to the churchyard corner and the usual gang was there. Adrian didn't know if Reg had arrived yet and we walked down to the bottom of the village. As we stood against the bottom bridge support a little boy shot out of a house and ran up to me and kicked me on the shins. I retaliated by cuffing him round the ears and he ran in, screaming. Out came his old man and told us to get back up the top and leave the kids alone. All common sense went out of the window as I told him in no uncertain tones to fuck right off and drive his boy in the arse. Off he went, saying he would speak to my father and how he had never been spoken to like that before. I gave him another barrage and he went into his house and peace reigned serene. Standing there that morning, I was content and looking forward to the next week in school, the first time for a few years, I might add, but I felt that a great weight had been lifted from me. No more homework, no more swatting for dreaded exams. Perhaps now they knew the dreaded pupil from the fourth was on his toes, they would have the common sense to leave me alone.

As we were standing there, the local builder and his sidekick appeared from nowhere and telling us to get out of the way, proceeded to dig a big hole by the side of the road. We stood there and watched them work, making smart remarks and generally taking the piss. This went on for about an hour and a half between cups of tea from a flask and considerable conversations, until they both decided to retire to the pub for some liquid refreshment, leaving a sizeable hole of quite some depth. We gave them half an hour to settle and grabbing the shovels, filled the whole lot in and stamped it down, chucking some old chippings on top. Unless you looked carefully, you would not see where it had been. About two hours later they emerged from the pub, somewhat the worse for wear and gaped in amazement at the spot where they had dug.

The builder then came up with a statement I will remember until my dying day. Pushing his cap to the back of his head and scratching his forehead he said to his man, 'Between me and you, Dan, we've just seen one of them oracles.' With that, they put their gear away and went back in the pub. To this day, I have never found out what they hoped to achieve in the bottom of that hole. That same gentleman had a job as sidesman at the church and was a longstanding member of the Parochial Church Council and to get out for a drink, used to write letters to himself about fictional meetings in the evening. When they arrived he would read them and throw them down, shouting, 'I'm not going down there again!'

His wife used to say, 'You must go, Fred; you're an important man.'

His reply was that he had to buy everyone a drink, being as he was so important, whereby he achieved a free night out a couple of times every week as she used to give him a fiver a time. (It does work because I've tried it).

Saturday night we headed for Stanner Rocks on our bikes to catch the seven o'clock bus down to Kington, where they showed films in the local church hall. Yes, it's true and half the young population of the town and surrounding area met here. I think we saw Carve Her Name with Pride but I cannot be certain. Anyway, we were all down in the dumps after it and very pleased to see the welcoming lights of our village at last.

Sunday morning and the weather was picking up, so I had a long walk after breakfast to see where the pools were after the long winter and if any new ones had formed. Although the sun was bright, I tried my arm in the water and it was icy, but I knew it would soon warm up now and we would be away again. Back at the house the old man had gone to the eleven o'clock service and I sat down with Mum and had a nice cup of tea and a chat. Asked if the film had been good last night, I said it was very sad and told her all about it. The house was strange and I asked her could we have another dog, to which she didn't make a lot of comment and I decided to leave it lie. Church service over and the old man back home, I walked down to the village but it was very quiet. Going past the pub, it was all shut up with nary a soul because of course we were in Wales, with no drinks served on a Sunday.

That night we headed over into England for a pint and a game of darts and I was thinking what I would meet the next morning when I showed my face in school. I thought to myself I might have a crack at Sylvia . . . well, faint heart never won fair lady and I was missing some female company. It was still relatively light as we walked down the Rabber pitch that night and I suppose we were making enough noise for ten instead of three. Back into the village, we quietened down and I left Reg on the barn meadow corner and hurried up the road and in through the gate. I let myself in softly and climbed the stairs, the ever present pear drop in my mouth. I wasn't many minutes getting undressed and I climbed into bed, put the alarm button on and hey presto, I fell fast asleep.

CHAPTER FIFTY
The Sound of Silence
(Simon and Garfunkel)

I was awake well before it was time for the alarm to go off and deep into thinking how the next change in my life would work out. Both my parents were up and my father walked down to the gate with me saying, 'Whatever happens, keep your cool, and for my sake keep the lid on anything you might feel needs saying.'

I could have hugged him for that, but just said they had no need to worry about me and I was gone through the gate and walking, alone with my thoughts. Standing waiting for the bus, my mind went back to my first ride to this faraway seat of learning.

With that, I heard the clank of the bus and with the hiss of brakes I heard that well known voice contesting my parentage, for I had a few things to say to him before anyone else boarded.

I thanked him earnestly for putting up with me, for his company and for his loyal friendship.

He looked at me. 'Johnny boy, you will be alright. I am well aware of the shit that's been thrown at you but you have seen it through and brought some good and loyal friends with you.'

Then with a clash of gears we went roaring up the hill and I was lighting up in a cloud of blue smoke. When we got to Sylvia's house, she smilingly got in beside me, telling me she was dreading today and we agreed to meet up for a walk in about two weeks, when she would be moving to London to start her University course. Although I felt a little sad, I was chuffed to bits for her.

Gradually the bus was filling up and I could hardly believe that in six weeks it would be filled with new people, and all those in the rear seats would be gone forever. I knew from experience that there would be a lot of meetings today and we, the older fraternity, would be left to our own devices. At long last, we pulled in outside the grey stone edifice that I hated . . . not the building, I hasten to add, but the hierarchy who clamoured to be heard in everything that might curry favour with the headmaster. Lessons today were put on hold and the whole school was in happy mode. I spent as much time as I could down in the playing fields talking to the groundsman. In fairness, I do not think they would have missed me, should I have walked out of the gate. Walking around the playground, my mind took me back to that far off meeting with a prior headmaster and all the hopes I had. Perhaps I was blaming the wrong people and it was, after all, My Fault.

Lunch came and went and it was off to the gymnasium for the speeches, the goodbyes to the staff who were leaving, The head girl and head boy, to end with Lord dismiss us with thy blessing, followed by the school song, Let us praise our benefactor, Good John Beddoes of Presteigne. There was much shaking of hands, wishing of good luck and many goodbyes aboard our bus that afternoon and Sylvia was very quiet on that last mile. All good things must come to an end and with a peck on the cheek she was gone, never once looking back and that was the end of that.

Walking up the village on that Friday afternoon, I was asking myself a whole load of questions and I have to admit I did not have an answer to any of them. I had left it all behind me, the piss-taking, the rivalry, the bus journeys through the lanes of Radnorshire, the quick smokes down in the bottom cloakroom. The arrival each year of the delectable and delightful, both shy and new first form teachers, wondering if they were as unreachable as they tried to show themselves. No more chatting over the day's events with Cecil, the bus driver. Just what had I achieved for all my trouble? I had to get up an hour earlier every morning with a six mile ride in front of me. Having already applied for my provisional licence and believe it or not you could purchase any make or model once you had it, I of course had my heart set on a Triumph Bonneville or Vincent model, the 1000cc Black Shadow and the Rapier. Some bloody hope. I would have been dead within the hour. Of course I had forgotten the return bike ride, mostly uphill, to get home from work. Anyway, enough of all this crap; I had five long weeks in front of me before I started my apprenticeship. I hadn't taken my satchel to school for some time now but today it was full of my belongings collected over the last year. Now then, Reader, you will be thinking this little sod is already regretting his decision. Who, me? Not a bit of it for I had the same hopes and fears of those I rubbed shoulders with. I now drive frequently past the school, which has been turned into a comprehensive and fervently hope they have as good a time as I have had. So no regrets.

As I neared the farm gate the geese were coming out led by the gander hissing and snaking his head at me. I knew he would not come too close but was showing off to the ladies of his harem. There was a time when he frightened me to death, but an old codger saw what was happening and shouted, 'Grab him by the neck, swing him around and let him go. Shaking, I did this but could hardly lift him; however he was as giddy as a churn, landed on his arse and never bothered me again. As I walked on up the road I was stopped by an old farmer who asked if he supplied the gun would I shoot a rookery out. I asked him who would supply the cartridges and he replied he only had a few, so that was the end of that. On reaching home I eased through the gate and here was my mother, asking was it too late to change my mind. Explaining that I would rather be kicked to death by spiders or flogged with a wet lettuce, I answered her.

'Listen, Mum, I have a chance to achieve something I want. Should I not like it or fail, I will do something else.'

She then told me we had a black Labrador puppy being delivered from Cardiff, a present from my auntie and I was chuffed after all. As I was already going to go down for a few days to the Cross, I asked if I could have a lift with them as they were going to Hereford station to pick up the puppy. Tuesday morning found us en route to Hereford and as my train left half an hour before theirs arrived, I waved goodbye as my train pulled out of the station.

I settled back in the carriage and watched the lush fields and streams gradually giving way to the hills and heather clad slopes of the Black Mountains. My mind was a whirl of mixed memories for I had made this journey so many times – once propelled by steam and now it was diesel. Arriving at Pontypool Road I was soon past the ticket office, under the tunnel and walking up the steep incline to catch the Jones bus down to the Cross. Standing at the bus stop I looked up the valley and stood breathing in the age old smells of industry.

Looking directly across the road stood the massive chimney of Pilkington's Glass Works, while further up the valley the various works were going full pelt and the blackened dust was visible at the roadside and inclines. Looking up, I saw the Jones bus and as I put my hand up he pulled in with a hiss of brakes and I hefted my case and jumped in. Finding a seat, I paid the hovering conductor as the villages of Upper and Lower New Inn flashed by. In no time at all we were sailing down past the Upper Cock as a voice called, 'The Highway!' and I was walking down the bus and then up my auntie's path.

After a hug and kiss from my auntie and a warm handshake from my uncle, we sat down and I related the happenings of the Rectory over the last few months. We then sat down to a very nice lunch and having finished, my uncle and I lit up a cigarette and had a chat and I then excused myself, for I needed a walk and wanted to see the new town centre.

Crossing over the road, I entered North Road, went past St Mary's Church and out into what used to be the Holly Lane. What a shock I had; it was now a dual carriageway with a huge roundabout leading to the new town centre.

Walking through one of the grand entrances, I found myself in a large square surrounded by shops of all sizes and descriptions. It was all very new and I could see the mountain and upper Cwmbran between the facades. I spent a little time walking around, but towns are not for me and never have been to this day. Walking back towards home, I wondered how the old folks appreciated the new landscape. Little did I think then that in a few years I would be fitting mahogany handrails around the main stairwell and up the stairs leading from the large carpark beneath us and working in conjunction with the Monmouth Chief Surveyor, who was a great man. The last time I saw them was at least twenty five years later, not a bad job, but they had the names of every youth who owned a penknife carved on every length of handrail.

I stopped off at my old mate's house on the way back but it appeared empty and although concerned, I made a mental note to ask about it. Totally disconsolate, I lit up a ciggy and sat on the seat in the bus shelter opposite, remembering how I used to go across the fields looking for mushrooms. It was now the Gwent Constabulary headquarters, a sea of glass bricks and concrete.

Grinding out my ciggy butt I got up, hitched up my belt and walked slowly up the hill. My last thought being: Well, Johnny boy, you had better catch the early train home on Friday morning. To be honest, I had left an awesome week behind me and my progress at this moment did not fit my bill. It was as if somebody had taken a giant paint brush and painted out, what was a lovely little community and then painted in thousands of houses, pavements by the mile and a grey stone monument to a new town. I was sure I would get to know it and also like it, but at this moment of my life I needed the quiet and solitude of the Radnor hills.

BOOK THREE

If I Were a Carpenter
(Bobby Darin)

CHAPTER FIFTY-ONE
Big Man
(The Four Preps)

Every time I play the song I have a laugh to myself over the words. Yes, I thought, I was a big man, but Jesus H Christ, was I about to grow up in the very near future. Those words, 'I was a big man yesterday but, boy, you ought to see me now' what a great line for a fifties' song.

The more I think about it, the more I feel it applied. My days in the Cross were fine but I couldn't wait for Friday as there was no one about that I knew. I called at my mate's home to be told by a neighbour that he had taken a job up the valley in Abersychan and had a flat and girlfriend up there. Well, one cannot stop progress and his folks had got a new but smaller house on a new development.

Friday morning came and after a nice breakfast and a cheery goodbye, I was waving off the Jones bus and heading for Pontypool Road station. Ten minutes later I was aboard the Hereford train. Arriving in Hereford, I caught a Yeoman's bus to Kington and knew there was a bus every four hours to Gladestry as it was market day in Kington. Sure enough, as I got up the road to where the buses pulled in, I found there was a bus at two o'clock, so I had an hour to wait. Thankfully, they put me off at the top of the village, by the bridge and I was soon up the alley, through the churchyard and through our gate to be welcomed by my dear old mum. I gave her a letter from her sister and climbed the stairs to have a wash and change.

Going into my room, I saw a letter addressed to me on the

dressing table and also saw that it bore a Coventry stamp. With my heart pounding, I tore it open and the single page said it all. Firstly, I was the biggest bastard that ever put a pair of trousers on. Secondly, she'd had a lovely boyfriend at school, but had finished with him because of me. Thirdly and finally, she never wanted to see me or the village ever again. Hiding it in one of my books, I thought, welcome home John, nice to see you. With that, there was a scrabbling sound at the door and into the room rolled the fattest, most adorable black Labrador puppy you could ever see. I formed an instant bond with him; he licked me all over and smelled as only young puppies smell. His name was Shan and he was really beautiful. Mum was laughing, as everywhere I went he was behind me. Of course, being carried upstairs was a one off and at that age he certainly couldn't get up there himself.

Back downstairs, the kettle was boiling on the Rayburn and Mum made a nice cup of tea. With a couple of chocolate biscuits each, we chewed the fat about the Cross and then I picked up Shan and took him down the paddock where he rolled about in the grass and it soon tired him out. The old man was apparently up in the other church at a PCC meeting and wouldn't be back until later so I jumped on my bike and took a tour around. Big snag; there was nobody about and I suddenly thought they were either in work or at school and I was Billy no mates. Bored to tears, I came back and went along the brook for a mile, and there were some fair trout about. Sitting on an old stump, I lit up a ciggy and contemplated the future. When I reached home the old man had returned and we took a turn around the grounds and had a good chat and before I knew it, it was time for tea.

The weeks passed quite quickly and my next move was to go to the Army and Navy stores and get a haversack. This had to be worn with one strap over the shoulder and I tried it out in the bedroom. I also had to get a Thermos flask, a big one, to last me all day. Out of the corner of one eye, I could see my mother shaking her head and thought, the realities of the working man, Mum, but said not a word.

Finally it was the weekend before I started work on the Monday and I stayed in on Sunday night to contemplate my future . . . and I would confess to not sleeping too well that night.

I had a received letter telling me to report to the Joiners' shop on Monday morning at seven-thirty prompt and ask for a Mr Logan, the foreman. Monday morning, I left home at six-thirty, so as not to be late and arrived outside the gates at seven o'clock to find the place deserted. At about seven-twenty the men started arriving and I asked them who was Mr Logan. Looking at me blankly, one man said that I meant Bill and he wouldn't be here until eight. I then asked where could I park my bike and one of them pointed to a tree, saying that would be alright. By this time, about a hundred men were assembled outside and at seven-thirty a big shiny car came down the road and the suited driver got out and opened the gates and gestured to the men to come in, which they all did. With a roar of different engines, lorries and vans appeared, the crowd climbed aboard the various vehicles, they all drove out of the yard and the place was deserted again. Seven-fifty and another gang of men started to arrive, taking up the same positions against the wall on the opposite side of the road. I tried to have a conversation with some of them, but to no avail; Mr Bill Logan seemed to be a fictional figure. I did notice, however, that occasionally some of them looked at my bike and sniggered. I noticed an old gent on an antique bike pass us and stop at the other end of the line. He wore a white apron and his bike had 'come to Jesus handlebars'.

At eight o'clock on the dot, the same man in the shiny suit came out and signalled. With that, we all walked across the road and one man pointed out the joiners' shop. As I walked in through the door I was obstructed by the old man in the apron, who asked me who I was. When I told him, he muttered about my being a priest's son and pointed out a chap, telling me to stay with him for a day. As I walked away, he called me in clipped tones to come back.

'My name is Bill Logan and I am Mister Logan to you. I've been here sixty years, not sixty fucking minutes,' he snorted.

Nonplussed, I asked him had I upset him in some way.

'Yes, you have, you've parked your fucking bike against my tree!' he fumed. Now I knew what the sniggers were all about and apologising profusely I backed away, afraid he might have an apoplectic fit. Well old mate, you have made a bloody great start, I said to myself.

The man I was to help, looked me up and down and said caustically, 'So you're the parson's son then? Glad to see you're staying in religion.'

When I asked what he meant, he looked down his nose and replied, 'Well, Jesus was a carpenter, wasn't he?'

I was dumbfounded; me, the big man, and half of Kington taking the piss in the first ten minutes.

About ten minutes later a younger man walked up, watched me for ten minutes, walked across and said, 'If I were you, I would walk across to the office and tell them you have changed your mind and want to be a painter.'

Again, I asked why.

'In the first place,' he said, 'anyone who can piss can paint and in the second place, if you make a mistake you can paint over it . . . and it looks like you'll make quite a few mistakes.'

And so the day continued. Every time the foreman appeared, he glared across at me and I was glad to see five-thirty. Leaving the workshop, I passed Mr Logan who said, 'Don't forget – it's my fucking tree.'

I left the yard and headed through the main street, up past the church and swung down the Hergest road, passing Hergest Court on the way, the once manorial seat of the Black Vaughn of medieval history, but more of that later. For now, my mind was in turmoil, I had never heard anything like it. I was covered in sawdust, it was everywhere from pulling timber off the saw and it appeared from the tellings off I'd had, I couldn't even get that right. The yard foreman was the boss's sergeant major and marched about the yard, shouting, 'Pick that up!' if he saw a piece of paper. So this was what the world was like, I thought. Should I admit defeat or stick it out? Surely it couldn't go on like this? I dreaded going home and facing the barrage of questions I knew would await me. Looking back, I saw that I was growing up into the real world away from the shelter of the rectory, plus the fact that Johnny boy was getting his comeuppance.

Passing around the side of the house, I put my bike away

and entered the back scullery. I must have looked like a grimy snowman and I saw the look of horror on my mother's face. As I removed my jacket she took it outside and shook it thoroughly. She handed me a brush and I stepped back outside, brushed the worst off and entered the kitchen.

My father appeared, smiling broadly. 'Well, Sunny Jim, how was your first day?' he asked.

I replied that it was very good and I had a great time and what a lovely place it was to work. My mother was trying desperately to get a word in edgeways, but my father, the wise one, kept me talking and for that I was eternally grateful.

The rest of the week passed by and I finally got to go upstairs where there was no dust and about eight joiners working, all in white aprons. I had to help a chap, who turned out to be the head joiner, to select some boards for a coffin, and then stayed to help him make it. When I say help, I stood and watched for most of the time but was fascinated by his skill, and when it was finished he asked would I try it for size. This I did, but spotted them carrying the lid over and scrambled out just in time, causing a lot of laughter. I have to say that over the years I worked with some good guys and was no slouch myself, but this man was the finest tradesman I have ever seen.

The week slipped away and the following week came along and I was still stuck downstairs in the machine shop. On Thursday afternoon I was summoned up to Mr Logan's office and he handed me an official looking brown packet,

'Do you think you've earned it?' he asked.

I replied yes, to which he sniffed and muttered that he fucking well doubted it. I began to think that he had something against me and wondered whatever could it be? Of one thing I was certain, I may have been the big man yesterday, but boy, you want to see me now. Mr Logan then gave me my orders for the following week.

When I got home, my mother told me over a cup of tea that they were worried about Shan, who was growing fast, getting out, and consequently would I tell Dad what he needed to complete the job of a fence and gate around the back of the house. I told her that I would give him a list and if he could get it delivered in the morning, I would do it for him. This was amazing news to the old man who toddled off down the village and the materials were inside the gate that very same evening. The next morning I was up with the larks and put the posts in position, started them with a bar and then drove them in with a sledge, leaving enough room for a sturdy wicket gate and posts. Hearing a cough behind me, I looked around and saw the old man standing there with a contented smile on his face.

'Anything I can do to help, Sunny Jim?' he enquired.

'No, thanks. I've only got this gate and posts to do and that's it, but thanks anyway,' I replied and he toddled off, the contented smile still on his face.

CHAPTER FIFTY-TWO
Man of the World
(Peter Green and Fleetwood Mac)

Opening my pay packet, I had received the sum of two pounds and six shillings and called in the tobacconist in the High Street and bought the old man two ounces of St Bruno rough cut and a box of chocolates for Mother. The sight and feel of this huge wage made me feel like a new man again. Once home, I proudly put my gifts on the table, only to be told, 'Well, it is very nice, Sunny Jim, but you must keep your money safe as we will be expecting you to put a bit in the kitty now you're earning. This really cheered me up and catching hold of Shan, who was growing fast, I grabbed his collar and we went out and down the paddock for a time. After some thought, I managed to make the gate to the back fence and hung it, if somewhat drunkenly to the post. However, the folks were delighted with it.

The weekend passed quietly with another trip to Kington pictures on the Saturday and a quiet pint in the pub on the Sunday night and before you could say whatever you felt the need to say, I was on my bike and headed for the dreaded work place. Little did I know it at the time but things were going to go a whole lot better than even I could hope for.

The great Mr Logan approached me about nine o'clock and showing me where he lived, instructed me to go to his house and explain to his wife that he had left a clean hanky in the bedroom and would she please give it to me. Tearing off on my bike, I found the house and knocked on the door, whereupon a lovely white haired lady answered and after listening, asked me to wait while she fetched it. Coming back with the hanky she then uttered the words which were to be my saving grace.

'Please tell Mr Logan that I've got a nice cup of coffee being made and would he come down for it.'

Talk about a gift horse, I couldn't get back fast enough. The great man himself was holding a meeting with four of his top joiners when I arrived.

'Took you long enough,' he grunted. 'Did you get it?'

'Yes,' I said and handed him the handkerchief. 'And Mrs Logan told me to tell you she is making a nice cup of coffee and would you please go down and get it.'

For a man of his years, I thought he was going to drop dead.

'What the fucking hell does she think I am? I'm a trusted foreman; I cannot run around the bloody country drinking coffee!'

The four joiners were grinning at me and as he stamped off, one of them remarked I had just got my ticket out of there. Within half an hour, he sidled up to me and told me that a man called Fred Wilson was working up the street and I was to go and help him and to tell him he had sent me. I was so pleased, I sang all the way up the street to meet Fred Wilson.

Fred seemed a cheery sort of chap although I think he had some problems of his own, but he loved it when I told him about my dealings with Bill Logan and said it would be a long time before he allowed me back in the joiners' shop. This pleased me even more as I had now got the freedom I wanted, meeting different people every day. The job we were doing was repairing floorboards and skirting in a ladies clothes shop. This was quite easy and I enjoyed it, especially when Fred showed me how to cut the joints on the Torus skirting. Even better, about four o'clock he told me he had an appointment at the dentist, to bugger off home and to come straight there in the morning at seven-thirty, not eight. This didn't bother me as I was always early and hanging about with the eight o'clock start. We worked at the shop for three days and then did various things all over town, where I learned to fit sash cords and many other small jobs and I felt really professional when I got a Sturmey Archer three speed chain which all the veterans had, and knotted it on a length of builder's line. This became known as a mouse and was used to pass through the pulley at the top of the window and thread the sash cord with it. Believe me, in 1957 you were a 'nobody' in the carpentry world without a mouse.

I was settling in well with Fred and we – please note the word 'we' is totally untrue – put a roof on a new house, so I learned how to set a roof out on the ground. Just after this, we were sent to put a new length of fence in along a road on the outskirts of town and I noticed this girl riding by on her bike. I didn't give it a thought, but she came by a few times that morning and Fred said she kept looking at me. I said not to be daft and he replied that she obviously fancied me and leered, saying I'd be alright there. That afternoon, she came past about five times and she was a nice looking lass. As we were finishing up that afternoon, I stopped her and she just smiled and asked did I go to the pictures on a Saturday night? Replying yes, I arranged to meet her outside the hall at eight o'clock. That week we moved on to Llandrindod Wells and travelled up in a van with some painters. Fred told them all I was going to get my leg over on the following Saturday and they all laughed, but I could have killed him.

The week flew by up in Llandrindod and I had a few more pennies to spend for the earlier start, so washed and scrubbed in my drainpipes and gear, we hit Kington on the Saturday. I must have been pretty quiet for a change on the journey to town, for my mate said I was in a strange mood. We got off the bus in town and walked up towards the square and guess what? This vision of loveliness was waiting for me by the hall door.

My mate commented, 'You bastard,' and I grinned and said see you later. As the lights dimmed we headed for the rear seats and some serious business. Finally we came up for air and before we knew it, were planning to meet the next weekend. Sally, as she was called, lived at the bottom of town and had to be home by ten as her parents were very strict, so I found my mate in the pub opposite and we had a couple of pints and it was time to board the bus to Stanner.

The bike ride home was pretty uneventful and after a five

minute smoke under the church wall we both headed for home and creeping inside so as not to wake the old folks, I was soon between the sheets and fell asleep wondering if I would ever keep up with this girl I had met.

Sunday morning and the sun blazed down through my bedroom window. Mother had brought me in a cuppa when she got home from church and I could hear her banging about in the kitchen, getting the Sunday lunch ready for my father's return from his other service. With Sally etched in my brain, I descended the stairs with my empty cup and put the gas ring on for another. My mother didn't want one so I sat there with my mind on a pair of glorious breasts and sipped my tea. Wanting to know how the last evening had gone and how the picture went and what was the film that we saw, I lied through my teeth and hoped she would not ask anyone else, as to be honest I did not see a bloody thing the whole evening.

I took a wander down the village after the service was finished and there was a big gang on the corner, so we had a smoke and a chat about who was in town the night before and after lying through my teeth once more, I headed over the style and across the fields, coming home through the paddock. Dinner over, washing up all done and they were off again, Mother to take the children's Sunday School and the old man of into the remoteness of the hill country to his other church for the afternoon service. I was left alone with my thoughts and dreams and I headed for the brook and sat gazing into the deep pools, watching the trout swimming against the current. Lighting up a ciggy, I thought about Sally and where I stood with her. I guessed I was the one at the moment and also knew half the lads in town fancied her. I also knew she would drop me without a moment's hesitation if someone else took her fancy. At my age, I also felt exactly the same, so I knew as long as it lasted it would be fun, and it certainly was. The year of fifty six was a good one and in those times we knew nothing about sex education, and treated the whole thing with an 'it could never happen to me if I was careful' attitude. However, I broke into a sweat on many an occasion, hoping that I was not going to get some very bad news and resolved to ask Fred about it at work.

CHAPTER FIFTY-THREE
Fire Brigade
(Roy Wood and The Move)

As I guessed, my brief time with Sally didn't last very long; no falling out, no recriminations, I just walked into town one Saturday night and she was propped against a wall with another lad. In a way I was quite pleased for I needed my space just as she did. At this time I was far happier with a beer in the pub and a game of darts. However, I did have my moments in the back row of the pictures but nothing seemed to turn me on at that moment.

I was now well into my apprenticeship and my papers were signed and I had to go to a meeting at Hereford Tech with the old man one evening. Suitably clad in a suit and tie we arrived and with about ten other lads and their parents, we were invited into a room and addressed by the deputy head. He explained that we had to come to the college twice a week, once for a daytime set of lessons and secondly for an evening class. This was exactly what I did not want and in any case, I had no way of getting there, especially at night. I went into school mode when I heard this and my mind shut down completely. My father had to sign a couple of forms and we were away, with me thinking the whole thing was a waste of time.

'Well, they can forget about me going to any night classes,' I said to the old man as we got back into the car. 'It's a twenty-five-mile trip with no buses after seven o'clock, and then there's nothing for the last six miles.'

His answer was not to worry, something would turn up and I thought, Christ, I'm sitting next to a modern Mr Micawber, some chance I've got, and left it at that.

On the way home I stopped and got us some fish and chips for supper and Mum was pleased as punch to see us home and we all had a nice supper, courtesy of yours truly.

I had nothing to worry about and was back to work the next morning. The term did not start until September and that was miles away, I told myself. I seemed to get on all right with Fred but found he was suspect to some very black moods, so I did my best to keep out of the way when I saw one of those coming.

I found myself working with another two men and Fred at a farm, way up above Knighton. It was right out in the sticks across a cattle grid, up through the fern, over a hill and down into a valley. We were putting an extended roof over the back of the house, a type of covered in walkway. In those days we had no electric drills and the joints in the brickwork had to be chopped out with a plugging chisel all the way along. Of course this fell to me, being the boy, but it was bloody hard work, although good for the arm muscles. We couldn't help but look inside through the windows and in the kitchen, the lady was working at something all the time. I could see she had a girl helping her and she looked quite attractive to me but try as I might, I couldn't catch her eye. Every morning at ten o'clock the lady would bring out the hot drinks and the same every afternoon, but no sign of the girl, which was really bugging me. We were finishing on the Friday and I was clearing up round the back when I heard a car start up. Looking up the drive, I saw the car pulling slowly away and in the back seat, looking through the window, was the girl and believe it or not, she was waving to me and continued until the car drove out of sight. I was manic about this but my mates told me that we would not be coming back there, so my ideas of a big romance crumbled into dust and I never saw the girl again.

Back home, she was on my pillow that night and also for a few nights afterwards, but thankfully I was deeply attracted to another, whom I idolised from afar, but that also went nowhere and for a long time I couldn't settle. I suppose, looking back, I was pretty horrible to some of the girls I went with at that time, but that was me, and I had an image to maintain. Besides, their parents were horrified when they saw me coming in my Ted regalia.

Monday morning at seven-twenty found me standing against the wall across from the yard, looking at my watch and wondering where the hell my mate had got to. Just as the gates were about to open, a lad called Brent, who had just finished his apprenticeship and who I admired from afar, came up to me. He asked if I was waiting for Fred, who was confined to bed with flu and I was to go with him to a local army camp up the road where some of the obsolete huts were being turned into turkey houses. My tools had been dropped off by the other chap we had done the roof with and I put them in the back of the van and away we went.

It was a deserted camp and we had to turn it into a comfortable abode for the rearing of hundreds of turkeys from the chick stage to adulthood, in this case for Christmas. Everything was erected in three by two partitions with wire mesh in the divisions and we really cracked on until, horror of horrors . . . who walked onto the site? Why, overalls, from my first meeting; remember the interview? Obviously he carried a lot of weight and after taking the piss out of me for ten minutes, which in fairness par for the course, we sat down to our bait. He showed his true colours when ten minutes into our allotted fifteen, he got up.

'Well, lads, I don't know about you, but my arse is getting sore and Mr Deacon doesn't pay us to sit on our arses all day.'

I thought, you would have a job on my friend, as yours is sitting on your shoulders, but just looked into space as I packed my half-eaten sandwich away, thinking, one day, my friend, you will find out how much you are thought of. Little did I know then how short a time it would be before he got a very sad wake up call.

The weeks passed and we were moved over to the county town of Radnorshire. Now, isn't life strange? But yes, I was back amongst the learned scholars of my not so old school. The contract was to take down some of the old offices inside the main factory, whilst building a whole new office block in the outside yard, this being adjacent to the main factory. Hey ho, I found a load of lads I went to school with working there. When I heard we were going to work at a factory, my mind went back to the Panteg Steel Works where my relatives all worked and I had been shown around by my uncle, but when I saw this I was severely disappointed as I felt you could put the whole thing in the rolling mill. But a factory is a factory and all metalworking smells the same, no matter the size. I have to say I have never seen so many girls in one place, but these were different. There were no downcast glances and simpering smiles here. You had it straight from the shoulder, as I was to find out in a very short time.

I got on well with Brent but he was a ladies' man alright and every minute of the day he was chatting up some bird or another in full view of the factory, but he really didn't give a shit. We were surrounded by other trades; electricians, our own heating engineers, who were very rare in those days, and plumbers and painters everywhere. I thought it best to keep my head down and say nothing, which was really not my style. The following week we had the roof fitted on the new office block and the floor was also finished ready for office divisions. Brent was off for a couple of days towards the end of the week, but I had plenty to keep me busy and I was now quite useful.

A gang of us, being a plumber, brickie, plasterers, Brent and yours truly used the office level as a bait room. The roof above us was finished and sheeted over with a tarpaulin, and the flat roofers were due to arrive that day. They finally arrived before lunch and lit their pitch boiler, stacking a wall of pitch blocks all around it with the rolls of roofing felt and a gas cylinder inside, and went up into town for some lunch. Ten minutes later, one of the plasterers called me and we settled down, backs against the wall, to have our lunch. With Brent being away that day, there were only the plasterers, painters and me eating our sandwiches. The building had no windows at this stage and with the boiler going, there was a strong smell of pitch pervading the place. However, before long, huge clouds of black smoke were billowing past the windows.

'Stick your head out of the window, John,' one of the plasterers said, 'and you'll become one of the black and white minstrels.'

Struggling to my feet I went across to the nearest window and was met by a fearsome sight. There was a raging fire down there, the boiler full of pitch had boiled over and caught fire, setting alight all the pitch blocks and the rolls of felt. Standing in the middle of this burning pitch was the gas cylinder, but far worse was the fact that two men from the factory had a crowbar through a roll of burning felt and with their backs to the burning cylinder, were trying to move the felt. Warning my mates, I shot down the ladder, hearing the factory hooter going off as I did so. This meant that the big sliding doors of the factory would be closed and all personnel were to go to a safe place. I came round the corner and screamed to the men with the crowbar to leave it, but I don't think they heard me. Looking up, I saw that the employees had reopened the doors and were all standing watching the fire. I shouted to them there was a burning cylinder but again they ignored me and I raced around the corner to find a manager. I hadn't gone twenty paces when I heard it go off and also the sound of women's voices screaming. It apparently blasted the two men straight through the open doors of the factory and blew the pitch boiler up, showering all the onlookers with boiling pitch.

Suddenly the place was alive with fire crews and ambulance men. One ambulance took the two badly injured men off straight away. The others were busy treating the spectators for their many splashes, and two girls came up to show me their bandages. The one I had seen many times before . . . whenever I looked around, she was smiling at me. I consoled them and they went off, giggling together. Everything was put on hold until the following morning and nothing could be touched, so we jumped in the van and headed for Kington, and arriving there, yours truly headed for the hills with a story to tell.

The next morning, we could do nothing in the way of clearing up until the insurers had been with their cameras and I was told that Mr Arthur was on his way to talk to the men. I was out in the front when I saw this big shiny car pull up and recognised it instantly as the man who opened the gate every morning. Quickly walking around the side of the burnt building, sighing with relief, I bumped straight into Mr Arthur head-on, walking towards me with the head plasterer.

'Is this the lad you told me about Stan?' he asked.

Being assured that I was the one, Mr Arthur called me over and asked if I had lost many tools in the fire. I shook my head, saying that this was not the case, but he asked me another twice, adding that this was what insurances were for. He then patted me on the head and looking back, he must have thought I was the biggest bloody idiot he had ever employed. Brent called me everything and come to that, so did everyone else, but it was too late and I was the biggest fool.

CHAPTER FIFTY-FOUR
God Only Knows
(The Beach Boys)

This is a chapter of uncertainties, of the frailties of humanity and the beginning of a new era.

I was now the proud owner of a Royal Enfield 150cc motor bike which I had at last scrounged off the old man. This was certainly no 650 mean machine and just as well, for it took me weeks to ride it without going off the road. I had seen Brent in town on Saturday night and he told me the factory office was on hold for a few days and to meet him in the yard on Monday morning. As I roared in on Monday he was there waiting and we carried our tools up to a new bungalow somewhere behind the hospital. Shock horror! Who was waiting there? Overalls himself, looking at his watch and stating that time was time. We ignored him and he got onto other things about his work on the bungalow . . . obviously the finest in Herefordshire, and finally got down to the fact that we were there to help him put the cedar shingle roof on. Being the boy, I was put to loading the scaffold and then got in the middle and soon settled into the job of nailing them. The thing that I liked most was the use of copper nails. We had a great day and covered a good deal of a very large roof and even Overalls seemed pleased with the day. Saying we would be there the next morning, on time of course, we headed for home.

I awoke the next morning and looked out of the window to find it was not only raining but it was pissing down. I make no apologies for the comment for that was exactly how it was. Climbing into my wet suit, I started the bike with a clatter and phut-phutted down through the village, wiping the rain from my eyes every couple of seconds. Reaching the bungalow at last I thought, well no shingles today, I wonder what has been planned? Going into the site hut, I was given a sack to put over my shoulders and told that Mr Deacon didn't pay us to sit on our arses just because of a drop of rain, we must get on with it. I turned around to see Brent who was already there, laughing at me. By bait time we were soaked through and it was running out of our trousers. Overalls seemed to relish our discomfort and I said under my breath that he should of course be committed to the nearest asylum. However, after our short break it started to clear and within an hour we were at full speed again. The next day there was no Overalls to be seen and another chap called Dai came to take over. This chap was a tidy fellow and within a few days we had finished our task.

It's a lesson too late for the learning, as the saying goes, but I was in the timber racks getting out some timber about a month later and who should be coming down the yard but Overalls himself, clad in his Sunday best, complete with scarf and trilby. At the same time, the head man was coming the other way.

'Hello, Bill,' he called out. 'Nice to see that you are getting over your nasty bout of pneumonia.'

'Yes,' came the reply. 'There was something I needed to ask you, sir, my doctor says I am improving with the days and I wondered could you possibly find me a light job until I am fully recovered?'

'Unfortunately, Bill, as you are aware, there are no light jobs in a building company and you mustn't come back until you are fit to do a full day's work.'

'Thank you very much, sir,' was the somewhat strangled reply and I had to head for the toilets and collapse with laughter.

This said timber rack was a marvellous place to hear good news, as sometime later I was again dragging out some timber as another carpenter was walking by. Suddenly, out of nowhere appeared God himself in the shape of Bill Logan.

In stentorian tones, he shouted, 'Jenkins! Was it you who hung those garage doors up at the upland last week? Or I should have said drowned them would be nearer the mark.'

'Bollocks! shouted Jenkins, 'What I do is fuck all to do with you, so mind your business.'

Disappearing between the racks I heard the reply.

'Right, I'll tell Mr Arthur about you speaking to me like this. I've been here sixty years not sixty fucking minutes and I was hanging doors before you were born!'

'Yes and I'll be still hanging them after you're dead, you evil old bastard, so go and tell who you want.'

Game, set and match to Jenkins, I thought, and if I were you, Mr Logan, I would give it up as a bad job.

So the time went on and I was learning more and more; not only how to be a craftsman but about life and how the mighty are fallen.

After finishing off various other jobs, we went to work on one of the most interesting jobs I ever worked on. It was at the Carmelite convent in the county town of Presteigne and it would seem that I was to spend all my time in Presteigne. Doctor Beeching's axe had just fallen and half the country's railway lines had been ripped up.

The convent, on the outskirts of the town, was completely enclosed by a high wall, which the nuns had built themselves some years before. The main house was very large and surrounded by lawns, gardens and paddocks where they had a good vegetable garden, chickens, tame rabbits and a couple of goats, all fenced in, of course. The nuns' sleeping quarters or cells as they were known, were old hen houses with domed corrugated roofs and cast wheels and were scattered around the lawns. Great in high summer but bad news in winter. We had to build a complete log cabin effect square of buildings with a corridor running right around the outside. The building divided into about thirty cells. Everything was being done with the use of railway sleepers; even the floors were one inch thick cut down sleepers, laid on bitumen and sanded down. All the windows were second hand casement windows and the inside walls were lined with Tentest board, which made them very warm and comfortable. We were working there for quite some time and of course my so-called mates told them that I was a parson's son. Well, this did me more good than harm as they used to come to me with all the messages.

I was involved in three very different incidents while I was there, the first of which I was quite ashamed of. I was sawing down a piece of timber on the saw bench in the corridor and one of my mates kept pushing past me, so I turned around the other way and, head down, carried on sawing. Next I felt a tap on my shoulder which made me jump and without straightening or turning, shouted, 'Fucking hell, Fred, you frightened the shit out of me then!'

Two nuns went past me like a shot and almost ran round the corner. I was mortified and immediately told Fred as well as Alf, the foreman, who gave me a good bollocking and told me to confess all to Mother Superior. It wasn't long before the two seniors came round the corner in the form of Mother Michael and her number two, Sister Anne. I walked up to them and explained how I had committed a cardinal sin.

'Whatever did you say, John?' asked Mother Michael, 'for I cannot foretell the consequences of the nuns' reaction.'

I told her and was sure I saw a flicker of amusement flit across Sister Anne's face.

'Now, John, what has happened is that they heard your profanity; remember that it is their sin for hearing it and they will have gone to pray and will miss lunch and supper for allowing their ears to hear your choice words. They will pray for twelve hours and that will be the end of it and thank you for being so honest, but do you really think that when we knew we would have a gang of builders amongst us for many weeks I told them all to close their ears to everything?'

I thanked them profusely and they went on their way, lovely people shut away from our world, but also praying for the sins of the world from dawn until dusk, seven days a week. At that same time, the Pope died and we felt we were treading on eggshells. However, Mother Superior came along to see us every day and my mate always asked if it was white or black smoke today. I used to cringe but they answered no, with a smile, until one day Mother Michael asked us to gather around and told us of her wonderful news . . . yes, of course, it was white smoke day.

Some time later we had a very hot day and took advantage of it and started ripping sleepers down on the circular saw for the floors.

I noticed earlier that the big bay window was open at the front but imagined they were clearing the big front lounge out and cleaning the windows while they were at it. With this terrible racket going on and a lot of effing and blinding as well, I looked up to see Mother Michael and Sister Anne waving frantically at us to stop the saw. We switched the saw off and peace reigned, while both nuns came tearing down the steps, bursting with happiness and explained that Lady Rennell the Rodd had lent them a radio so they could listen to the service of the induction of the new Pope. They were clearly very happy and invited us all in to share the service with them. Well, I had been to a good many services in my short life but never a one like this. There were eight of us scruffy builders in a semicircle and about twenty five nuns, including a couple in wheelchairs on the other side of the room. I would imagine that one half of our gang had never been inside a church and the icing on the cake was that most of the service was in Latin. Obviously the nuns were familiar with the service and joined in all the responses. I looked at the floor and just glued my eyes to a certain floorboard to keep myself from bursting out laughing. Finally it was all over and we all trooped out and back to the saw and sleepers, which sounds like a good name for a pub to me.

The job was finally coming to an end when Mother Michael came walking down the corridor one afternoon with no Sister Anne, but instead a most beautiful young lady at her side. Introducing the young lady to me she explained that the girl was from Ireland and wished to become a nun with this order. She also told me that there was another joining her the next week. I shook hands with the young lady whose name was Teresa and wished her well. She was one of the prettiest girls I have ever seen.

Strange as it may sound, some twelve months later I was sent back to the convent to carry out some remedial work. By now almost a fully- fledged tradesman, I obviously met the two nuns and we had a daily laugh with a cup of tea. They treated me like a fondly remembered relative, asking many questions of me as to where I had been and what I'd been doing, and I learned that BBC TV were going to film a programme on the convent with a candlelight procession down the corridor.

I had a young apprentice with me one day and I saw Mother Michael coming down the corridor on her own, but I then saw that she had Teresa with her, and I warned the apprentice to keep quiet.

The Mother Superior asked if I remembered Teresa. I thought, I'll never forget her, and she then announced that Teresa was getting married that week and would I still be here? With that, the lemon I had asked to keep quiet asked Teresa who she was marrying. Before I could kill him, Mother Superior, with a knowing glance at me, replied instantly that she was getting married to God. This didn't sink in, but with a strangled 'Oh!' he shut up, probably thinking she had met him at the Saturday night dance.

I walked on a bit up the corridor when she said, 'As you were here when she came, John, as long as you are on your own, after the ceremony I will let her come to the end of the corridor to show off her wedding clothes for a brief moment.'

Thanking her profusely, I said that I hoped Teresa would have a happy and fulfilling life and we said goodbye. On the Thursday, I was finishing my lunch and heard the singing from the church and I realised that this beautiful young lady was now a bride of Christ. I then heard the shouts of celebration from the grounds and coming along the corridor, I saw her as she came to the far end and stood there and waved. My breath caught in my throat as she was covered in wild flowers from head to toe; even the memory of that sight brings a burning to my eyes after all these years. I was told afterwards that she didn't have a stitch on and that was how she went to her God. True or not, she made a most beautiful sight that afternoon.

CHAPTER FIFTY-FIVE
Paranoid
(Black Sabbath)

On the Friday I had finished everything, cleaned up and once more saw the figures of Mother Superior, Sister Anne and a nun that I hadn't seen before, approaching me and looking rather serious. I thought, Jesus Christ, don't say they have found some more work, but no, they had come to say thank you and goodbye. We chatted and I kept looking at the new nun as there was something about her that was somehow familiar. Mother Superior, sharp as a tack, picked up on this.

'John,' she said, 'let me introduce you to Sister Teresa, who you saw yesterday.'

As I shook hands, the penny dropped and gulping, I made my apologies. Gone forever was the raven-haired beauty that I once saw and standing before me was a serious nun with head dress, coarse brown robe and bandaged legs, and who would now spend her life praying for the sins of the world, with no outside contact. I said my goodbyes and never saw them again, but some things never leave you, and a couple of years later we were asked to go to an old manor house, which was being knocked down and take up an oak floor which had been bought by the Carmelites in Presteigne for their refectory. I had just saved up and bought a new Disston panel saw, which was like gold to get hold of. Plus it cost a bloody fortune. Anyway, I was using it flat through the first board and suddenly a shower of sparks shot out and I found to my sorrow that the beautiful old oak boards had cast iron tongues which completely ruined my saw teeth. After ten minutes of effing and blinding, I got an old saw and managed to get the first board up. From then on it was easy, but beneath this floor was a polished marble floor and it had a complete circle with the pentacle signs around it. I immediately had visions of witches' covens and wondered what the bloody hell was going on here a few centuries ago. I also wondered how the nuns would take it if they knew what their new floor was covering up. Finally on this subject, the order moved to France many years ago and anyway, ninety percent of them would be dead by now. I called by there recently and all that remains fifty-six years later are the Roman Catholic church and part of a concrete block wall.

Time was marching on and I had been working on jobs all over the country, but the only cloud on the horizon was our Technical College at Hereford, where I will confess I spent too little time. Firstly, I had no means of transport, which they were aware of, to get me home at nine o'clock. Secondly, it was boring as most of the course I had done years ago at school. Thirdly, I had only been there a few weeks and we had technical drawing and were given homework. This involved drawing a plan, side elevation and end elevation and having a drawing board and squares, I did this and also added a perspective.

Our tutor was called Mr Lane, nicknamed Bronco. At the next lesson he asked if this drawing was all my own work. When I told him it was he said I was wasting my time at carpentry and I should think it over and he would get me in a draughtsmen's class. This, however, would mean a lot of study and hard work. The answer was an emphatic 'no way'. This really sickened him and I think he gave up on me completely. Coupled with my mode of dress, the fact that my mate dropped one of the teaching staff in the canteen and then three of us were caught by Bronco coming down the steps of the Ritz at five o'clock. The following Monday I was duly summoned to the head's study and it wasn't a nice chat. I tried to get my side of the story over and was told that the pugilist had departed.

Next question: did I like working in wood? Replying yes, I was advised to bugger off and join the Forestry Commission, his words not mine. I was not thrown off the premises, but I just didn't go any more. By this time I was fed up of being public enemy number one, but still enjoying work and leisure. Talking of leisure, I had just got myself engaged to the young lady from the factory, mentioned earlier. However, it was doomed to failure as I was pissed almost every weekend and could always be found with a glass in my hand. Another problem was I could now drink an awful amount of beer and this cost an awful amount of money. I was working up in a small village just outside Kington, putting a new roof on their village hall. This was all showing from the inside and all put together with mortise and tenon and then oiled, and I loved fitting the mortises, racing with other older and more experienced tradesmen.

Getting home that day, I was in a jubilant mood and after wrestling with Shan I walked in the sitting room and it was deja-vu all over again.

'Cup of tea, son? asked my mother.

'No, thanks, I replied and sat opposite, waiting for the shit to hit the fan. The old man was at his best.

'Now then, Sunny Jim, as you know, your old dad is not getting any younger and I went to see the bishop only yesterday. I need a quieter life to continue in office and he completely understood, to which end he has offered me a parish in a lovely little village down in Herefordshire.'

'Good for you,' was my reply. 'I hope you will be very happy, but don't expect me to come with you as I have had too many outings with you to put up with another,' and I walked out of the room.

Getting my shotgun on the way out, I picked up some cartridges and down the paddock I went and God help anything that got up in front of me. Mother Nature must have put the word about, for nothing got up in front of me and I sat down and had a smoke and calming down, set off for home. Things were quiet when I got in and putting the gun away, I had a quick look around but they had obviously gone out.

I let Shan out of the kitchen and into the sitting room with me and gave the latest news some thought. Six years of happiness getting to know all the surrounding farms and houses. All my friends and suddenly work; I had another turn when I thought about that, as it was plain I couldn't travel a long distance to get to Kington. I heard their voices as the came up the drive and into the room they came. The old man went on about it being good for all of us and Hereford area was the place to be, and then the question, what did I think?

Keeping a cool head, I told them exactly what I thought, but added they had given me no thought. First it was school, but they didn't know the damage the constant moving had done. Now it was my apprenticeship that was going to suffer and right at a critical time. The old man was on it like a shot and said they had a branch in Leominster and would allow me to go there. I jumped straight down his throat and asked who had given him these facts. He told me the people in the village where he was going. This put me into swearing phase, but my mum was sitting there so I just asked if he had been telling my business to a bunch of bloody strangers, and in return I would now broadcast his business all around the village. This got him going and I walked out of the room without a goodnight and went up to bed to sort my mind out.

Next morning, I got up early and left before anyone was about and called at the tobacconists to get a couple of pies and a bottle of pop for my bait and dinner and was in a pig mood all day, and glad to be off when five-thirty arrived. Arriving home, I saw the car was out and walked round the back to be confronted by my mother, who once again was protecting the old man's decision. I was older now and not in the mood for any small talk, but what put the icing on the cake was she told me they were off the next afternoon to meet some people in the village and find out all about it. I am afraid I was very rude and said I wasn't interested. That evening when I got home from work, all I heard was what a lovely place it was, what a marvellous vicarage it was and how some of the ladies had said they could find me a nice friend when I moved there. Can you seriously believe anyone could talk such crap? I replied in icy tones that I wasn't interested in any of it and whoever the ladies were they should be committed to an asylum immediately and I didn't play with anyone and if I needed a mate, which I didn't, I would go and find my own, and once more picked up my smokes and lighter and buggered off down the fields before there was a tragedy in the house.

At work the next day my mate who also came from the village, asked me what I was so grumpy about and in the end I told him and although I swore him to secrecy, I knew it would be out before the end of the week.

CHAPTER FIFTY-SIX
Blowin' in the Wind
(Bob Dylan)

I had set my alarm clock for six o'clock, but was awake before five and up and dressed by five-thirty. It was still dark outside and I thought to myself, I must be off my bloody head, the men don't get here until eight-thirty, but I wanted a bit of quiet time to myself before we left. Shan was having a fit as I switched the kitchen light on and made a cup of tea. I still couldn't believe I had agreed to this lunatic move, but by now, I thought wryly to myself, the old man's genes must have taken hold. Lighting a ciggy, I fondled the dog's ears and seriously contemplated what lay in store. In the first place I didn't know the area, but felt it was somehow grander. I didn't know a single soul around the area. I was starting work in a town which was known to be full of fighting men and who weren't too keen on the place I had come from. On a scale of one to ten this gave me, at best, minus two. Having given it some thought I was thinking I had moved from here to there and met a huge amount of people and nothing fazed me in the slightest. I had run with a pretty rough crowd for a long time and found if I kept my eyes open and my mouth shut, I should be alright. Hearing the floor boards creaking upstairs I thought that was the end of my peace and quiet and walked through the back scullery and checked everything was gone from there and it was clean and tidy. Also the outhouse and toilet and I thought they could be locked and finished. Back in the house, apart from the kitchen table and chairs, there was only the crockery and cooker and the small electrical appliances to go.

'Morning, Sunny Jim,' boomed down the stairs. 'My word, you're up early, we didn't expect to see you downstairs yet.'

I briefed him on the state of play, but knew it was a complete waste of time, he would carry on regardless and probably redo everything. Well, so be it, I thought. Five minutes later Mum appeared and informed me that tea and toast would be ready in ten minutes.

It was breaking daylight and a time I loved so, putting Shan on the lead, we went down the paddock for the last time and I looked across at the bulk of the hill, Glanescob and the Cwm wood below it and realised I would not see it again from this position.

I could hear Mum shouting and went inside. Kicking off my boots, I sat down for toast and Bovril and another hot mug of tea. All the carpets and lino squares were rolled up and the furniture stacked ready for the men as of yesterday's hard work. Tea chests were everywhere and I don't think we could have moved at all without them. This was the old man's domain, with all the china and ornaments wrapped in newspaper and double wrapped again in the chests. Upstairs, Mum had stripped the beds and packed them in baskets and cases which I carried it out to the old man's car. On the return journey I saw the lights of the removal van coming up the road and thought with distaste, I hope he's happy, here we go.

I saw there were three of them jumping down from the cab and the old man was showing them the furniture that was going to the temporary house and the rest to the vicarage where it would be locked in a room until we moved down there. I thought, well, even if there are any mistakes, we only have to drive down the road to get it. By mid-morning we were all having a cup of tea and everything was packed on one or two lorries, dependant on where it was going.

I said to the old man, 'You go in the car in front of the first lorry and see it where you want it and I'll go in front of the second one to the vicarage, but give me both the keys to the vicarage.'

I thought he was going to argue, but he saw the sense of it and gave me the two sets of keys which I checked and pulling on my coat and helmet, I was ready for the off. With the second lorry tight behind, we had a convoy. To be truthful, I was glad to have something to busy myself with and I didn't even look back at what was once my favourite home. With the lorry following me, I had to go quietly and we went down the Wern, through Kington and across through Pembridge to Golden cross, turned right and past the temporary house, down into the village and turned left into the vicarage. Up and along the winding drive with a Yew shrubbery on the right and up to a big turning circle and the huge front door. The key to this door was the biggest house key that I had ever seen and it was a double lock, so turning it over with a rusty squeak, the door opened with much groaning and we were in the big hall. I have to admit there was an eerie feeling on entering this house and in later days, I would not have gone in on my own, but that is for much later.

Opening the door into the large front room was a whole lot easier and the three of us carried the whole lot into the room, stacked it tidily and I locked it up again. The driver and his mates started out to finish at the new house and I had a good look around the grounds again before riding up to the other house. I got there just as the last vehicle was pulling out. Giving the keys of the vicarage back to the old man, I could see he was about knackered and told him to sit down for ten minutes. Sitting with him while Mum was making a cup of tea and dusting everything in sight, I remarked how well it had gone and he smiled and said they couldn't have managed without me. Strange how a few little words like that can turn you upside down when you least expect it. Well, we did not do a lot that night, not that there was a lot to do, but with no TV and a very poor reception on the radio it was not too long before I wished them a goodnight and hit the sack.

Looking around the room, which was quite bare, my last thought as sleep overcame me was that Mum had put curtains up in my room.

CHAPTER FIFTY-SEVEN
Looking for Somebody
(Fleetwood Mac)

I woke up the following morning with the sun streaming through the curtains and the most unusual noise of heavy traffic on the road outside. Gradually, I remembered where I was and for a minute thought I was back in Nottingham with this bloody traffic nonstop on the road.

Pulling on a pair of jeans and a T-shirt, I quietly crossed to the bathroom and had a good wash before descending the stairs. It was plainly obvious that no one was up and looking at my watch, it read seven thirty-five. Yawning, I put the kettle on and was licked all over by Shan, who must have thought he had been deserted after spending the night in a strange kitchen. I made a cup of hot sweet tea and opened the back door, letting Shan have the run of the newly-fenced back lawn. Lighting up a ciggy, I pulled a chair out from the kitchen and sat on it with my tea and smoke, enjoying the delights of the morning. Looking around, my mind went back to my village and I wondered what it was like this morning. Deserted and horrible, I thought, as I could visualise my mates going about their normal day. This brought me to thinking about the following week when I would be starting in my new part of the firm, wondering what they would be like and if I would get along with them. I certainly hoped it would be so. I thought that later I would go into the town and have a walk around and get my bearings. One thing . . . I would make sure I didn't park against somebody else's bloody tree! One thing I sincerely hoped was that the old bastard didn't venture down this far. Hearing a movement from upstairs I called the dog up and shut the door just as my mother came in from upstairs with a tentative smile and asked what I would like for breakfast. What indeed? As I was hooked on Bovril toast there wasn't anything else that I needed. She told me that old man was having a lie in, as he was tired out from yesterday's events and this I completely understood, with his heart condition.

As we sat there, she asked me what I thought of it so far, and I replied that apart from the noise and density of traffic for a country road, I supposed it was alright, but I did point out that I had no option anyway, but also that this was the last time for me. Little did I realise that those words would prove to be so true; that it would be the last time for him before too long. I hung around, putting things away for her and moving other items until at last I could hear the old man moving about upstairs and then I went out to my bike and headed down the road to the vicarage to have a scout around the new gardens. I had given them a quick look over, but I thought I would have a good look around this morning. Going up the drive, I thought to myself, well, old man I can see the attraction, but how the bloody hell are you going to keep these grounds under control?

To the left was a huge area of grassland with three massive trees growing, two of beech and one of yew. The mast from the beech was thick on the ground from last year; this area was bordered by the main road as it wound through the village. The immense hedge dividing this was a bit of everything, including two acacias. To the right of the drive was a tall and very overgrown yew shrubbery which divided off the grounds from the small cemetery for the churchyard on the opposite side of the road, which had been full for several years. The width of this shrubbery was about twenty feet and it followed the drive right along to the house where it opened up into a large sunken lawn which bordered the front of the house and at the bottom, the Glebe lands which were rented by the church. This lawn was extremely large with flower borders to the sides and was probably used as a tennis lawn generations before. To the whole length of this lawn on the left hand side ran a very overgrown hedge which divided the lawn from the vegetable plot, again huge and untended for years, and to the left of this, the red brick wall of the orchard which had been already noted.

Again there was no one working inside and I laughed, thinking typical builders, but there, it was nothing to do with me. I walked down to the orchard and there was still blossom on most of the trees and I noticed several clumps of mistletoe hanging from various branches and wondered if the old man would hold a séance to ward off the evil ones. I checked around the back of the old part but nothing was disturbed and anyway, there was an occupied coach house against the road, so nothing going on there. Back around the front I lit up a ciggy and sitting on an old stump, regarded what was going to be my new home. I imagined the old man would have to get a gardener in as he would never manage this lot and I certainly intended to be away for most of the time. There was no doubt about it, he had done well for himself but also brought on a whole shed load of hard work. Stubbing out my butt end I pulled on my helmet and was out through the gates and up the road at maximum revs which, believe you me, were not a lot.

Back at our new home I had a hot cup of tea and a biscuit and after answering all their questions I gave a hand shunting various items of furniture into the places required by my mother. Promising I would put up some shelves and pictures tomorrow, I sat down and had a civilised lunch with them and explained I was heading for town to find my new place of work.

As I approached Leominster it was quite a bit bigger than Kington and finding a car park, I paid the fee and headed up the street. There appeared to be several olde worlde alleyways off the main square with a lot of folk drifting about for a Monday afternoon. After some consideration I realised that this was a lot larger than I imagined and there were a lot of pubs scattered around, which I had heard about from the lads back home.

I walked down a little avenue off the square and came out onto a cricket pitch with a pavilion and the square in the middle freshly marked so I assumed they were playing here tonight. Hearing a clock play a hymn and chime the hour I looked to where it had come from and saw an amazing old church surrounded by trees and vowed to come and have a look around it when I had time, but I had other business at the moment. Asking where Deacons builders were, a man pointed out the way to me and I thanked him and followed his directions up a long street with trees growing along it at intervals. Suddenly I saw it there between an old house and a pub and was amazed to see the size of it. Apart from anything else, it looked deserted and very small, not like a working yard. There was only one entrance I could see and I walked on hurriedly in case someone came out of what I supposed was the office block. Little did I know at the time that this was the place where I would grow into a man. Sow my wild oats and finally leave with, if nothing else, a huge knowledge of the finer parts of joinery and hold my own anywhere and with anyone. Without appearing to be nosy, I walked back down the street a few yards where there were another two pubs and a couple of small shops and a café. Pretending to browse for a few minutes, I ambled back up the street for another look at the hub of the building industry, which was to be my new place of employment. Nothing moved that I could see and I thought perhaps they had moved. Suddenly I heard a saw working and it appeared to be coming from a place over which I assumed were the offices. A door slammed and a man with glasses, carrying a boxwood surveyors' ruler came out of the door, jumped into a Morris Traveller and passed me as walked hurriedly up the street. So this was it and I would learn the full extent of it all come Monday morning at seven-thirty am, shit or bust.

Back at the ranch I was subjected to a hundred questions, but in truth I had nothing to say at this moment in time. On Wednesday evening I set sail on the new route to the girlfriend's house and figured it was about a fifteen mile ride. We went out for a long walk and I told her all about the things that had happened over the weekend and also broke the news that as I was starting a new job on Monday I would not stay on after the dance on Saturday. Needless to say, this went down like a lead balloon, but in fairness I had a good deal on my mind at the time.

CHAPTER FIFTY-EIGHT
Let's Work Together
(Canned Heat)

Friday afternoon was the big day for my parents and look out anything that got in the way . . . like me for example, for I had firmly said I wasn't coming to this one. On Friday morning the house was cleaned from roof to footings in case His Lordship the Bishop dropped in on his way to the church. I spent the morning as far out of the way as was humanly possible. The old man would have killed any unsuspecting moths from five hundred yards with the camphor fumes issuing from his best suit. The service was at three and the tea was at four o'clock and I couldn't help but wonder how many times he would toll the bell this afternoon. I thought he should have some automatic ringer attached, then perhaps he may stay here forever, which was to happen on down the line.

I bade them every success at their big day and at last relaxed. At quarter past three I had a wash, shave and change, donned my dark suit, jumped on my bike and headed down to the vicarage. Parking my bike in the shrubbery, I checked my watch and headed for the Crown Inn and the getting-to-know- you crowd. Spotting the hero of the hour, the new vicar of Dilwyn and his lady wife, deep in conversation with he who rules the world dressed in purple, I dived up the steps into the bar area before they could see me. As I sat down at a spare table, a very commendable young lady came up and asked if I would like tea or coffee. Responding in my nicest manner, with my best smile, I replied that I would love a cup of tea. Off she went and returned bearing a pot of tea and I thanked her profusely. I was in the act of pouring myself a cuppa when three people came up and asked if anyone was sitting there. I replied in the negative and they asked if I minded if they joined me. I could feel their eyes giving me covert glances and eventually, one of them gave in to curiosity.

'Are you from his old parish?'

As all three studied me intently I replied yes, that was the case.

Now hungry for further information, another asked what he was like, adding, 'He seems a nice sort of chap.'

I replied that I had known him for a long time. 'He's an alright guy,' I nodded, 'but he spends most of his time in the garden, so no one really knows him.'

This seemed to dampen the conversation and they wandered off, but I could see them muttering to themselves and I thought, well that's one I owed you, get out of that one. Finishing my cup of tea and demolishing a large slice of Victoria sponge, I headed to the door marked toilet and from there out the back and up the road. Back at home I changed quickly into my old clothes. I heard the car pull up sometime later and in they came, full of enthusiasm.

Asking how it went, they replied it was lovely, the people were so friendly and two ladies came up out of the blue and asked your father would he come round and give them some tips on their gardens. I thought to myself what a strange question to ask a vicar, but as I said to him, 'Well, you don't know anything about gardening do you?'

I went back up to the dance on Saturday, but she who knows everything was in a mood so I thought in all honesty it was better if I shot off back. I had a few beers that night but there was no limit or breathalyser in those far off days. I couldn't settle at this moment and needed some time to myself. Anyway, I got home safely, switched the bike off twenty yards down the road so as not to wake the natives and pushed it through the gate. The folks were in bed and I made a quick cup of tea and headed up the wooden hill myself.

Sunday was the day when I supposed the old man had to make a good impression on his flock, so I left them to it and lounged around reading all day. That night after Evensong they came home, worn out but happy, and I was glad they felt they had made the right move. About ten o'clock I bade them a very good night and up to bed I trudged.

My alarm awoke me at six-thirty and after the bathroom, I entered the kitchen to find my breakfast cooked, sandwiches made and flask filled. After finishing my food I packed them in my valise, gave my mum a kiss and it was look out builders' yard, I'm on my way.

I rode into the yard at about seven-twenty and a guy said to park my bike in the dry in the large garage. The yard was already a buzz of people running here and there and climbing into vans and roaring out of the gates. I saw the chap with the ruler that I had seen on Friday and asked him where I should go.

Speaking in a strange accent he said, 'Bliddy, bliddy hell, you must be from bliddy Kington? Mr Bliddy Arthur said to bliddy will expect you, but yous is miles too bliddy irley, so go up to the bliddy chippy shop and wait till summon bliddy will arrives!'

I was slightly confused by this gibberish and wondered if he meant the chip shop or the carpenters' shop, so I decided to go to what I imagined was the latter. Opening the door, I was confronted with a flight of damaged stairs and at top of these, found myself in a broken down old shed with three benches in it and across the front wall, a row of windows I estimated must be fifteenth century.

Gazing through the cobwebbed and sawdust spattered panes, I looked down on the circus that was performing below me. You must understand that one of the Mr Deacons who owned the company ran a very tight ship in Kington. He had been a decorated hero in the last war and also a Captain in bomb disposal. Working for him were his Sergeant Major as yard foreman and his batman, who ran the offices. They ran the whole place like a Quartermaster's stores and woe betide anybody – and I do mean anybody, who dared to step out of line.

You weren't even allowed to think of a cigarette in Kington, but here, eighty percent of the workforce had a fag going. The one thing Bliddy (I will call him that from now on), was obsessed with, was getting out of the yard by seven thirty and all the vehicles were gone by this time. The melee gradually quietened and the last van sailed out through the gates and Bliddy disappeared, no doubt to have his breakfast. This left one man in a blue overall and cap, who I was to learn was the yardman by the name of Herby.

I sat on my bench and waited for the arrival of the eight o'clock gang with some trepidation. Bang on eight, I heard the door downstairs open and running up the stairs, in came a chap of about thirty, smartly dressed, well spoken, and asked was I John? He introduced himself as Gerry and said he normally worked in the shop and around the town. He obviously knew his stuff and on top of that he was a real gent and I was sure we would get along.

This shop was also the meeting place of the local men who were working around the town and who came up for a chat. I shook hands that morning with bricklayers, plasterers, painters, plumbers and labourers, all of whom seemed to want to know how were all those bastards up at Kington doing, and assured me how well I would get along down here. After they had gone about their duties I asked Gerry was it all right to smoke.

'Listen, John,' he replied, 'this is not Kington and you can smoke as many as you like.'

I explained that I had none with me and he sent me to find Herby who would know where to get some. Herby was relaxing in his hut and after introductions, sent me down the street with instructions to tell Margaret, who was a friend of his, to give me a nice cup of coffee on the house.

I obviously thought I had died and gone to heaven; compared to Kington, this was magic. I walked down and got my cigarettes and a box of matches and on returning, Gerry told me we had a pair of framed, ledged and braced doors to make. While he was cutting the mortises and tenons, I cut the boards to length and painted the tongues. We then found out that the roughing out of the mortises had already been done, so we cut out the tenons and haunches and also cut the wedge room for the wedges and glued up the joints, squared each frame, drove in the wedges and dowelled the joints. They were now ready for boarding. A message was then sent up asking me to go down to the office as they wanted my details. Gerry said he had to go up town to check on something or other and said we would board up the doors after lunch.

Going downstairs, I knocked on the main office door and a voice shouted me to come in. I was met by a young chap who looked about thirty and introduced himself as Tony. I entered his office which he shared with a Mr Midwinter, who turned out to be his stepfather, and he took all my personal details and told me I was so lucky to have come to them, as it was nothing like Kington and a lot less regimental. He then asked me if I enjoyed a drink and I said I had been known to have one. He told me not to worry about the time sheets, reiterating that he always did them. Bliddy then came out of another office and Tony introduced him as Jim, the manager. Bliddy had certainly got over his morning panic and shook hands, saying that Mr Arthur had told him I would do the work of ten bliddy men, so I must steady down a bit.

Back outside I looked at my watch and it was ten to one so I went upstairs and ate my lunch and had a smoke. This had to be too good to be true, I thought, I had really made it at last. Gerry arrived back about ten past two and I had laid out all the boards and cut the starters and finishers, so we nailed them up between us and fitted the braces loosely as we didn't know their hanging positions.

'Well, that will do for today,' said Gerry, 'Did you know the fair was in town?'

'No,' I replied, 'I didn't.'

'Come on, then. I'll show you around.'

We went up the little alleyway known as School Lane and out into the Square which was now crammed with kids of all ages and the bumpers, Noah's ark and waltzers, and I also noticed the Three Horseshoes, which looked quite handy. We then walked down another alleyway called Drapers Lane and out into the wide, aptly named Broad Street. The music was blasting and this area was filled with rides and sideshows. We had a good nose around and Gerry filled me in on what was what and who was who and we then headed back to the yard.

'Well, my friend, that's enough for a first day so you shoot off home and I'll see you in the morning.'

I couldn't believe my ears, but jumped aboard the bike and was heading out of the gate for home at three forty-five. Oh! Mr Arthur, Oh! Mr John and all your gang . . . if only you knew. I had landed in Heaven.

CHAPTER FIFTY-NINE
The Times They Are a-Changin'
(Bob Dylan)

The times were definitely going to change for me in the not too distant future.

I was standing in the timber rack one morning and heard a shout.

'Just the bliddy man I want to see!' Sure enough, it was himself brandishing a sheet of paper and an official looking document. The document was my stamped and signed official completion of my indentures, which I had forgotten about. Looking down at the entry from the Technical College I could see the remarks bordered on disgraceful.

'Bliddy, bliddy hell you have not been to the bliddy place for twelve months and got me in the shit with Mr bliddy Arthur.'

My apology to him prompted some expletive and, 'Read this,' handing me the sheet of paper.

It was a letter to Dear Jim, saying this report is dreadful and I want you to speak to this lad in no uncertain terms.

Looking at me, he said, 'You're going out into the country tomorrow, so you can keep out of his bliddy way until he calms down.'

It was then that I saw the good in him and knew he would protect his men to the end, wherever possible. Personally, I was glad to be getting out of town; apart from the fact that I was drinking far too much and the town was full of pubs, a few amusing incidents had happened. We used to go and grab the job sheets early before anyone else. This gave us the pick of all the good jobs. I grabbed one on the Wednesday with instructions to go into the Grammar School field and erect a stile over which the pupils took a shortcut from the school. That morning we got all the materials ready for loading and set off to the said field. We had worked it out that it would be finished by Thursday afternoon, giving us all of Friday in the pub. Working like Trojans, we ripped out a long section of high hedge and inserted the stile, and were screwing the rails to the posts each side when the sports master came running up with a class of lads. He asked us what we were doing, we explained, and then he advised that we were in the wrong field.

We worked like demons that afternoon and filled the hole with post and rails, which we smuggled out of the yard. We then cleared up the mess with the help of our lorry driver and started again in the right place. I think we got it all done by four o'clock on the Friday and finally got to the pub. We never heard a word from the farmer and I expect he was delighted to have twenty feet of post and rail fencing erected in his hedge line.

The following Monday I dived in at first light and retrieved an order for a new floor in a bungalow about five miles away. We knocked on the front door and told the householder we had come to renew the main bedroom floor. His answer was that the wife had nipped into town but we could come in and start; however, he didn't realise there was anything wrong with the floor.

'Oh yes,' we replied, 'you have dry rot, I'm afraid.'

He showed us in to the bedroom which was full of furniture and left us to it. We humped wardrobes, chests of drawers and everything else outside on the landing and were rolling up the carpet when I remarked that the floor looked all right to me. As we were debating this, I heard some talking down stairs and then the wife appeared, looking rather flustered. She asked to see our order and instantly told us the house we needed was along the lane about fifty yards. Talk about egg on your face! I felt about two feet tall, but we put it all back and she made us a cup of tea before we proceeded onwards.

So it was a relief to climb aboard a Morris J2 van driven by a lunatic bricklayer, heading across the Shropshire borders to a huge

Georgian mansion in its own grounds of several acres. Kington had also put in for the job but Leominster had been awarded it and a few Kington lads were working there. The Kington lads got jealous and put a big sign up in the hedge which said Butlin's Holiday Camp. This it was, as we had a huge room for our bait and office and there were fry-ups every morning and afternoon and a serious Brag school after lunch. The foreman was from Kington but our lot were too clever by half. My task was to reccy the grounds and find as many different birds' nests as I could, This took a lot of my time and I found some quite rare species.

One incident made me laugh. Rick told me he needed a sheet of eight by four oak faced plywood to finish a job he was doing at home. Later that day I heard the Kington foreman ordering the very same to be delivered the following day. From the scaffold, we could see the lorry coming down the drive for at least a quarter of a mile and Rick parked his van at the back of the house. Because the sheet was four feet high, we took the beads off the sash window and the sashes were loose. We saw the lorry coming and surprisingly, it was our Leominster lorry with our favourite driver. We laughed and said we would give him a lift and guess what? The plywood was the last bit to unload. Straight through the house we carried it, past the stores, through the sash window and into the van, no problem. Rick took his van and parked it at the front, I beaded the sashes back onto the van and the job's a good 'un. Rick was then away from there to his appointment with the dentist and I was telling the foreman that I had not seen a sheet of oak faced plywood on the lorry and that was the end of it.

Something happened the next day which made me realise that the lady of the house was not the demure little creature we thought she was. The ten o'clock fry-up was in full swing when she walked into the bait room. As she looked around, a sudden silence fell and choosing her moment, she spoke in a loud and clear voice.

'Who's been shitting down Pheasants Walk?'

Ten men engaged in various acts of cooking stopped dead, frying pans poised. Standing in various poses, mouths hanging open and frying pans suspended mid-sizzle, these men, from all walks of life, froze on the spot, deathly silent and completely lost for words. I looked into her eyes and saw they were like chips of marble and recognised then the cold menace in her. This lady would take no prisoners and woe betide anyone or anything that got in her way.

Up spoke our brave foreman who, in his gentlest voice, enquired what was the problem.

Without turning a hair she asked again, 'Who has been shitting down Pheasant's walk?' Then, in an ice cold voice, she said that she had been walking with her Pastor Jack Russell terrier through an area of shrubbery known as Pheasant's Walk. Apparently, she could not walk through there for piles of faeces and tumps of various coloured paper on every tussock. She then warned that it must stop instantly and she would be checking it on a regular basis. With this final remark, she walked off to leave the bait room in stunned silence.

We mere mortals were under the impression that she fancied the foreman. However, this was to come to its horrific conclusion a day or so later, when he came to us as white as a sheet.

'I've really done it now,' he said. Apparently, he had been engrossed in the day sheets with his head down when someone nudged his arm. Thinking it was his mate, he told them to fuck off. He looked up to see the lady scuttling through the door and ran after her to apologise, but it was too late and she never spoke to him again.

I was up on a scaffold a few days later and I heard her husband call out, 'Tweetie Pie?'

'Yes, darling, what is it?' she answered from the herb garden.

'Our windows have all just arrived and none of them fit.'

'Who measured them, darling?' from the herb garden.

'The foreman, Tweetie Pie.'

From the herb garden, 'Well, darling, what did you expect?'

I nearly broke my neck descending from the scaffold to tell the foreman what I had heard. He turned a queer shade of purplish-brown and hit his desk so hard it collapsed in a heap and I heard him effing and jeffing as I walked back out.

The following bait time he spoke to us, saying he had to go to another large house, miles away, to take charge of the workforce and that was the last we saw of him. One of our brickies took over and that was that. Strangely, the Butlin's sign had disappeared as we turned up the drive the following morning. Within a couple of weeks the job was finished and we headed for town. Mr Arthur must have forgotten about me, as I bumped into him a week later and he just nodded and said, 'Alright lad?'

I didn't bow my thanks but gave him a nice smile. We were alright, me and Arthur.

Two things were about to happen which were to affect my life, both in different ways and I was to experience a very rude awakening. I had found a completely different lifestyle in my new area and I was thoroughly enjoying myself. I will freely admit that I was drinking a lot more and my consumption levels had gone up considerably.

My fiancée had changed her job and did not get home until later on a Saturday and not until three o'clock on a Sunday. The result of this was that I would arrive at her home about three on a Saturday and go straight into the pub, resulting in being half cut by the time I got to the dance. On the Sunday, I would go over the border with my friends playing brag, and not get back until about four o'clock. This lifestyle was a no-win situation and one Friday night, going to the pictures, I was told in no uncertain terms that it was all over.

This added to my downward spiral and for several weeks, I must confess I was not good company to be with. Gradually, I saw the light and pulled myself together, going out with a lot of girls, but never getting too serious. Although my weekends seemed to hinge around the pub, I kept myself tidy.

Finally, after a roaring few years, I met a young lady who, after some time, as by now I had a terrible reputation, decided to risk going out with me and we finally got engaged. About six months later she told me one night that she was 'late' and . . . you've guessed it, I was about to become a daddy. Bad news for the vicarage, I'm afraid, but worse things happen at sea, or so I was told.

I finally got married and tried to settle down; I did say tried. Becoming a member of the local village I soon got into the cricket, darts and quoits teams and was a regular customer at the local inn. So one would imagine I was a happy chappie but, like I always say, do not believe everything that you are told.

We had a new landlord at our local, who turned out to be the best I ever met and I used to go out with him killing pigs on a weekend, as this was one of his many jobs. He was a top sportsman and was never serious and people used to come to our Local from miles away. I also became a proud father and sadly, was also made redundant from my long term employment. Also at this time, about the month of November, the first epidemic of Foot and Mouth hit our county and so everything was closed down in our locality for fear of this dreadful disease spreading around the area.

CHAPTER SIXTY
Walk of Life
(Dire Straits)

It was a Sunday morning in early June 1987 and I was sitting on the crest of a hill in the heart of Eastern Powys. That is what they tell us to call it these days but to me it is Radnorshire and always will be. Sitting by my side, lost in wonder was my friend Christopher Fletcher, known to all his friends and workmates as simply Fletch. His wife, Judith, had dropped us off early that morning and the plan was to walk over the hill to my old village and spend the day having some liquid refreshment and enjoying ourselves until Judith picked us up in the village much later that day. As we sat on the final peak eating our rolls and drinking our tea, Chris was in awe of the view. I pointed out to him the various places and the haunts of my boyhood, the farms and told him of the folks that lived there.

He was really fascinated with the place and felt that it was like looking down on Switzerland. The peak we were sitting on was the final peak of the Hergest Ridge and all my boyhood memories came flooding back to me. Finishing our rolls and tea, we started the steep climb down the hill into the village. Strangely enough, Chris's grandfather and grandmother were buried in the chapel graveyard that lay at the bottom of the hill. I then took him up through the village and through the churchyard and showed him the house where I had lived for six years. He was well impressed with it and although I could see a lot of changes had happened since we had left, I was also pleased.

As we were walking back down to the Royal Oak he remarked

it would be a good place to spend a weekend in a tent and I agreed. I had only known Chris for a short time, having seen him around town a lot but somehow our paths never crossed. However, I was in the club one Friday night and a big mate of mine introduced me. From that moment on we never looked back and went to a lot of places together with our wives and other friends. They were both brilliant company and we got on really well together. That Sunday we sauntered into the pub and I introduced him to the folks that I knew. We had a great afternoon and Judith came to pick us up about six o'clock. Both well in our cups, we must have been a bundle of laughs for poor Judith. At the time I was playing a lot of golf and we spent many evenings around the local course. How he put up with me I will never know, as he was a very good golfer and I would lose all concentration after about three holes. The following week, I bought a small three-man tent and put it up in the garden. When Chris saw it he couldn't contain himself and that weekend we were off to erect it at The Swan pub in the next village.

In truth, we had a great weekend and I introduced him to all my old mates that I'd had since boyhood days. The biggest shock I had was when we walked around the churchyard looking at the various headstones. I must have gone really quiet as we sat on a seat and I lit up the ever present cigarette and said that I had suddenly realised that a great number of the stones were for people I knew and in lots of cases had spent time on their farms. It brought me up with a jolt to think I was now middle-aged and the days of my youth were long gone.

That first camp was so enjoyable that we asked a local farmer if we could go into his field. He agreed and found us a great spot by the brook in a small copse. We were now staying in my village and started going up every other weekend through the summer months. It was during these first few months that we talked about my life and the places I had lived and the different folks and schools I had gone to along the way. Whatever else I am known for in my life, I am very well aware of the frailties of my makeup and character. We had been for a cup of tea and a chat one Saturday morning with old friends and it went like magic as I brought back the memories of years long past. Some of the stories brought tears of remembrance and after we had left, the oldest son came round to see me and said how much his folks had loved it and we were welcome back at any time. Sadly, the three of them are at rest in the churchyard now, but it was a lovely experience on that morning of nostalgia. Chris was deep in thought that morning and said later, 'You had those folks in tears; you really are wasting your time, why don't you do it? Why don't you write a book of your times?'

I had now purchased an old caravan and during the winter months, parked it on Chris's car park and refurbished it. The following Easter we were raring to go back up. I drove up on the Good Friday morning and it was starting to snow as I left Leominster and getting up into the borderland, it was snowing heavily. I rang Chris from the phone box in the village, saying the sun was shining where I was and he said he was just leaving. He would have a hell of a shock crossing the border and climbing the hills. We had a day of days in the pub with the walkers who did not want to leave our warm bar and walk back over the hills to Kington.

The next morning after a fry up and a gallon of hot tea, we set sail back down into the village and . . . you've guessed it, the local and started all over again. Although I didn't know it, I was heading for disaster on golden wings, but that was a short while away. Smoking upwards of sixty cigarettes a day was not helping my robust health, but all this was for another day. That morning, the sun came out and the foul weather disappeared and we had a change of heart and walked up onto the Ridge and Chris, always full of questions, asked me about my later years and what happened after I got married, so I told him the story as best I could, and what had happened to me since 1965.

It appeared that I was to become a father, which was a shock to me and I secretly wondered how I would cope with the situation. However, I was responsible and no one else and I felt strongly that I should get married and move away from the old folks and save them, especially my father, any embarrassment. Not that I would be doing it for their sake, but I was quite happy to settle down and become a reasonable citizen at last.

My eldest daughter was born in the summer of sixty-five and she was much loved and still is to this day. Settling down was no easy task as I was mixing with both married and single people who did enjoy a drink. I had suffered a redundancy and decided to take a change of career and went into a factory learning specialist grinding and did very well at it, but I missed working in different places, with different people and I gradually began to feel trapped so I handed in my notice. I took various positions all around the country wherever the work came up and earned fair money but still couldn't settle. I was offered a full-time job working up in Scotland, putting in new laboratory benches when I had helped a guy out at a local school during the holidays. He was starting as foreman joiner up there, but I declined. Whitbread's area manager offered me all the work on their bar fitting side and I did a few jobs for them, and I finally finished up working for a company fitting out new computer rooms which were becoming all the rage then. I worked all over London, Liverpool and Manchester and eventually settled in a local joinery company.

It was around this time that my second little girl was born and I settled for a time. An American knocked my door one evening and asked would I do some work for him as I came highly recommended. It turned out he was a nutcase and finished up in dire straits, but paid me a lot of money at the time. Again, I was working on medieval buildings, mostly houses, making both bay and bow windows for some of these houses. I also fitted them and finished up running what was left of the empire, and went out to measure up some windows for a large black and white cottage which had been bought by a retired ex-SAS soldier. I made all the windows for this house and also fitted them and both he and his wife asked me what I thought of some of the work done. By the look on my face they could see my answer without going any further. I said nothing, but one evening when I got home there was a letter waiting for me. On opening it, they had offered me a position working for them, and after a long chat I thought it might work, so we shook hands on it.

I was well aware that they were not ready for me to join up for a month or so as they were building up their portfolio. This gave me the chance to finish all outstanding works where I was and I thought it should benefit us all.

About two weeks before Christmas, I had a phone call from

my boss one night around nine o'clock and he was obviously pissed, but asking me to go to a large country house with him, where, unknown to me, a kitchen had been delivered and fitted by us and boy, was he unhappy with the outcome. So was I, as I didn't know a thing this devious bastard had set up. He was in no fit state to drive but demanded I meet him in my local and in the end I agreed. Appearing at least half an hour late and clearly out of his tree, I asked him if I should drive, but no, his common sense had deserted him and he drove. We finally reached the house, some eight or so miles away, miraculously unharmed, and were met by a very irate owner. My companion was burbling so, taking over I asked what the problems were and without further ado he showed me.

The offending kitchen was a very nice looking Elizabeth Anne in bottle green and cream. Strange how something can be visually wrecked by poor fitting and this one certainly had been. After a long look at it and the spares that were left over, I agreed to refit it on the proviso that I had a mate with me who had joined the company to help me. The owner said there were some other small jobs to be done as well, and after a lot of haggling it was agreed, and I guaranteed that it would be finished within a week.

The following Friday was the night of our gang's party at a pub in Ludlow and I had one last piece of laminate to glue and fit and asked my mate if I gave him a hand to rear the double extension ladder, would he hack out the broken pane in the top sash window of the bedroom. He said he could do it on his own and I could finish the kitchen. I was just finishing the last edge when I heard a terrific crash and thought he must have killed himself. Running round the corner, I looked up at a huge, gaping hole. The ladder had struck and gone through both huge sashes, completely smashing them to bits. I shouted Dave, who suddenly appeared at the opening and we both effed and blinded until we were breathless. Going upstairs, the room was a total shambles with wood and glass everywhere. I was absolutely speechless; the weekend before Christmas and he had wrecked the master bedroom completely.

I sent my mate down to the local builders' merchant where we had an account, for some batten and sheets of hardboard, found a vacuum cleaner and while he was gone, cleaned and hoovered the bedroom of glass and wood splinters. Dave arrived back and we weatherproofed the opening, double checked the room was clean and I wrote a note explaining what had happened and we locked up the house with my promise to ring him later. We went to the party that night and had a brilliant time. I rang the owner of the property on Saturday morning and was dreading it. However, he said accidents happen and as long as it was fixed after the holidays it was fine. He also said his wife was overjoyed with the kitchen, so that was it.

While everybody else was getting pissed and enjoying their break, I was the one making two sash windows.

CHAPTER SIXTY-ONE
Five Hundred Miles
(The Pretenders)

It was the middle of January and I gave my notice in and joined the opposition. While there I did some very good work for the owners and at this time, four of us old friends went over Hereford way to where our previous landlord had a pub. He really was the salt of the earth and everyone who knew him got on with him, but he was a shit for a good laugh and a legend in his own right.

We had only been there about an hour when I visited the Gents and coming back out, I could hear singing and here were my mates giving The Northern Lights of Old Aberdeen full throttle. I thought to myself, bugger my old boots, we've only had three pints. But then fate took a hand in the shape of a twenty-stone lorry driver.

'You buggers will never see the skies over Aberdeen,' he sneered.

Quick as a flash, I was on to him. 'Well, that's easily solved, old mate,' I said. 'Just put your money where your mouth is.' I was watching for a right hand to come looping over.

'I'll have a tenner on it,' he said, looking at me.

The landlord was shouting, 'I will hold all the bets!' and everybody in the pub wanted to have a bet.

The following morning, I walked in our local and told of the happenings of the previous night.

Instantly, a chap stood up and said, 'I'll have fifteen quid on John o' Groats.'

Our landlord said he would hold the bets at our end and it

started piling up. I thought, Jesus H Christ, if we back out of this now, I'll have to leave the country.

On the Monday morning my mate who was out of work drove out to a country garage and asked if we could hire a car for four of us to go to a wedding at Gretna. After a lot of argy-bargy he agreed to it for twenty-five quid and we had a Riley Kestrel for our trouble and it had to be back on the forecourt by Sunday night. On Friday at approximately six-thirty pm, we left the village with a huge load of cheese rolls, flasks of tea, an old map and a tank full of petrol in our old mini with wings, bound for the end of Britain, but in those far off days it might as well have been the end of the world. Travelling through the night, we reached Carlisle and the last services where, after emptying out, we topped up with tea and headed for Gretna. I must have fallen asleep for a loud cheer woke me up in time to see the Blacksmith's Shop and on again until we crossed the border. Heading for the Tay Bridge, we stopped and wearily asked a couple if we were on the right road. Pissed out of their brains, we might as well have asked for the nearest chip shop. They had a bottle of Red Biddy each and were swigging and swinging and we buggered off before they launched one through the windscreen. Carrying on, we saw a sign for Montrose and stupid prats as we were, decided to have a look round it. At about three o'clock we saw the sign for Carnoustie. Somebody suggested stopping for a piss but cool head said just get the hell out of here. More by luck than judgement, we saw a sign for Stonehaven and away we roared. We passed through Stonehaven at about four am, as dawn was breaking. It looked truly beautiful and on and on we went, to Aberdeen.

Here we were at the Granite City at five thirty on a dull morning, taking our first view of the buildings that made up that majestic city. Red-eyed and dry with thirst, we drove around looking for a café where we could relieve ourselves and have a brew. We finally found a little café with about ten trucks parked outside so we knew we were safe and sat there soaking up the atmosphere, drinking hot sweet tea and listening to the conversations flowing around us, but not understanding a word. Lighting up a ciggy I thought, I'm going to get my head down for a while in the back and we changed over drivers with our number two saying he knew the area and we had to cut across to Inverness, Capital of the Highlands. Far too tired to argue, I clambered into the back, but first remembering to find a phone box and make a return charge call to our local and to the New Inn where we had our other bets before we left the city. With all this accomplished I was soon in the land of nod. I must have been extremely tired as I woke up in a daze, wondering where the hell I was and what this continuous bumping and swaying was all about.

Looking out of the car window, I could see a chairlift in the distance and realised we were up in the mountains. I asked our driver, who said we were on the way to Inverness and up in the Cairngorms, obviously near a ski run, judging by the lifts I could see. Our navigator was now in a dozing state so we stopped and I took over while he settled down to sleep. That was some road in the early seventies and Colin, who was driving, was doing a marvellous job. Biting into a cheese roll from the depths of my bag, I realised the remainder were getting stale, but beggars can't be choosers and as a lover of scenery, this took some beating, I can tell you. Mile after mile of peaks and valleys with snow still on the tops and I was chuffed just to be there. On and on, mile after mile we went, until we found ourselves on a kind of main road and saw the sign which read Inverness, Capital of the Highlands, and my breath surged in my chest for I had read about these places but never seen them. Skirting the main area we picked up the coast road and this was beyond belief.

If my memory serves me correctly, we travelled one hundred and forty miles to John o'Groats, following a road of sharp bends with the sea to our right and various islands and lochs. Looking up, I saw in the distance what I thought was a company of men all looking out to sea. As we approached, we could see that it was a graveyard or cemetery with the cylindrical stones all facing the sea. To us, it was very eerie and we passed more of them on our journey until the hills or mountain flattened out and we felt as if we were on top of a plateau. After a couple of miles we saw the sign, John o'Groats. The only features we could see were the hotel and the post office, so we all had our photos taken under the sign.

We entered the hotel and had a hot drink and a sandwich with a great feeling of a job well done. Two reverse charge calls to two licensed premises in England confirmed our arrival and the bet was won, but how long it would take us to get home and how far or which way was anybody's guess. We walked around the side of the hotel and all threw a stone in the sea which I thought the locals, if there were any, would think was some Sassenach ritual. As we walked back to the car, I heard the throb of a powerful engine and thinking it must be a plane, scoured the skies for it. However, it got louder and we could see in the distance a big car coming along at speed. With a roar, it pulled to a halt outside the post office and I couldn't believe my eyes, for the driver was about twelve years old and wearing a full Stetson. Ignoring us, he disappeared into the post office and came out with a large bundle of daily papers, reversed round and roared off at maximum throttle. One of our company, made a remark about the police and I said I would imagine they were virtually non-existent up here and would come when needed in a Chopper.

We checked our watches and it was two-fifteen as we retraced our steps back along the eerie road. Although we had travelled along it, the scenery was totally different on our return, with two very large lochs as we rounded a bend; they were behind us on the upward journey so we would not have seen them. I thought the one was a sea loch it was so vast. Finally, we made it back down into Inverness and saw a sign for Glasgow. As it was my turn to navigate, we followed the loch all the way down to its end and saw many Nessie viewing platforms and various countries' search centres. I could have been romancing but I thought I saw the Japanese one. At around this time there were a lot of sightings and fresh interest in the loch and its famous occupant. Derek was driving and we were motoring along this road when I suddenly saw a sign for Oban and shouted, 'This way!' and off we roared. We were now following a mountainous road and the sun was slowly dying on us, when I saw another sign: Glencoe seven miles. Derek called me everything he could lay his tongue to which amused me, especially irresponsible bastard, for a detour right down the Western Highlands. The sun was setting as we entered

Glencoe from the Loch Leven end crossing at Ballachulish and I have never seen anything like it in my life. That mystical height of those mountain peaks, the vastness of the glen; the whole scene held a feeling of foreboding and mystery. Above us but on the lower crags, the huge Red Deer stags looked down in distain and circling high above, the first Golden Eagle I have ever seen in the wild. Tearing myself away from it and climbing back into the car, I was trembling with the rawness of the natural world I had seen, and vowed to come back in the summer. We drove off down the glen very slowly, past the Great Herdsman and away from those mountains, bound for Glasgow which, a sign told us, was some seventy miles away. It was now getting towards dark and with hardly any trouble, we finally reached the outskirts of Glasgow at about ten o'clock.

Well a good few things had happened of late but nothing compared with our arrival in Glasgow that Saturday night. We did our trip around part of the Gorbals and it was something else. After reading No Mean City I could have imagined anything around there. We then drove past Bishopston Cross and Colin was driving and I was watching for the drunks. We were in a dangerous situation; unknown to us, Rangers had played Celtic that afternoon and whoever had won, everybody was pissed. They seemed to be drinking a type of red wine out of bottles and when finished, threw them onto the road. I found out later it was the dreaded red biddy. They were staggering all over the road and I thought if we so much as tapped one, they would turn the car over. The place of their desire was a huge dance hall with neon signs flashing and I thought, who the hell would be a bouncer in that place? But we had cracked it and were through the worst and heading for Carlisle, so the sign said.

We pulled into a service station on the outskirts and had a welcome drink and a sausage sandwich and heading back to the car, Colin, who knew about such things, said the subframe was going and so we got off the main drag and headed down the old road for home. I walked into the house at six forty-five that Sunday morning and went straight to bed, waking up at eleven, had a cooked breakfast and headed for the pub at eleven forty-five to face all the doubters. The poor old Riley Elf was left on the forecourt of the garage with the milometer reading 1483 miles, and to my knowledge was never seen again.

Back to my local, I was the hero of the hour and probably drove everyone nuts with our tales of derring do. As the rest of our tour party were still in bed it fell to me to regale them with stories. The landlady told me we were all expected in that night for a steak supper and believe me, it was the best. Our old landlord dropped in and left our winnings, plus a round of drinks for us and that was the end of it all.

I was asked by the lads to plan another, but everything seemed a bit tame after Scotland. However, one of our travelling company approached me the next weekend and after telling me he had the wanderlust, said that he was planning a trip around the world. I didn't take a lot of notice at the time but fair play, come the autumn he was away. Sad to say, it nearly killed him and although I have seen him a couple of times, he never came back to the village, which was a great shame as he was a great lad who could always be relied upon.

CHAPTER SIXTY-TWO
Keep Searchin' (We'll Follow the Sun)
(Del Shannon)

'So that's the story so far,' I said to Chris. It was a lovely day and we were sitting high up on the ridge, looking down on the village.

'What happened next?' he asked.

Replying that it was going to get interesting, I said we should go down and have a pint and I would tell him the next part of my journey. He was hard on my case about the number of cigarettes I was smoking a day and that morning we had counted them up and unfortunately arrived at the total of sixty a day. It didn't bother me in the slightest but I have to say that he was appalled. At today's prices those cigarettes would have cost me about one hundred and sixty pounds a week. What a good job I packed it in about sixteen years ago, then.

We had now moved on a piece and had an up to date caravan with all mod cons in a small field next door to the pub and I had dozens of CDs and books there and we were laughing. So after constant questioning by Chris, I started on the next phase.

Writing it down, it seems to be a catalogue of disasters. The chap I had gone to work for and his wife were very nice people and we had some good times and I did some very good work for them, especially a panelled oak bar in a medieval gallery in the city. But to quote Shakespeare in Julius Caesar, there is a tide in the affairs of men and one evening, a very old friend of mine knocked on my door and told me that the headmaster of a private school several miles away, where my friend was caretaker had some cabinetry jobs he wanted someone to look at and give him some advice, and would

I be interested. I agreed to go and meet this gentleman and we agreed the Thursday evening.

He showed me several small jobs and asked if I would be interested in doing them, and I gave him a price. This agreed, we set a date for two weeks ahead on a weekend when the school was closed for half-term. I did the jobs and both he and his wife were extremely pleased and he offered me some other jobs. Again, he was pleased with the outcome and we talked for some time. He asked me if I was interested in teaching basic skills to the classes of the day and I told him I would be and was competent to teach to O level standards, both technical and practical. We agreed to meet again the following week in term time, and both of us would think it through until then.

At our meeting I agreed to a contract which also included small maintenance work around the school and a Clerk of Works job on any works done by outside companies. The only part I was not sure of were the small maintenance jobs, which I was told would be a couple of blackboards here and there, but nothing major. Shaking hands, I agreed to commence in approximately one month.

I spent a few nights browsing through some old O level papers. I also brushed up on the various tools and the intended use of and sharpening and grinding angles and sharpening angles which, although I had a few apprentices, one has to be aware of all things, especially with youngsters. My employers of the day, although disappointed at my decision, were alright with it and we did not have my sort of work in abundance in the near future, so finishing off what I had left, I found myself with a free fortnight on my hands. I did a small job for a farmer friend of mine, but found plenty to keep me busy around the house.

My friend the caretaker dropped in and said the head would like to see me if I could slip up there and I went up one evening at close of school to see him. It is funny, but I have an inbuilt sense for trouble before it starts and sitting in the study with a cup of coffee did nothing for my hopefulness for the start of a new job.

'Now, John,' said this charming man, 'we have a slight problem with your teaching at the moment; nothing at all to worry about but I'm afraid it may take a little time to sort out.'

The door opened and his wife walked in, something I would get used to as time went on. No messing about with her, straight from the shoulder.

'You see, the trouble we have is with brother Fred, his brother being assistant head . . . over to you, Headmaster.'

I thought, good job his name wasn't Dominic, I would have thought I had joined a bloody monastery.

'The problem I have is brother Fred has been looking after the woodwork side of things while we found someone new and he appears to have heard that we are now getting a new teacher. To be honest and between these four walls, it hasn't been going too well, but we need to change over very gently. We have plenty of items for you to do throughout the school, one being a new Governors' room. We feel that would be marvellous, and we can leave things run their day in the woodwork area.'

Nice one, I thought, it's a bit late in the day now to give me this news, but I said I would give it a try and see what happened. Well, I found I was the general odd job man, that's what happened, and asked to do everything from putting handles in cleaners' brooms to wallpapering the head's children's snug. The only thing that was going well from my point of view was the Governors' room which was looking a treat. The next problem I had was that the boys were seeing me working around the school and were starting to call me 'mate'.

On the Monday morning I had just put a pane of glass in one of the dormitories and walking back down the path, bumped into a bunch of lads out of Remove. They addressed me like an old friend, saying, 'Hiya mate, how you doing?' As I turned the corner, I met the caretaker who asked how I was.

'How the hell do you think I am?' I said. 'Your mate the headmaster has stitched me up and I am on my way to see if there is anything about where I can earn some proper money and not be messed about by these degenerates who think they are better than anyone else. I'll see you later.' And away I went, heading for the local employment office.

Needless to say, there was sweet bugger all going on at the time and after a beer and sandwich, I headed for home. I got back to the house and as I went through the door my wife said that the headmaster had been down and asking for my whereabouts, that there had been a misunderstanding somewhere along the line and would I be kind enough to go up and see him tomorrow morning.

I'm afraid I cannot put down on paper how I replied, but I fetched the gun and a few cartridges and went across the fields to get everything out of my system. It was beautiful across the eighteen acres as I walked the hedgerows. I have always found that a solitary walk through the fields with a gun under your arm does wonders for your state of mind and by the time I got through the bottom gate I was at peace with myself again. I had put all my issues, all my problems in little boxes and felt I should just make a note of them for the following morning's showdown.

Next morning, straight after assembly, I was pushing the button on the study door and a green light came on immediately. We sat down and I calmly laid down my points of view, saying that our ideas were totally different and I was not prepared to continue as a handyman to anyone, pointing out that I could be doing far more constructive things for a lot more money than I was getting, concluding with the fact that the older pupils were thinking of me as an odd job man and addressing me as such. I felt that I had handled it well and the head was smiling and nodding and asked me would I go down to the town with him to meet the school's accountant. This I agreed to on the understanding that I could carry out my work as the woodwork master with immediate effect. I felt that brother Fred could get on with his other subjects, but that was not my business. Driving into town, I expected things to be awkward, but we seemed to get on fine. What I did glean from the conversation was that the caretaker and he had a long conversation in which he had said I would be earning a lot more than him, and didn't want to upset him by causing another problem. I slowly began to understand the intricacies of a small conclave of adults living and working in a small area.

Arriving at the offices I was introduced to the man who controlled everything within reason. The head laid out what he wanted and how he envisaged it working. When they included me in it for my ideas, I put up my case and they both nodded their agreement. This also made a big difference to my salary and I was given a copy of what had been agreed and given three days to sign it, or otherwise and bidding a good morning, we headed back to the car. It appeared I was to start with the first classes on Thursday. The only small annoyance was that there were two classes on a Saturday morning, but this was small potatoes and I was quite happy.

Looking at the schedule for woodwork I saw that classes started at nine-thirty am on Thursday, going through to three-thirty that afternoon and I also noticed this last double period was the class who were leaving that summer. Thursday morning found me filled with anticipation. Nine fifty-five and the door opened and the first pupils entered the woodwork shop, a little unsure of themselves and of me of course, and within minutes the whole class had arrived. Putting them at their ease I firstly introduced myself and they in turn did likewise. I then heard what they had learned so far about the subject, explained how the year would now run, what it entailed and the benefits of the skills, especially if they considered taking it for O levels. We then talked about the importance of wearing aprons for practical work and finished with a short quiz about the names of the tools available to them, their names and purposes. This instantly told me that although they were an A stream class, their knowledge was very limited. The most rewarding experience for me was that twelve months later, we were interviewed by a handicraft inspector, and the same class came through with a brilliant hour of their knowledge of the tools and their uses, I was asking the questions and was met by a sea of raised hands. At the end of my day with the inspector, he told me I was far ahead of any craft teacher he had ever come across.

The morning went on with both A and B streams and I felt good but was acutely aware there was a lot of work to achieve, especially on the practical side. Looking at some old exam papers, I was amazed at how the standard had moved upwards over the last ten years and how much work there was to do. Looking at the schedule I had been given, I saw that it was the sixth form at two-thirty; double period of practical. Two-thirty and gradually they wandered in, some carrying chairs and other things they had been working on which were supposed to be done in woodwork club. Within minutes I knew I had problems and also that they couldn't give a monkey's. After introducing myself, I asked what they were working on for O levels and they simply said that they were mending chairs and doing their own things which were club items. My response to them was to take the stuff back to their studies and we would settle down to making a mortise and tenon joint. With that, five of them said they were finishing with woodwork immediately. I'm afraid this culminated in me telling them to get out of the class and they went, carrying their work and muttering. This left about ten pupils and we had a long conversation during which they expressed an interest in staying on, learning all they could and taking the exams.

As soon as the bell rang I shot across to the head's study and the green light came on. I thought, this is the end of it, and told my story. He went quiet for a minute and then said if I had not done what I had, he would have been worried and that I had proved myself.

Back in the shop, within minutes the five trooped in and apologised and told me they wanted to make a table tennis table for the school; would I please help them? Peace reigned once more.

CHAPTER SIXTY-THREE
EVERYBODY HURTS
(R.E.M.)

That weekend was a glorious time to spend up in the hill country. Chris and I went up to a village called Colva where the old man had a parish all those years ago. It was up there that I got the blame for stealing his motorbike on a Sunday afternoon; however, I do not remember the incident. Chris was amazed at the little church and as if by magic, a donkey came trotting down between the tombstones to welcome us. There were just the two of us, the donkey and the constant calling of the birds, and I told him that just above us on a hill called Gwaun-Ceste, the river Arrow had started to flow out of a spring and flowed all the way down to Leominster. We had a can of Cola each and drove down into Kington for some fish and chips on the way back to our camp site. That night we went over to the Swan at Huntington, a lovely little pub which had been a haunt of mine on Sunday nights as it was in England and therefore opened on the Sabbath. I will remember for ever how we used to walk over the top as we called it, and planned our future and what we expected out of life. We got back to our site about twelve-thirty and I just knew Chris would want to know how I came to leave my village. Sure enough, I lit up a ciggy and the questions started.

Funnily enough, his nephew was at my school and one day he called into the woodwork shop to ask if he could do O level woodwork. So it was with some trepidation I told him he was welcome, that it was very hard work and I could not and would not put up with any disruptions from anyone who did not want to do the course.

The woodwork shop was always full of pupils and out of the blue one morning, a red-headed woman came in carrying a broken broom. No embarrassment this one, and she calmly told me that she had broken the broom and gone to the headmaster who had sent her over to me and wanted it back straight away. I laughed at this and told her to go back and tell the head that I had far more urgent things on hand than mending a broom. Off she went and I could tell from her body language that she was not a happy bunny. Apparently she was working with a friend of mine in the dormitories. She told me she would complain to the head and I told her to go right ahead.

About an hour later, in walked the headmaster and asked about the broom. I completely lost the plot with this and asked did he want the new blackboards finished and in place or should I spend an hour on the broom? With this, he laughed and said his wife was also on his back as this cleaner had been pestering her as well. After lunch I got a new handle, glued it and screwed it in and took it over to the dormitories and gave it to the lady in question. With exams to set and O levels to contend with, I was far too busy to think about it any more. There were also the many and varied displays in the woodwork shop to be prepared for the annual Speech Day, which signalled the end of term with many fifth and sixth formers leaving.

However, I was in town one Saturday and bumped smack into the broom lady, whose name, I discovered was Joan. We had a peaceful chat and she was all smiles. But I'm afraid that something stirred inside me that afternoon. Although I was busy, I always took a little time out to have a chat with Joan and we got on well together.

As well as all the displays the pupils prepared, I also made a couple of things to help it along as we had a lot of parents and governors walking through. One of these items was a Fox on the Run which I had carved from a piece of mahogany. He looked a bit special with his brush sailing out behind him and I took it over to the canteen during a break to find out what the ladies thought of it. One of the ladies commented that it was beautiful and could she buy it. Answering five pounds, I just laughed and there was no reply. On the Speech Day afternoon, however, the school doctor was walking round and offered me one hundred pounds for the piece. I explained that it was not a sale item but offered to carve one for him at a later date.

After everyone had left for home I walked across to the ladies who were washing up and said, 'Here is the carving that you wanted; give me five pounds and it's yours.'

She was suitably thrilled, Joan was pleased and so the term ended with a bang.

A few weeks later I was outside the workshop talking to the Geography master when the head appeared around the corner. On his approach, the Geography master walked back into the woodwork shop, but the head came straight up to me.

'We were very pleased with the feedback from the parents about your work with the pupils and the display that you showed everyone who wandered through,' he said.

I thanked him and he then asked, 'I suppose you would like your results from this year's O level Practical? My stomach did an immediate flip but he continued.

'You entered five pupils and the results were four of them had a Grade 3 and one of them had a Grade 2,' stressing, 'and would have had honours if he could spell his own name correctly. So that is very well done and try to keep up to this standard.'

That same morning I was in the top dormitory measuring up some broken glass when Joan and her mate walked in. In conversation, I opened my big mouth and told them it was my birthday and as I was going down the stairs, Joan ran up and said she would give me a birthday kiss. My fate was sealed from that moment and thirty-nine years later, we are living back in Herefordshire and also very happy.

However, that was just the start and a lot of traumatic events were to happen before everything was sorted out. We both had the sense to carry on as normal during school hours but spent time together in the evenings, thinking we could get away with it for ever, but were soon to have a very rude awakening.

Everything was now completed and ready for the new term and I walked up the empty driveway on the evening before they all arrived back at school. I was meeting Joan that evening and being all alone, took the time to take in the silence all around. Tomorrow the pupils would be arriving from their various abodes, including some from Iran and Saudi Arabia. Some would be happy, some in tears and the really unhappy ones would be the juniors, but they would all settle down in a few days and hopefully enjoy the camaraderie. My friend the caretaker came round that afternoon and I told him I had bumped into the head earlier and he had squeezed my shoulder and asked if I was alright, but seemed miles away. Don the caretaker said he had found him the same and said in all the time he had known him had only seen him like that once before.

Don's parting words were, 'Watch out, because one way or another, the shit is going to hit the fan before the end of the week.'

Time passed quickly and before we knew it, the yard was full of both young and older pupils. I was very busy with the new intake plus the remove who would be taking O levels before the end of the next summer term. When I got home that evening, I realised that I had left my pipe and lighter and managed with cigarettes for the evening. The following morning, I searched in my office in the woodwork shop but all to no avail. I must have looked everywhere and then I noticed the head walking trance-like across the yard. Catching him up, I asked if my pipe and tobacco had been handed in. Totally ignoring me he walked on and I asked again.

Spinning on his heel to face me, he was white with temper. He spat out the words, 'Certain rumours have reached me concerning members of my staff and have no proof, but if I find they are true and causing a danger to my school, I will take very firm action!'

'What rumours?' I asked, 'and why are you shouting at me?'

He ignored this and was looking up into the sky.

I was incensed and shouted that I did not have a clue what he was talking about, 'But listen,' I told him, 'no one . . . no one shouts at me in the playground, and if you haven't got the guts to tell me what you are talking about then you can stick your job as from today!' With that, I turned on my heel and as I walked back inside the woodwork shop I found I was shaking with temper. All of that day I waited for a phone call to come to the study but as of four o'clock, nothing; nil; zilch, so I sat down there and then and wrote my notice to take place with immediate effect and gave it to the caretaker, asking him to deliver it into the head's hand and nobody else's.

Ringing Joan later, I explained the situation to her and told her not to worry. I said that although I didn't know, it might just concern us, so it was quashed with my resignation. She was obviously worried but said she would keep in touch and also keep me informed.

I was in the pub later when the caretaker walked in to inform me that he had handed my letter personally to the head, who asked if he knew what was inside and he had answered that he did not have a clue.

Joan's fellow worker and her husband were having a new bungalow built in the grounds of the farm and she came to see me the following night to ask if I was interested in painting the rooms, laying the carpets and general alterations that she was not happy with and this kept me busy for quite some time. During this time, Joan and I were getting a lot closer and I knew that it wouldn't be long until the balloon went up.

My old friend the builder came to see me one evening and told me that he had some classic work in a big house in the Hereford area. I duly finished it and was praised for the standard of work I had completed. During this time, I noticed a job advert in the local paper for teaching woodwork. Apparently the previous holder of the position had passed away after a heart attack and they urgently needed a replacement. I rang the number in the said advert and was advised to reply to them and after a brief conversation, went off suited and booted for an interview. With my background and experience I was awarded the job and started a week later. The first thing I realised was that my pupils, or lack of them, would need watching very carefully. Coupled with this, I had to wear a white coat and was given a tour of the hospital by a senior doctor. Secondly, during this tour I was told that one female and one male ward was kept permanently locked as the inmates could be, and sometimes were very dangerous. Thirdly, that afternoon a tremendous fight broke out during the tea break, resulting in swollen eyes and bloody noses resembling a pitch battle on display. I began to wonder what I had let myself in for and marched along with my key as all the doors were self-locking.

Never one to give up, I stuck it out for six weeks, framing over one hundred pictures brought in by the local population and tidied up the workshop and stores all with one helper. The following Monday morning, I knocked on the Matron's door and explained that it was not for me. She fully understood and we had a long chat and on the Friday afternoon I said goodbye for the last time and that was that. I have to say that the staff I knew were some of the kindest, professional people that I have ever worked with. I would be pleased to work with them again anywhere, as long as it was under different circumstances.

On Saturday morning I caught the bus to town and bought some items of clothing I needed and called in the pub back home for a pint and look at the local news. I had just sat down with a pint when in walked a lad I knew from Hereford. Having worked with him previously, he brought me over another pint and asked if I had anything going on work wise. He explained that he had just taken on a contract in the Middle East and asked if I was interested. The money was excellent and we agreed that I would be part of a three-man team and would be leaving in three weeks. He also confirmed that his wife would bring housekeeping over to my wife, and considerably more than she had been receiving of late, so we shook hands and sealed the deal. The only fly in the ointment was that we were going to Iran, which came under the World Health Organisation. This meant I would have to have a smallpox vaccine and it took three weeks to erupt and could cause me a problem over there with the medical situation. I decided to chance it; of course, my travelling companions had theirs some years before.

Two weeks later it was Terminal 3 at Heathrow and we climbed aboard an Iran Air Boeing 707 and prepared ourselves for a nine-hour flight. Complete with passport and World Health confirmation document, I confess that I had a nagging doubt about all this but have to say the stewardesses looked after us brilliantly and having done my fair share of flying, the service would take some beating. Although tired as we crossed the mighty Bosphorus river, looking down I saw the country below changing. As far as I could see the country was barren and bare and I knew from previous perusal it must be the Steppes. Next, it seemed there were many miles of heavy gun emplacements as we dropped at a steady rate until the seatbelts lights came on and we landed. Not a bump, this boy, and we taxied to a halt outside the airport building. Collecting our luggage, we then cleared passport control and were met by dozens of ladies in national dress who were presenting their fellow countrymen with a flower.

There was quite a crowd waiting at the gate and I noticed a man holding up a board with my misspelt name on it. Shouting to my two friends, we walked across to these men and seconds later were introducing ourselves. Their names were Ami and Slomo and they were the two top men, it appeared. As we left the airport it was getting dusk and so humid that I could hardly breathe. Jumping into a Pecan 1725, Iran's version of the Hillman Hunter, we headed up a main boulevard into the grand courtyard of the Intercontinental Hotel which was possibly the finest hotel in the country. Explaining they had to teletext Israel and leaving us with a note for God knows how much, disappeared and we were getting Tom Collins's down us as it was the only alcohol on the menu.

Eventually our two companions returned, all smiles, and as we went outside I could see it was almost dark. Wondering how long a ride we had, I little realised that in a few minutes I was going to get a big lesson in how to get out of a car on an Iranian forecourt.

CHAPTER SIXTY-FOUR
It Takes a Worried Man
(Lonnie Donegan)

It is not in my mind to go into vast details of the months spent in the Middle East. Suffice it to say that it was the hottest summer for many years, and on returning I laughed when I saw the vast fields of ripening corn in Herefordshire. Everyone was moaning it was too hot and I thought, you should have been with me. In fairness, the main contractors were from Israel and a better bunch of people you would not have met anywhere. I had a postal friend who set up my correspondence, both sending and receiving letters from Joan, so I was up to date with everything back home. After scouring the local news, we managed to find what was advertised as the only English pub in town and were seen to head to Tehran every Friday, which was the holy day off and anyway it was much cheaper than the Intercontinental. The one thing we enjoyed was sitting out in the garden every evening, talking with the Israelis, drinking 7-Up and eating tons of pistachio nuts. We were just putting the world to rights and learning from each other of the differences between us. Needing something to occupy my time, I took charge of getting the gallons of water boiled and refrigerated for the following day. This water had to be boiled against the nasties which it contained. The water with which to make ice had to be boiled also. Mosquitoes were a serious problem and we had a machine to keep them out of our room. Working some ten hours a day, travelling through the most horrendous traffic you ever saw, took its toll. We finally saw that the end was in sight and Ami, the head man, took us to downtown Tehran to book our flight home, making sure that we had a British flight so we could have bacon and eggs for breakfast.

The following Friday, Slomo, who was our big mate, told us he would drive us to the Caspian Sea through the mountain passes. He was true to his word and we left early in the morning, travelling right over the Alborz mountains through tunnels, which were hewn from solid rock; one we were told was seven miles long, with no lighting whatsoever. The air in the tunnels was shocking and we could not have the windows open. Finally, we came out into the daylight and a different world. A land of villas, swimming pools, tropical fruit trees and date palms, while in the distance could be seen the Caspian Sea. This was a vast inland sea, being the biggest fresh water lake in the world, the home of the famous Caviar Sturgeon. After our journey through arid desert-like areas and barren mountains, this was surely heaven. Parking on a quiet street, we had a walk to stretch our legs and looked round the shops. Further down, we came to a café with the most expensive cars and motor bikes imaginable. Looking around, we could see that they were all super bikes, notably Suzukis and Hondas. Wandering down to the shore, the weather was very hot and windy and guess who burned?

After a few hours, we headed back to the car for the journey home and Slomo took a different route through the mountains where there was deep snow on the tops. We stopped in a grand, impressive ski lodge hotel which had a helicopter pad and we were told it was the then Shah's winter sports lodge. Then it was downhill all the way to our villa. Slomo must have been extremely tired and we couldn't thank him enough. Saturday, being our last day, we did not kill ourselves and that night we all went to a farewell supper at the Chattanooga restaurant, which was well known to the Israelis.

These people who had looked after us so well, who were marvellous company and who we sat at the table with on that last night, were the best. Looking at the huge menu I saw ham and black olives as a starter and really fancied it, but remembered that our compatriots could not eat pork. Declining to order first, I was amazed that they all ordered the ham and black olives. I looked at them and Ami was laughing and explained that the food was completely safe in a modern restaurant but it had been made law not to be eaten in the heat of Israel as it went bad very quickly and caused many thousands of lives to be lost in the days before refrigeration. Yet another lesson learned, we enjoyed a wonderful evening with our hosts. Back at the villa, we shook hands with them all with promises to keep in touch and Slomo, who was driving us to the airport the following morning, agreed the time to leave and it was goodnight.

The following morning around six o'clock as the sun climbed in the sky, we tiptoed out of the villa for the last time and were away to the airport. Saying goodbye to Slomo was the hardest thing, but despite all our worries we boarded on time and took a last look at the surroundings from the window of the plane. I was then privileged to see one of the greatest sights of my life as we taxied out, for the pilot said we had to wait for a German 747 Jumbo to land and all in the starboard seats would see an amazing sight. Sitting there, the sky suddenly went dark and this huge plane landed in front of me with some flame and smoke as it hit the runway. Even in our plane, the noise was amazing and it was indeed a sight I will never forget as its vast bulk roared down the runway and we were cleared for take-off, climbing steadily over the vast mountain ranges and onwards, crossing the Bosphorus, over Turkey and London bound.

CHAPTER SIXTY-FIVE
Sunday Morning Coming Down
(Kris Kristofferson)

Rocketing up the runway of Heathrow airport some ten hours later, I realised I was completely knackered. We had breakfasted on bacon and eggs, heard the English number one of the moment, which I am sorry to say was, I've Got a Brand New Combine Harvester. We had been informed of the very hot weather in England, with no rain . . . there was a laugh; they should have been where I was to experience hot days, I thought. Clutching my samovar, which was filled with ciggies and my cases which were also filled with the same, I headed towards the green gate and passport control. Proceeding on with nary a question, we hit the exit gate and Tony was immediately covered in a huge embrace by his wife who, with her friend, had driven up to collect us.

Once outside, I was aware that although quite hot, it bore no resemblance to our recent weather and after loading up the car we were away up the motorway, heading for my village which was the first drop. Looking out of the window at the countryside, I was amazed how green it all was; totally different to our recent scrub deserts. I must have dozed off for the next thing I was aware of was Kevin shaking my arm and saying I was almost home. I rubbed my eyes and found we were coming down the bank into the village. Turning right, I got out of the car as it stopped, hauled my cases out of the back, said goodbye to the lads and I was away up a strange garden path. Everything looked different; somehow dull and overgrown and I opened the back door to find no one at home. No change there then, I thought, and suddenly the door burst open and my youngest threw herself at me, telling me that Mum was working over at the shop.

I left everything on the floor. 'Come on,' I said, and we walked down by the school, through the gate and into the fields. This was just what I needed . . . some space and with my little one jabbering in my ear, I sat there looking across to Bircher, still amazed how green it all was. This was the product of the hottest summer for years, but it all seemed perfect to me after the sun-scorched land and oppressive heat I had just left behind. Slowly we walked back towards home, where I learned from my garrulous youngster just what had happened during my absence and found it all quite humdrum.

I unpacked my case and put all the dirty washing in the scullery and hung the rest of my clothes away. Looking into the mirror, I realised I had lost a couple of stones, which I knew would do me more good than harm. Hearing the back door open I next had the dulcet tones of my wife for an hour before tea as she moaned and told me what a terrible time they had all had during my absence and how everything had to change from now on. This barrage was seemingly never going to end and I began to wonder if I had done the right thing in coming home at all. After tea, I had a wash and change of clothes and was off up the road to the local to meet all my mates and enjoy a few pints of good old English beer.

I was very grateful to the Israelis for keeping us out of the sun but was also very grateful for the morning by the Caspian Sea on which I had managed to get a deep wind burn so, although it wouldn't last very long, it showed I had been in hotter climes for the last few months and shut the wits up. What a night! The beer was wonderful, the conversation great and I was dead beat by the time I climbed the wooden hill to Bedfordshire.

The next morning I was going into Hereford with a mate to get a couple of pairs of jeans and sweaters, as I was feeling the difference in temperature and was also very tired and listless. We called in the local on the way back and I had a long conversation with my lady and was glad that nothing had changed. I also had a chat with my builder mate who had a few jobs waiting and so it was back to work on the Tuesday and with my lady coming to pick me up everything, as they say, in the garden was wonderful. However, the storm clouds were gathering at a great rate of knots and life was going to change in a very short space of time. Strangely enough, the work was piling up and from that point of view it couldn't have been better, but things back at the ranch were not good and I was aware that it couldn't go on for ever.

That Sunday I was playing cricket again and thought I could just run up and shout, 'Howzat?' and they would be walking. Bearing in mind that I had not turned my arm over for weeks, I had a dreadful shock when I opened the bowling at a batsman who looked familiar, but who promptly carted me all over the ground in the first over. Suddenly realising who he was, I took stock and steadied down in my next over. With a beautiful Yorker it was bye bye and as he walked past me he said I only needed one straight one, and I recognised him as a good bat with a good reputation. I found out later that it had been the hottest day of the year and I had enjoyed the game and the drinks in the club and felt I had got my own rhythm back again. My last thoughts as I closed my eyes were that this little island of ours was not such a bad place after all. Little did I know that behind the scenes all hell would soon break loose. But for now I kept quiet, knowing that my mother was coming to stay for a while, and thought how I could avoid it as I knew relationships were teetering on a knife edge.

I had some work to finish in Richard's Castle and Monday morning found me catching the bus up to my friend's new bungalow. They asked me could I fit the carpets and various other things that needed doing and I thought it was going to be at least another two or three weeks to finish it properly. Needless to say, Joan brought her mate back every afternoon and the world was back on the track.

From conversations I had with my mum, I understood that everything wasn't right at home and I was also aware that I was being talked about as soon as I left the house. Another worry I had was that my mother's sister was rapidly going downhill back in the Cross, and was becoming too much for the sisters to cope with. This was a shocking end for a lovely old lady who, having lost her husband some months previously, kept wandering off at all hours and was in a very bad place with dementia.

Hey ho, it was good to be back, but I knew it was all coming to a very hasty end. I had some long conversations with my mother and told her not to worry as I was not as far away as she imagined and knowing the situation with my wife, explained that I would sort it and also I would come down to Croesyceiliog and sort out the mess down there. This seemed to mollify the situation and I hoped that peace would reign again for a short while. However, the best laid plans of mice and men and all that jazz certainly fell upon my ears on the following Sunday, with my mother and my wife having a terrible bust up. I knew she was going back home on the following Friday, so having had a gutful of everything I packed up my belongings and my mate came to pick me up that morning and I found myself on the Intercity from Ludlow heading for South Wales.

CHAPTER SIXTY-SIX
The Gates of Eden
(Bob Dylan)

Arriving at Pontypool Road station and smelling the air conjured up all those childhood memories. Struggling through the underpass and up the hill onto the main road, I wished I could have brought less. My suitcases contained everything I owned in the world at the time, but I was to look back a few months later with bitter regret that I did not bring more of my personal stuff.

On reaching the main road and the bus stop, I took in the scene before me up the valley. Immediately I saw Pilkington's big chimney belching out smoke, and many of the works leading up the valley towards Pontypool and beyond. As I stood there breathing in that air I felt at home, but realised it could never be the same and once more I wondered if the first bus down would be a Jones's or a Western Welsh. Jones's, I was told many years ago would be the cheapest.

Sure enough, I spotted the bus behind a stream of traffic and sure enough, it was a Jones's, as with a hiss of air brakes it glided in, the automatic door swung open and I and my two large suitcases clambered aboard.

The conductor was on to me like a flash.

'Croesyceiliog, the Highway,' I muttered and paid her and we were speeding through New Inn and heading for Crossy by the time I had pocketed my ticket and sat down. Studying the many other passengers, for the bus was almost full, I saw the same complete disinterest on the same type of faces. Not the interest of country people looking over the stock in the fields and who was ploughing, haymaking or harvesting, depending on the season. This was the dividing line between town and country; smart appearance smart dress and a love of walking down endless malls looking in shop windows. However, my reverie came to a quick end as we sailed down past the Upper Cock pub and with another hiss of the brakes, the bus came to a stop outside my auntie's house on the Highway.

Struggling up the front path, I ignored the gully and knocked on the front door, which was opened about an inch by my mother and then swung wide to give me a big hug. Entering the front hall I was met by my Auntie Gertie, but Uncle Bill, who had suffered a bad stroke, couldn't get out of his chair.

Instantly I found myself answering a lot of questions as to my visit while being given a cup of hot tea, plus a cigarette from my uncle. I tried as best as I could to answer the questions being fired at me from all sides. It was obvious that Mum had told all at great length to them when she returned yesterday and so I was not public enemy number one, but welcomed with open arms and told I could stay for as long as I wanted or needed.

Feeling the need for a nap and with the start of a heavy cold coming on, I must have looked worn out and my auntie said, 'Go and have a lay down, John, for you look totally tired and a sleep will do you the world of good.'

So next thing I was trotting up the stairs I had been carried up as a baby and I blissfully pulled the bedclothes over me and I was gone. No ducks quacking at the bottom of next door's garden; just the monotonous, steady roar of early morning commuters going to their daily workplace.

I opened my eyes the following morning wondering for a fleeting instant where the hell I was. I had left the curtains open and had a quick look through the bedroom window. Although it was many a long year since I had scrambled up into the old willow tree, I could see that it was still there, although looking a little ancient now. I gazed intently at a sight that had been my whole world back in those childhood days, now all changed with different people next door and no one to keep our garden tidy any more. Lighting up a ciggy, I contemplated my future and my past and blowing a plume of smoke, wondered where the road was going to lead me. Joan was coming down the following week and we would be long gone to wherever and whatever the future.

There is something special about going down stairs that you have been going up and down since you were a babe in arms and as I opened the door into the front room, I could hear the same sounds from the grandfather clock ticking and smell the same wax polish and the aroma of breakfast cooking. Both the ladies were scurrying about and laying the breakfast table and I was given a fresh cup of tea and asked if I had slept well. My uncle would not get up for a while, I was told, and I sat down to a lovely breakfast. Finishing off, I lit up a ciggy and gazed out of the window onto a scene of cars, vans, lorries and an occasional bus heading up and down the Highway as some medieval councillor had christened it. The pavements were a mass of people, including school children, all busily going about their daily business. Looking over their heads across the valley, I could see the chimneys of the various works and far above them the mountain, with its mighty tump of Twm Barlwm looking out over everything below. This, I thought, was the only thing that never changed in the faraway scenery.

Somewhat at a loss, I wondered just what was going on in Herefordshire and thought there would be 'Wanted' posters all over the place. Mother asked me if I had anything planned for the morning and I replied I thought I might take a walk around the Cross and probably have a look around the town centre. Breakfast over, I helped clear away the dishes and thought it would be a good time to go and have a look around the Cross and see what else had gone on, with the building of the new town still not finished. Also, I realised that my uncle needed time to get up, wash and have his breakfast and knowing he was a very private man, he would like his own privacy and after all, it was his house. So, wishing them a cheery farewell, I set off on my tour of the village where I was born, spent some time in the school, sang in the choir and probably often made a huge nuisance of myself over the years.

CHAPTER SIXTY-SEVEN
All By Myself
(Fats Domino)

Yes, reader . . .I know we have been here before, but I would say that time and tide wait for no man; also the changes that had taken place astonished me and I realised then that I could never live in this place for any length of time again. Well, here I was on a Saturday morning, heading into the great unknown and not knowing what tomorrow would bring, but one thing was certain – the shit was going to hit the fan big time before too long.

Lighting up a ciggy, I exited Auntie's gate and headed down to Turnpike to see if there was any sign of life at my other auntie's house, but all to no avail. I retraced my steps and cut off down Woodland Road or the Black Road as it used to be called on account of it being surfaced with cinders long ago. I passed the huge school entrance which was built in the fields behind my auntie's house. It must have catered for a lot of pupils, close on a thousand, I thought to myself, but again what did I know? And a thousand is a lot of people.

I was now heading for the grocer's shop where I had been snubbed a few years back, and wondered idly was she married? Probably, and with a few kids as well, I thought to myself. Crossing the road, I passed it with hardly a glance and headed for the new town of Cwmbran.

Climbing up the steps from the car park, I was amazed to see the mahogany handrails were still in place and although seeming to have every Cwmbran resident's initials carved deeply into them, they were still looking smart. Leaving at the top of the steps by Boots the chemist, I turned right into the square and stood looking at the plethora of big names that had opened for business since I was last here. To the left, the pavements led to a huge building with the name Woolco across its entrance. I thought this must be the store recently opened, which was the main topic of conversation, and had a wander round before hitting the street. Shops and retail held nothing for me but I thought Joan would love it all.

I was feeling a bit thirsty so I bought a newspaper and headed for the Moonraker, which was still there, with no name changes; so much for progress. With a foaming pint of bitter, I settled down on a bench to read what was going on in the eastern valleys. Lighting a cigarette, I scanned the pages for something of interest but on drawing a blank, finished my pint and headed for the door.

On leaving the town, I thought I would take a turn around old Pontnewydd, a small village with some mining history, now long gone for ever. When passing Tynewydd Road, I remembered the times when, just a squirt, I used to visit my relations with my mother and auntie. Now, many years later, I mused the occupants were all dead and no one was left to know of their passing.

I took a leisurely stroll up the hill and there it was: the White Rose Cinema obviously closed for some time, but with the tattered banners of the last pictures shown. My thoughts took me straight back to Doris Day singing The Deadwood Stage, the illicit ciggies and the furtive glances at some teenage girl that didn't want to know . . . all long gone and never to return. Somewhat crestfallen at my view on all things past, I wandered down the hill, past Jones the corner shop, where my other auntie shopped, also long gone, and turned up the hill up to St May's church, which long ago was the start of it all and on those polished pews had sat my grandparents, uncles and aunts, cousins and people I knew and people I would never know, whose lives had been lived and now lay 'neath the hallowed turf of Llanfrechfa, which was the parish church.

'Come on, old mate,' I muttered to myself, 'pull yourself out of this. Joan is coming on Monday and it is the start of a new life for us both.' I idly wondered what they would think of me now?

Would they smile or frown at my antics? Lighting up another ciggy, I then quickly doused it and realised that I was not feeling too good, and was sure I had the signs of bronchitis coming on. I thought, you can't go sick, John, and take it back into the house full of elderly people . . . besides, Joan was coming on Monday. After coughing my way up the Garw, I turned right into North Road and instead of heading straight across to the Highway, turned left up to old Florence Place. My mother had never taken me there as I remember, but it was hard to conjure up the stories she had told me how, as a young girl, she grew up here with her sisters and brother and also a very ancient grandmother.

I must have stood there contemplating the stories that my mother had told me by the flickering flames of the firelight in the front room of the Parsonage and the Rectory and last of all, by the fireside of the vicarage at Dilwyn; tales of Christmases of long ago, before I was born, and I felt strangely sad.

Pulling myself away from these memories, I headed back into North Road across the Highway and in through Auntie's front gate, up the gully passage and into the warmth of the front room, where a smiling uncle offered me a cigarette as a cup of hot tea was thrust into my hand. When these were finished, I fell asleep in the easy chair and awoke some time later to a fit of coughing. Refusing food, I decided the best thing for me was an early night and as I pulled the covers over my head I fell into a deep, deep sleep.

CHAPTER SIXTY-EIGHT
All I Have to Do Is Dream
(The Everly Brothers)

I must have tossed and turned all through the night. The bedclothes were soaked in sweat and I looked at the bedside clock which said it was nine o'clock so I checked my watch, which agreed. There was a knock on the door and in came my mum with a cup of tea and a plate of biscuits. I lay there and assessed my health, or lack of it, and I must confess I did not feel any great shakes. I drank my tea which I couldn't taste but which soothed my chest, gave the biscuits to the birds outside my bedroom window and contemplated my day. Sunday. I've never liked Sundays. When starting out on life's big adventure, I acted as I had seen my parents, with sombre mood and nothing to laugh about as Sunday was hallowed. Now grown up, I spent my Sunday mornings in the local and my afternoons on the cricket pitch, if it was summer. If not, it was spent on the golf course, but now I hadn't a clue what I would do with myself.

After a good wash and a change of clothes, I felt somewhat better and refusing bacon, I managed some fried egg on toast, washed down with several cups of tea and then walked down the garden to have a smoke. Standing under the willow tree I remembered those far off days when I used to climb up into the branches and sit for hours, whittling various bits of wood and contemplating my future. Now I noticed if it was twenty-five feet high to the very top, it paled into insignificance against the massive oaks and beech in the Pamber Forest.

Wondering idly what my mates were doing down in

Hampshire, I finished my ciggy and wandered back up to the house. Never mind, Joan is coming tomorrow morning; I could think of nothing else and without a doubt, she would never let me down.

I decided to go down the Highway past the Turnpike and take a look at the new South Wales police centre and get some fresh air in my lungs as I had a wracking cough. Against all warnings, I set off and told them I would be back for lunch but not to wait for me. Passing the row of houses at the Turnpike where my other auntie and uncle lived, I regressed to happier times when I used to play in the garden. Sadly, their only child had died at a young age and left behind a husband and two young boys. They never got over this and my uncle had died about nine months ago and my auntie was badly afflicted with Alzheimer's and could not recognise anyone. She was in the hospital in Caerleon and was in a very bad way. I stood and just looked at the house, remembering those days. Past the houses, I came to the little copse where an old thatched cottage used to stand. Now, nothing stood above a foot above the ground.

I remembered they used to keep chickens and sold eggs and I used to go there on a Saturday morning with my uncle for some eggs. They always made us welcome and if I remember rightly, their name was Owens. No chickens here now, I thought, only desolation. Somewhat nonplussed, I walked on for a few hundred yards and there it stood in glorious splendour . . . a huge brick and glass building surrounded by police cars. Again, memories of collecting mushrooms and nuts during the autumn flashed through my head. Ah well, it cannot ever come back now, I thought and taking a long look, walked away with a heavy heart. But strangely, in years to come, I drove past it many, many times and didn't give it a thought.

I passed the police headquarters and crossed the roundabout, carrying on until I reached a turning with a sign saying Edlogan Way. Following this, I eventually came to some recreation grounds with seats at regular intervals. Walking along past the seats I heard the rush of running water and there it was, still flowing, the dear old Afon Llwyd or the grey river in English.

No longer the sluggish brown water smelling of countless spoil dumped from the works up the valley, but a frothing white river as it cascaded over the boulders, chuckling and bubbling along as if happy to have been released from numerous years of industrial waste. I sat on a bench and lit up a ciggy. Wonder of wonders, I espied a fisherman with rod and line, casting into a pool. This meant only one thing: that there were fish living in the river and that meant there were other forms of life in order for the fish to survive.

I was happy as could be and thought there were some good things to come out of the new town. Dousing my cigarette, I walked along to the newsagent on the North Road and bought a Sunday paper. I then proceeded onto the Highway and walked up the hill to the Upper Cock inn and with a pint of bitter, settled down to read the news. I must confess that the sight of the Afon Llwyd, turned from a works dumping ground into a clean and healthy river just as it must have appeared to my forebears long centuries ago, had cheered me up considerably. Feeling somewhat better in health, I drained the last dregs of my bitter, folded my paper, wished everyone good day and I was heading once more down the Highway and home for lunch.

Sitting down at my auntie's table to have lunch was a step back in time for me. As a youngster in the final war years it was spam and mashed potatoes and with the elders always having salad, there was always tinned fruit and ideal milk to follow as I sat there, pretending not to listen to their conversations, but believe me, I didn't miss a thing. Not today, however, for the war had long ended and it was roast potatoes, roast beef and Yorkshire puddings. After lunch it was a stagger across to an easy chair, fall asleep and then back to reality as I had to repack my case . . . for Joan was coming in the morning.

CHAPTER SIXTY-NINE
Travellin' Light
(Cliff Richard)

I was awakened the next morning, although it was the first week in October, by the birds in my auntie's laburnum tree carolling fit to burst. It took me a few seconds to familiarise myself with my surroundings and only half a second to realise that my chest was wheezing like bagpipes and I was due for a bout of bronchitis or at the least, a heavy chest cold. Opening the bedroom window, I lit up a cigarette and coughed my way through it, washing it down with a cup of scalding hot tea which had mysteriously appeared on the bedroom cabinet. Suddenly, I realised that it was Monday. Today was the first day of the rest of my life and Joan would be arriving in a few hours.

Coming out of the bathroom, freshly shaved, scrubbed and polished with enough aftershave on me to poison all the wildlife in Gwent, I put on my best shirt and sweater, trousers with knife-edge creases in them and coughed my way to the breakfast table. Mother looked me up and down and smiled as only mothers can, but I knew she was proud of me and I also knew she was worried to death about the coming storm from Herefordshire. It appeared that the two great friends of my uncle and auntie had called round to see them and I was to find out far later, had their say over the matter. However this did not come to light until after my uncle's and auntie's funerals and as the lady in question had also lost her husband, it was too late in the day to say anything. But in a sense I was glad as I knew I would have told them to keep their own counsel and not interfere. Anyway, least said, soonest mended and I'll leave it at that.

Strange, isn't it, how two people can sit in a room where something monumental is about to happen and the subject is not spoken of, hinted at or mentioned in a roundabout way? It has happened before and without doubt will happen sometime again, but hopefully not in the same context. Auntie Gertie had not come downstairs this Monday morning and was giving my uncle his morning wash and dress for the day ahead. I dived into the bathroom and cleaned my teeth, then upstairs, opening my case and checking its contents for the umpteenth time and away downstairs once more.

Asking why my auntie had not put in an appearance, I was told that she thought it was more diplomatic to stay upstairs until we had left as she felt we had a lot to talk about. This suited me as I knew Joan would be on a knife edge and also I was sure that my mother had a lot of questions to ask and many tales to tell . . . if allowed, the whole history of our family going back to William the Conqueror's days, so I knew I would have to handle the meeting with great care.

At last my constant glances through the front room window were rewarded as I saw the green Morris Traveller come to a halt outside the front gate. Funny how life sets its own rich patterns, and I must confess that when I saw her coming up the path I knew for a certainty that this was the one for me and I hoped it would be forever. Did she look the business? I was so proud of her and have been ever since.

After a long kiss I opened the door and there stood my mother with a cup of tea in one hand and a pile of photographs in the other.

'Come in, child,' she said and gave her a kiss.

Joan sat down on the sofa, trying to answer the torrent of questions, drink her tea and look at the decades of photographs which my mother had accumulated. It was time to rescue her and put an end to the questions so I broke it off by commenting that we had a very long ride ahead of us and we would have to go, but would be in touch as soon as we reached journey's end.

So, after kisses and hugs and with my suitcase in the back, we set sail with my mother waving until finally she was a little speck in the distance. I would also explain here that I had briefed my mother that on no account was she to tell anyone that she had seen us. It was somehow strange as we drove back through the county of Herefordshire, picked up the M5 and then the M6 and we were soon heading for Lincolnshire and a little village called Wragby, where I had booked a hotel. Now I would be back on familiar ground as I had stayed in Bardney and Horncastle many years ago with work.

We stopped several times for a break and a cup of tea on the way. Joan was a perfect driver and companion and we were comfortable in telling each other the things that had happened to us along life's busy way. It seemed as if we had known each other for a lifetime. She told me about her life in service when she left school, working as both a nanny and household help and I explained my past life as a vicar's son and my achievements, or lack of them, so it was an extremely informative journey out into the wilds of Lincolnshire.

Joan had already noticed that I wasn't very well but I tried hard not to be a damp squib on the long journey. At last we were entering the city of Lincoln with its beautiful and imposing cathedral and I knew where we were and directed Joan onto the road for Wragby. Seven miles to go, out into the countryside until we saw the village sign and there it stood, a large, imposing red brick, three-storey building. We pulled into the car park and took our luggage into the hotel where I signed the register. The lady behind reception took the room number which was already booked and we both struggled up the stairs with our suitcases. As we reached the top of the first flight I saw our room number and said, 'Thank you, Lord,' because I did not think I could walk much further.

After a night spent coughing and spluttering and being cared for by Joan, we awoke to a most beautiful morning and after a hasty breakfast, set off to explore Lincolnshire. Having worked around the area some time ago I was keen to show Joan the places I had been to and the surrounding villages. We were amazed by the fen country and stopped for lunch at a pub called The Jolly Sailor, where I had put up for bed and breakfast a couple of years earlier.

On the way back we called at a small town called Horncastle and both thought it was lovely little place. Having a walk around, I spotted a nice Bed and Breakfast tucked away, with a vacancy sign up. We both agreed and found the lady of the house who showed us round, whereupon we agreed to stay for a few nights and that was that.

That night found us in the local cinema, followed by fish and chips and we were finally enjoying ourselves. I happened to be in the fish shop about four days later and got talking to a lady behind the counter. Asking if we were enjoying our break, she said she had a friend who kept a Bed and Breakfast in Skegness and it was empty all winter, with a path in the back garden going down to the beach. Next morning found us with the keys and a choice of three large flats, of which we chose one and paid for three weeks.

So the Saturday found us loaded up and heading for 'Skeggy' as it was known locally. That night we went to the pictures in Boston and watched *The Outlaw Josey Wales* which I thoroughly enjoyed. We went to see the gaol where the Pilgrim Fathers were kept until they were sent aboard the Mayflower on their journey to the New World. We also visited Boston Stump, both of us climbing to the top and looking out over the fens.

The flat we had in Skeggy was very nice and we found we were only a couple of doors from the Lifeboat station. We had some lovely walks along the beach at Ingoldmells, past the Butlin's holiday camp and found some lovely walks. All too soon it was time to pack up, load the car and head back to South Wales and, I suppose, reality.

After a very long drive with Joan at the wheel, we finally arrived at Croesyceiliog to a nice tea and a rest. The conversation was mainly about Joan with the police looking for her but it made me laugh that no one enquired about yours truly. We were going to look for a Bed and Breakfast somewhere close but were told that we should stay here for the time being. So as not to be idle, we papered the lounge/diner and it looked very nice. Meanwhile, I was writing to different companies on a daily basis until one morning I was asked to go for an interview in Haverfordwest and secured a job in Llanelli as a kitchen designer.

Of Times Long Past . . . Or Are They?

The hair dye stands unused on the cabinet shelf
Accompanied by the gelatine for the famous D.A.
The combs and twin mirrors are covered in dust
And the old sideburn trimmers are rusting away

The velvet collared drape jackets, all of different hues
Hang down from their hangers, so once proudly worn
The black drainpipe trousers, so immaculately pressed
The belts and the buckles now just lie there forlorn

The bright brocade waistcoats, the prized Slim Jim ties
The row of brothel creepers, lie in various shades
Pairs of luminous socks coloured lime green and pink
Laying there in white tissue paper to save any fades

Still caught up in the fifties, their owner now gone
Was like thousands of others who will never give in
A Rock 'n' Roll dinosaur who was there from the start
When the Teddy Boys swaggered and Bill Hayley was in

The cobweb covered collection of the fifties LPs
Now unplayed and unwanted by the youth of today
The rock and roll history from five decades ago
When the coffee bars rocked to the Wurlitzer's play

When pretty young things in their Jayne Mansfield tops
With petticoats starched used to jive around the floor
Then great roars of approval met a suspenders flash
To the Devil's own music, so the kill joys would roar

When the world came alive, when Elvis Presley was king
When dance halls were packed to hear a Fats Domino song
As the great Buddy Holly with the Crickets would play
With his Fender Stratocaster he could never do wrong

The killer Jerry Lee Lewis and Gene Vincent's Blue Caps
Frankie Lymon, Little Richard set the whole world alight
Larry Williams, Eddie Cochran all gave it their best
As the Teds rocked in the dance halls on a Saturday night

But although that great era has long come to an end
The great songs of that decade will not fade and die
For the purists and their concerts still live on in our lives
And the gigs still take place neath a rock and roll sky

But there on a tombstone in an old country churchyard
Are written the inviting words of an old rock and roll song
By one of the greatest, Jerry Lee Lewis, a king of the fifties
Saying 'Come on over, there's a whole lot of shakin' going on!

EPILOGUE
Dear Mr Fantasy
(Steve Winwood)

To those who have read this book I make no apologies for the content. In 1956 the world was a very different place and growing up as a local parson's son made it totally different. Everyone I met expected me to be an angel or, later on, a saint and I was always set up as an example, or very much under the microscope. Being moved around the country with different schools every year entailed some horrendous work with all the copying up of class work to be done every evening as well as the homework for that day. How I remember sitting down and copying up a full year's term work until my eyes were closing, all this to no avail, however, and not even glanced at by the staff.

Everything was drab in those days after the war. The cars were mostly black, the wireless programmes dreadful, no street lights in the rural villages, in fact no mains electricity or water in some cases. Then along came rock and roll, the music, the stars and the clothes they wore. A whole new world was there for the taking and I for one was not going to stand back and let it all go by. I make no excuses for my lifestyle and now at the end of it all, I look back and wonder what would my old folks be thinking? Are they looking down with feelings of love or disgust? I would fervently hope that it would not be the latter, and feel the experiences I shared, the marvellous folks I met along the way and the whole rich pattern of my life can be enjoyed by others who followed my pathway and maybe even those who didn't.